Inside Private Prisons

INSIDE PRIVATE PRISONS

*An American Dilemma in the
Age of Mass Incarceration*

Lauren-Brooke Eisen

Columbia University Press
New York

Columbia University Press
Publishers Since 1893
New York   Chichester, West Sussex
cup.columbia.edu

Library of Congress Control Number: 2017027653
ISBN 978-0-231-17970-6 (cloth : alk. paper) |
ISBN 978-0-231-54231-9 (e-book)

Columbia University Press books are printed on permanent
and durable acid-free paper.
Printed in the United States of America

Cover design: Milenda Nan OK Lee
Cover image: © Shutterstock

Contents

Acknowledgments

THIS ENDEAVOR WOULD not have been possible without the guidance of many colleagues, the support of my family and friends, and countless cups of coffee.

This book owes so much to the thoughtful and careful editing of Stephen Wesley, who believed in this project from day one. His vision of the book guided me along this journey, and his patience with my late night emails filled with bullet points is very much appreciated. To my agent and dear friend, Stefanie Lieberman, thank you for spending hours on the phone explaining the ins and outs of the publishing world to me and continuing to serve as one of my chief advocates. I also appreciate the detailed feedback from peer reviewers at the Columbia University Press, all of whom had thoughtful and important critiques of early chapters.

To my Brennan Center colleagues, thank you for your support of this project. I owe a huge debt to Inimai Chettiar, who blessed this project from the beginning and challenged me to explore the powerful role of incentives to change public policy. To Fritz Schwartz, thank you for reading early chapters and providing feedback and for your encouragement to dig into the subject matter more deeply. To Michael Waldman, for teaching me how to fight for our democracy and inspiring me with your own tales of all-nighters to finish books. To Dorothy Samuels, for taking the time to think through some of the book's challenges with me, and for your invaluable advice on this project. To Elisa Miller, for reviewing the manuscript and for her continued support of this project. To John Kowal, Vivien Watts, Mike German, Beatriz Aldereguia, Nicole Fortier, Ames Grawert, Matt Menendez,

Grainne Dunne, Natasha Camhi, Vienna Tompkins, Alicia Bannon, Chisun Lee, Rachel Levinson-Waldman, Diana Kasdan, Jaemin Kim, Faiza Patel, and Kim Thomas, thank you for your support, advice, and pats on the back. To Jen Weiss-Wolf, thank you for being my partner in crime and commiserating with me on how hard it is to write a book and hold down a full-time job. To Jeanine Plant-Chirlin, for reviewing my book proposal and for her effusive encouragement; to Jim Lyons, for his editing assistance and always making the time to review my materials; to Erik Opsal and Rebecca Autrey, for editing countless articles I wrote on this issue; Jessica Katzen and Mellen O'Keefe for their help with this book's rollout; and to Andrew Cohen, who pushed me to ensure that this book included the perspective of everyone that a private prison touches. A number of colleagues and New York University Law School clinic students have made significant contributions to this book, including Jay Cullen, Adureh Onyekwere (who is a whiz at finding esoteric information), Noah Atchison, Jon Frank, Leah Romm, Carson Whitelmons, Jason O'Conner, Nicole Lieberman, and Danielle N Vildostegui.

I am grateful for the conversations I had with so many colleagues and mentors in the criminal justice field over the past few years about what we should expect from our correctional system. Martin Horn, thank you for your guidance on this project, introducing me to your colleagues, and providing insight into this complicated world. I am especially grateful to Rick Raemisch for opening up his prisons to me. Thank you to Michael Wishnie, for reviewing an early chapter of the book, and to Sarah Serafin, who transcribed many of my interviews.

My conversations with Jeremy Travis, Michael Jacobson, Jim Austin, AT Wall, Justin Jones, Rick Seiter, Jack Donson, Suzi Wizowaty, Frank Smith, Tiffany M. Joslyn, Leonard Gilroy, Daniel Hanson, Erik Schlosser, Barry Friedman, Scott Schuchart, Glenn Martin, Khalil Cumberbatch, Rabbi Ammiel Hirsch, Bernie Warner, Alex Friedmann, Bob Libal, Lisa Graybill, Dan Carillo, Sawy Rkasnaum, Barbara Hines, Andy Mannix, Donald Cohen, Marc Mauer, Reggie Wilkinson, David Wagner, Bret Bucklin, John Pfaff, and Jimmy LeBlanc were invaluable to my research.

I owe a deep debt of gratitude to Peggy McGarry and Alison Shames for their mentorship and guidance in this field and to former colleagues Ram Subramanian and Danyelle Solomon, whose friendship and sage advice mean so much to me. To friends who supported this endeavor and gave me feedback on early chapters, Lauren Brody, Brian Elderbroom, Jessica Mederson, Jen Millstone, Jennifer Suellentrop, Emily Turner, and Joanna Weiss, thank you for making the time!

For those who shared their personal stories with me, I am grateful to Bob Thompson, Ron Ronning, Ella Every, Joseph Gaylin, Lindsay Holcomb, Gary Hendricks, Chadwick Syltie, Kathleen Culhane, Michael Ingram, Richard Gagnon, Greg Turner, Eric Daley, Layne Pavey, Khalil Kumberbach, Elizabeth Cree, so many undocumented immigrants who I spoke to in detention centers in Texas, and inmates at private prisons in New Mexico and Colorado who spoke to me when I visited. For those of you who spoke to me on the condition of anonymity, please know how grateful I am to you for opening up about your experiences in prisons and detention centers.

Thank you to my daughters, Hadley and Phoebe, who continue to inspire me with their kindness, wisdom, energy, and unconditional support. Thanks also to my husband, Elias Levenson, who provided a valuable sounding board, many illegible edits, and even more nights of entertaining Hadley and Phoebe while I was researching and writing this book. To my father, Charles Eisen, who cheered me on during this process and passed down to me his belief in the power of laws to improve the world. To my big brother Scott Eisen, for always looking out for me. My mother-in-law Isabella Levenson deserves a special shout-out for her relentless support and wise counsel, making it possible to work full-time and write a book with two young children running around. Thank you to Bob Shapiro for your support and unabated interest in my work, to Amy Singer and Conrad Levenson for your support and ideas, to Harriet Singer for your hugs, to Jackie Pletcher for making my father smile and laugh every day, and to Madonna Park for your energy. Georgia Levenson-Keohane, thank you for opening doors for me and serving as a role model who gets even less sleep than I do, and to the rest of the Keohane Clan (Frances, Eleanor, and Nat) for their support. Finally, to my mother, Ruthie Eisen, the kindest and gentlest person I have known, who left this world far too soon and continues to be the quiet inspiration for everything I do.

Inside Private Prisons

Introduction

The subject of prisons and corrections may tempt some of you
to tune out. You may think, "Well, I am not a criminal lawyer.
The prison system is not my problem. I might tune in again
when he gets to a different subject." In my submission you
have the duty to stay tuned in. The subject is the concern and
responsibility of every member of our profession and of every
citizen. This is your justice system; these are your prisons.

JUSTICE ANTHONY KENNEDY, AUGUST 9, 2003[1]

THE PRISON SITS on a road not heavily traveled unless you work
in corrections, know someone in prison, or are an inmate yourself.
It is a short drive but a world away from Colorado Springs, where
the Colorado Department of Corrections is headquartered. The road
unfolds in front of the blue-gray Rockies, the land gradually flattening,
the houses smaller and farther apart, and the vegetation shifting from
green shrubs to brown grass peeking with cacti. Riding with Colorado
Department of Corrections Executive Director Rick Raemisch, we
pass bison on our right and train tracks on our left. We are headed
to the Crowley County Correctional Facility, a private prison run
by CoreCivic, formerly known as the Corrections Corporation of
America (CCA). The medium security prison is situated in remote
Olney Springs in southwestern Colorado, about a hundred miles from
the New Mexico border. Olney has a population of about 345, but the
prison can house up to 1,800 inmates.

I was in the car that day to examine an industry that had long
intrigued me, and I wanted to see for myself its practical effect on the
ground. It was one visit of many I would make to untangle through

first-hand experience how exactly private corporations operated prisons and immigrant detention centers. I needed to see the everyday reality behind a roiling debate that had preoccupied me and my colleagues for many years: the federal government's and states' growing reliance on corporations to oversee American incarceration. When Governor John Hickenlooper appointed Raemisch, he asked him to limit the use of solitary confinement for mentally ill inmates and generally to reform the practice for state prisoners. The director Raemisch replaced had been shot and killed by a former inmate who had spent a good portion of his eight years in prison in solitary confinement.[2] Within seven months of taking the reins as head of the Colorado Department of Corrections, Raemisch spent twenty hours in solitary confinement. The cell was only 7 feet by 13 feet. He didn't sleep at all. The lights were on, and every half hour guards would yank on his door. "I couldn't make any sense of it, and I was left feeling twitchy and paranoid. I kept waiting for the lights to turn off, to signal the end of the day. But the lights did not shut off," Raemisch said. "I began to count the small holes carved in the walls."[3] Raemisch has since devoted himself to reforming solitary confinement policies across the nation.

On this June afternoon, Raemisch, talking to me about private prisons, said "private prison companies are not the demons they are made out to be," candidly sharing his complicated view of the role of private prisons formed from his experience.

Raemisch spoke slowly, choosing his words carefully. "Private prisons filled a void when politicians did their 'tough-on-crime' thing. Our relationship with them in Colorado is good, and they are receptive to our needs. I came from Wisconsin where we didn't use private prisons though." Before taking the top job in Colorado, Raemisch was head of the Wisconsin Department of Corrections. After nearly two years at the helm of Colorado's prison system, Raemisch was still open-minded about the partnerships with private prison corporations, but he understood the discomfort many have about a corporation profiting from running a nation's prisons.

As we headed up the access road to the Crowley County Correctional Facility, withered peach, apple, and pear trees flanked the road, victims of Colorado's struggles with a decade-long drought. A CCA guard stood watch on the roof, scanning the 21 acres that surround the medium security prison, the border lined with barbed wire. A few days earlier, the Netflix original series *Orange Is the New Black* aired an episode depicting private prisons as Keystone-cop ventures run solely to turn a profit. The episode prompted Carl Takei, attorney at the American Civil Liberties Union (ACLU) and a thorn in the side of the private prison industry, to publish a blog claiming that "life in many real private, for-profit prisons is actually worse." That week Columbia University announced it would become the first university to divest itself of private prison stocks, selling $10 million worth of shares in the industry, including a stake in CCA.

We walked into the prison, a low-lying brick structure enclosed in razor wire, and passed a row of lockers where correction officers store items from their transparent backpacks. CCA staff ushered us into a conference room where CCA's chief executive officer was waiting. I had spent time in dozens of prisons, but the receiving line of CCA officials took me aback. Damon Hininger, CEO of CCA, had flown in from the company's Nashville headquarters for my visit. Beside Hininger stood CCA's director of public affairs, Jonathan Burns. I had spoken to Burns a few months ago when I was at my wit's end trying to gain access to CCA's facilities in Texas and Louisiana. One call to Raemisch and I was invited out to tour a CCA prison.

The Crowley County Correctional Facility was built in 1998 as a speculative undertaking by the Dominion Group, a collection of real estate companies. Among other things, Dominion specializes in leasing properties to the U.S. government, with holdings in Oklahoma, Texas, Kansas, and New Mexico. At one time Dominion had been a major investor in private prison construction, claiming it had "developed more high-security prisons than any other privately owned company in the U.S."[4] Whatever its holdings once were, Dominion is now out of the private prison business; it sold the Crowley County Correctional Facility to CCA in 2003.

We sat awkwardly around the large table, sipping bad coffee out of black CCA mugs. On the wall was a map of the United States showing CCA's eighty-nine correctional facilities. Crowley was marked with a thumbtack. With a total design capacity of approximately 88,500 beds in twenty states and the District of Columbia, CCA is the nation's largest private prison operator.

Another private prison titan, GEO Group, oversees the operation and management of approximately 87,000 beds at 104 correctional, detention, and reentry facilities worldwide. It is the seventh largest correctional system in the United States by number of beds in its capacity. With operations in the United States, the United Kingdom, Australia, and South Africa, GEO Group is the second largest provider of privatized correctional and detention facilities worldwide. America's third largest for-profit prison corporation, Management and Training Corporation (MTC), founded in 1981, is privately owned and operates twenty-six state and federal prisons in Arizona, California, Florida, Idaho, Ohio, New Mexico, Mississippi, and Texas.

In the conference room I asked about this private prison, trying to understand how it was different from Colorado's state prisons. Warden Michael Miller detailed the strides they have made toward reentry. In criminal justice argot, *reentry* is the transition of inmates to civilian life. Decades of research indicate that the better prepared prisoners are to reenter their communities, the less likely they are to be rearrested. Miller spoke highly of the reentry pods where inmates nearing their release dates lived together and received services to help them acclimate to life back in the community. The prisoners participate in specialized programming such as classes that instruct them in how to find housing. "I didn't become a warden to house inmates behind walls," Miller said.

A lawyer who works to eliminate private prisons warned me before my visit to look out for perfectly polished floors but grime on the walls and ceiling that the cleaning staff might have forgotten to clean in their haste. He said these clues would reveal the naked truth about the conditions of the prison. As I walked around the prison, I noticed that the floors were clean, as expected, and that the ceilings were not covered in grime.

I was ushered into a classroom where GED classes are taught. With its wooden tables and desk chairs, it didn't look very different from any high school classroom in the United States. Inspirational words were painted on the walls: "Failure is not an option." "Success (sek ses), n. a favorable result; wished for ending; good fortune. 2. Person or thing that succeeds." In the computer room, ten inmates sat at monitors, dressed in matching green pants and green tops. Some wore baseball hats. They were learning skills they would need upon release. One man was reading about renting a car. Across the room, another struggled with a computer exercise on money management. This education program is highly sought after: 136 inmates were on the waiting list that day.

Director Raemisch explained to me that this programming was part of the reentry initiative for the Colorado Department of Corrections. He introduced himself to the inmates and asked whether they had any questions. One of the inmates complained he had not finished his reentry programming and was about to be released. "I feel like I am being set up for failure," he said quietly. Raemisch listened to his concerns and wrote down his name.

Once a farming area, Crowley County's economy turned to corrections when crop and cattle prices dramatically declined in the 1960s. Two state prisons operate within the county's borders: the Arkansas Valley Correctional Center (Arkansas Valley), owned and operated by the state, and the Crowley County Correctional Facility, owned and operated by CCA. Together they make up 46 percent of the estimated 5,823 people residing in the county. CCA's private prison in Crowley contributes more than half of the county's $1.6 million annual property tax revenue.[5] Most prison employees live outside the county, commuting from larger towns and cities. Like many prison towns, the unemployment rate is high: 16 percent of Crowley residents are unemployed and almost 30 percent live below the poverty line.[6]

Crowley prison has 1,894 beds for its all-male population and is one of four CCA prisons in Colorado, but CCA's footprint in the state is expanding beyond prisons. Like its rivals in the private prison industry, CCA wants to run drug treatment facilities and halfway houses too. In 2016, CCA bought Boulder-based Correctional Management Inc. for $35 million, a company that managed seven community treatment centers in Colorado.[7]

As we left the building and continued our walk around the prison grounds, men in their green prison uniforms passed by in pairs, walking from one location to another without guards. "They have a certain amount of time to get where they are going," one of the correction officers told me. "If they don't show up, then we start looking for them."

We entered a building where inmates worked with solid oak, wielding hammers and belt sanders, building homes for Habitat for Humanity, a program started at the facility in 1998. Seventy-five inmates were enrolled in the job training program. Working in the program is something of an honor. Inmates must first complete their GED, take a safety course, and then be referred by their case managers. They earn 74 cents a day plus a portion of the sale of their work. Although neither CCA nor the Colorado Department of Corrections tracks the job placement of inmates in the Habitat for Humanity program who leave the prison, CCA officials said a recent participant had started a cabinetry business in Denver.

We toured a housing unit next. On the wall, painted in huge red and blue characters, was a phone number and information about how to report prison rape. "One of the inmates painted it," a female correction officer said. In 2012, the Justice Department issued rules for all prisons to follow in preventing, detecting, and responding to sexual abuse. Both public and private prisons have come under fire for not enforcing these standards, which were promulgated to curb sexual abuse in prisons.[8] On we went into the pods, the housing units where the inmates sleep. A female correction officer entered first and yelled "Female on the floor!" I sheepishly followed behind her and asked whether I could speak to some inmates. An older white man who wore his hair in a ponytail sat alone at a table playing solitaire. He said he'd been a prisoner in both state run and private facilities. "They aren't that different," he said. "But I'm on the waiting list to go back to the state prison because I want to get into Colorado Correctional Industries. There is just not enough programming here."

One of the persistent objections to private prisons is their financial incentive to keep costs to a minimum to preserve profits. Prison vocational and educational programs are expensive, especially now, because best practices for these initiatives can require large outlays of cash. It is difficult to tell whether private prisons truly do skimp on these programs. Every state and private prison offers a different array of programs, obscuring easy comparisons.

Nearby, three inmates sat at a table talking. One mentioned he had been at the prison for ten years and that his family visits every other week. His favorite class was a parenting program that taught him how to be a better father. He climbed the stairs to the second floor to retrieve the highlighted and tattered parenting book he used in his class. His cell had the typical debris one might find in a freshman dorm room: books strewn about the bottom bunk and Ramen noodles stacked high on the shelves.

After about three hours at the Crowley County Correctional Facility, we left to visit the state-run Colorado State Arkansas Valley Correctional Facility, which can house more than 1,000 inmates of mixed security levels (low, medium, and high). Inmates in a culinary program had prepared a lunch of cold cuts, pasta salad, and fruit for us. Raemisch and I walked around the prison and passed inmates wearing green pants and shirts; the same clothing inmates at the private facility down the street wore. In one building forty-five prisoners were building modular furniture for Colorado Correctional Industries; in another room inmates worked at a call center for the Department of Motor Vehicles. They wore headsets and spoke to customers, many of whom had no idea someone in prison was on the other end of the telephone line.

The facilities are difficult to compare because of the different security levels, but the state prison certainly offered more educational and vocational training than the CCA prison we had just toured. CCA's prison in Crowley doesn't have the state prison's coveted culinary arts program, where inmates learn catering skills such as cake decorating and how to serve food, which they practice by waiting on visitors in a dining room. Although the CCA prison in Crowley offers the chance for seventy-five inmates to participate in woodworking through its Habitat for Humanity program, the state run facility down the street offers advanced training in modular furniture building, jobs packaging canned goods for food banks, web design, an auto call center training program, a license-plate-making program, a law library, and a lending library. Inmates at the private prison in Crowley don't have keys to their cells, a privilege for certain inmates housed at Arkansas Valley. Still, the private prison didn't feel that different.

As Raemisch and I headed back toward the Rockies, we discussed some of the challenges facing Colorado's growing prison population. On that day, no state prison in Colorado was over design capacity, a balanced status many state corrections chiefs can only wish for. Raemisch was deflated that the legislature had just passed a new law requiring intoxicated drivers to spend time behind bars. Worried that this might bloat his prison population, he pondered whether he would have to rely on private prisons to keep his facilities from overcrowding. "It has somewhat of a chilling effect when you think that private companies are housing inmates for profit," he said. "But if you set that aside and start looking at some of the voids that they fill, it can be a good system."

After thirty years of intense debate, this book endeavors a fair-minded look at an industry that raises profound questions about state responsibility, economic development, morality, and the nature of punishment. What does the increasing reliance on the private prison industry since the 1980s mean for American justice? Some find themselves behind bars, others hope a private prison will open in their small town and employ them, and some policy makers or corrections officials may see them as a vehicle, providing a safe way to relieve overcrowding at other prison facilities. Others active in the criminal justice sphere have long criticized the use of private prisons. Some argue that they create perverse incentives that drive overcrowding by cutting costs and reducing the quality of life for inmates. Others point out that the corporations that run private prisons earn additional revenue when inmates serve more of their sentence, which encourages private prison officials to hand out extra infractions. Still others take issue with the concept of a corporation profiting from the nation's predilection for incarceration and rewarding companies for the sheer number of inmates they can house rather than for successfully rehabilitating and reintegrating prisoners into society. For decades, some legal scholars and policy makers have contended that certain state functions cannot be delegated—and that one of those is punishment.

The private prison industry provides a safety valve to meet demands from taxpayers for more incarceration, which allows policy makers to avoid thinking through the implications of imprisoning so many Americans or to confront the hard decisions about how to safely downsize prison populations. The industry is a mixed blessing, providing newer facilities to jurisdictions that can't keep up with the demand for more bars. Yet it is important to understand that the tremendous growth in the private prison industry is a direct result of the equally tremendous growth in incarceration, inextricably linking the two in political debates about whether incarcerating so many for so long benefits society.

The stories and voices in this book offer a glimpse into the challenges and experiences with the privatization of corrections through the eyes of incarcerated individuals, their families, local government, directors of state departments of corrections, private prison officials, legislators, and criminal justice experts. This story comes at a time in the American narrative when correctional populations have begun, finally, to flatten out. The number of prisoners in state and federal prisons decreased by 35,500 (down 2 percent) from 2014 to 2015, but the United States still has a higher percentage of its population behind bars than almost any other country on the planet. The story of America's prison growth remains complicated. In 2015, twenty-nine states and the federal Bureau of Prisons saw decreases in total prison populations, but eighteen states saw increases. In fact, Oklahoma increased its number of inmates by more than 900; Virginia grew its inmate population by 840 people.[9]

What does the future look like for the world's biggest jailor? <u>Will we rethink how we punish individuals who break our laws?</u> As Marie Gottschalk, member of the National Academy of Sciences Committee on the Causes and Consequences of High Rates of Incarceration, wrote, "The construction of the carceral state was the result of a complex set of historical, institutional, and political developments. No single factor explains its rise, and no single factor will bring about its demise."[10]

Today 126,000 inmates are held in private prison facilities across twenty-nine states and the federal Bureau of Prisons, accounting for 8 percent of all inmates.[11] (Private prisons hold almost 7 percent of state inmates and almost 18 percent of federal inmates.[12]) Six states currently house at least 20 percent of their inmate population in private facilities.

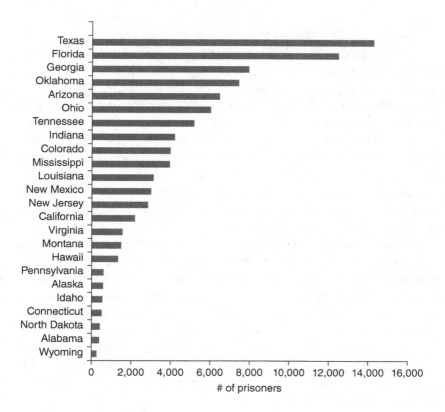

Figure I.1 Number of prisoners in private prisons by state, 2015 *Source*: Bureau of Justice Statistics, "Prisoners in 2015" (States with less than 30 inmates in private prisons are not listed.)

New Mexico houses the largest percentage of inmates in private facilities with 42.2 percent of its almost 7,000 inmates housed in private prisons.[13] Recently private prison corporations have contracted with Immigration and Customs Enforcement to manage more than *half* of the immigrant detainees being civilly held behind bars in immigrant detention centers.

The for-profit prison industry and the vast prison industrial complex did not singlehandedly drive the growth of mass incarceration, but their emergence reflects a deeper punitiveness in U.S. society. For-profit prisons and the broader prison-industrial complex that surrounds corrections today are not the engine behind the growth of mass incarceration. Private prisons have become ground zero for the anti–mass incarceration movement that sees closure of these prisons as a concrete step toward reducing the number of people behind bars. We can't ignore the influence the private prison industry has had on the carceral landscape, but eliminating private prisons entirely would only shrink the state prison population by 7 percent.

This book explores the impact of the for-profit industry—whose lives it affects, where it is harmful or helpful, and what it means for the country. This book is in no way meant to endorse the private prison industry; but it seeks to recognize a controversial reality. Private prisons are unlikely to go away any time soon. What are the industry's flaws and how should they be addressed?

I recognize that even asking that question has worrying, moral ramifications. If as a matter of principle, it is wrong, as some say, to profit from punishment, anything short of abolition—including proposing reforms—risks complicity in an indefensible industry. In the meantime, tens of thousands of inmates pass through the doors of private prisons. How the institutions function—whether they make it more or less likely that these inmates end their sentences ready to rejoin the community—matters a great deal, to those prisoners and to us, and it is the concern that drives this book's inquiry. As the broader debate rages, are there ways to improve these institutions, to shift the incentives that shape them? Or is the current misalignment between humane values and an often-brutal justice system simply too ingrained to be changed?

After researching the history and efficacy of for-profit prisons and traveling the country to meet with inmates and immigrant detainees, speaking to their families, interviewing correctional staff, criminal justice researchers, private prison officials, lobbyists, private prison abolitionists, criminal justice reformers, policy makers, and elected officials, I have come to conclude that the industry suffers from a significant opaqueness and little accountability given the power it has over the lives of so many. And for those who care about reducing American mass incarceration, the industry is an enormous hurdle.

Chapter 1 examines the nation's prison buildup. Chapter 2 surveys the history of the privatization of many government services, from policing to garbage collection. Chapter 3 looks at the privatization of crime and punishment in the United States and the sudden birth of private prisons. Chapter 4 goes inside the $80 billion prison industrial complex that has infiltrated corrections in the United States. Chapter 5 examines prison towns and the attractions of the private prison industry to impoverished rural America. Chapter 6 focuses on divestment campaigns and activism against private prisons. Chapter 7 covers the political debate, everything from presidential campaigns to the introduction of legislation to curb the industry's growth. Chapter 8 looks at the arm of private corrections that may provide their best chance of growing more profitable—housing of immigrant detainees. Chapter 9 compares private and public prisons. Chapter 10 considers the incentives and perils of these prisons, examining whether they play an outsized role in incarceration rates and recidivism. Chapter 11 offers some recommendations on how we might improve private prisons in the United States.

CHAPTER ONE

The Prison Buildup and the Birth of Private Prisons

The fact is that the criminal justice system is not enough—or even the most relevant institution—to deal with our crime problems. It makes about as much sense to look to prisons to solve our chronic crime problem as it would to build more funeral parlors to solve a cholera epidemic.

ABNER MIKVA, FORMER ILLINOIS REPRESENTATIVE AND FORMER WHITE HOUSE COUNSEL UNDER PRESIDENT CLINTON

ALMOST NO ONE is ambivalent about private prisons. Justin Jones, former Oklahoma director of corrections, doesn't see a place for private prisons in American corrections. In 2014 he stated that private prisons "create demand for their services much like drug dealers ensure that their customers are addicted, but not so addicted they die. . . . CEO profits and shareholder returns have no place in our criminal justice system."[1] But former New Mexico Governor Gary Johnson, who oversaw the construction of two new private prisons in his state and ran for president on the Libertarian ticket in 2016, stated: "Private prisons stepped in and offered the same goods and services at about two-thirds the cost."[2]

This issue engenders so much discord that students across the nation meet weekly to plan divestment advocacy campaigns, Democratic presidential candidates refuse to accept campaign donations from private prison corporations, and hundreds of people gather to protest private prison corporation shareholder meetings. With a little less than 10 percent of the correctional footprint across the nation, why do Americans care so passionately about who runs their prisons?

Perhaps it is because the private prison debate has become entangled with the growing call for an end to mass incarceration. Today, more than 2.1 million Americans are behind bars; more than 1.5 million people are held in state or federal prisons, and more than 720,000 people are held in local jails. This is more people than live in Belize, Fiji, Luxemburg, and the Maldives combined. These inmates are locked up in the nearly 1,800 prisons and 3,000 jails across the nation. At the end of 2016, upward of 40,000 undocumented immigrants were held in immigration detention facilities on any given day. Adam Gopnik wrote that more people are incarcerated in America today than were imprisoned in Stalin's gulags.[3]

Prisons provide little rehabilitative programming and often release individuals into communities with little or no reentry support. Without this support, prisoners sometimes turn back to crime. In addition, more mentally ill people are in the nation's prisons than in its mental hospitals.[4] Based on these findings, it should be no surprise that recidivism rates in the United States are so high. More than half of all prisoners released return within three years.[5]

Punishment's Roots

Prisons did not always dot the American landscape. In colonial America, jails housed those awaiting trial or who were delinquent on their debts. Early settlers relied on the laws and practices common in England, which focused on banishment, corporal punishment, and public humiliation. Once convicted, jails were irrelevant; those who were convicted of crimes were subject to swift and severe sanctions. In colonial America, communities were small, and society could not afford to imprison those who violated the law because their labor contributions were needed. Those with means paid fines as punishment, and colonists with little money were often publicly humiliated, thrown in the stockades, or whipped in front of crowds.[6] These punishments aimed to deter future wrongdoers and simultaneously allowed convicted individuals to quickly return to work.

Incarceration as we know it today began just after the American Revolution. The Walnut Street Jail in Philadelphia, Pennsylvania, built in the 1770s, held pretrial defendants and others awaiting sentences handed down by a judge. By the late 1780s, a group of prominent

Philadelphia men began to discuss crime as a disease of the mind and advocated for a house of repentance where prisoners could meditate on their crimes. In 1790, a portion of the jail was converted to accommodate convicted criminals. At the Walnut Street Jail, contractors created cells for separate and solitary confinement, a new form of punishment that would eventually become known as the "Pennsylvania System."[7] With Philadelphia's population on the rise, its capacity to house criminals was at a breaking point. The jails were overcrowded, and to achieve the goal of complete isolation a bigger building was needed.

The Philadelphia Society for Alleviating the Miseries of Public Prisons, also known as the Pennsylvania Prison Society, which counted Benjamin Franklin and prominent physician Dr. Benjamin Rush as members, was instrumental in convincing the Commonwealth of Pennsylvania to authorize construction of a more suitable building. British-born architect John Haviland designed the building, the first of its kind in the Colonies. Seven wings of individual cellblocks were built, replete with central heating, toilets that flushed (not built for the luxury of inmates but to eliminate contact with other inmates), and baths in each private cell.[8] "The penitentiary boasted luxuries that not even President Andrew Jackson could enjoy at the White House."[9] Construction began in 1822, and by 1829 inmates moved into the newly constructed Eastern State Penitentiary in Philadelphia, famous for fully implementing the "separate confinement" theory of incarceration.

Eastern State Penitentiary offered a radically different type of punishment, leaving behind corporal punishment in favor of the Quaker-inspired belief that criminals could benefit from spiritual reflection, which could lead them to see the errors in their ways and live a life devoid of crime. The prison reformers in Philadelphia believed that "for the criminal already imprisoned, isolation from his fellow men was to prevent harmful corruption, protect his good resolutions, and give him ample opportunity to ponder on his mistakes and make his peace with God."[10]

Inmates were separated from one another and did not engage in any communication with fellow prisoners. The wardens combined a system of isolation from other prisoners with labor. Inmates were given Bibles to read in their cells and were forbidden to write letters to friends and family members. To keep busy, prisoners spun wool or made shoes in their cells. Prisoners wore hoods when they left their cells to enhance their isolation and to ensure they had no knowledge of where they were housed in relation to the rest of the prison.

Thus was born America's first "penitentiary," from the Medieval Latin "paenitentia," the root of which means "repentance." Motivated by the Quaker belief that this form of punishment would create "genuine regret and penitence in the criminal's heart," Eastern State Penitentiary quickly became a tourist attraction.[11] It enticed French political scientist and historian Alexis de Tocqueville and English writer and literary critic Charles Dickens to separately visit the prison soon after it was built.[12]

Dickens visited in 1842. He spoke to men in their cells and wrote down his impressions of America's earliest inmates.

> There was a sailor who had been there upwards of eleven years, and who in a few months' time would be free. Eleven years of solitary confinement! "I am very glad to hear your time is nearly out." What does he say? Nothing. Why does he stare at his hands, and pick the flesh upon his fingers, and raise his eyes for an instant, every now and then, to those bare walls which have seen his head turn grey?[13]

Dickens was wholly unimpressed by this new form of "penitence": "I hold this slow and daily tampering with the mysteries of the brain to be immeasurably worse than any torture of the body; and because its ghastly signs and tokens are not so palpable to the eye, . . . and it extorts few cries that human ears can hear; therefore I the more denounce it, as a secret punishment in which slumbering humanity is not roused up to stay."[14]

Ironically, as American ideals of freedom and independence became celebrated, prisons became more isolating and sterile. David Rothman, professor of Social Medicine at Columbia University College of Physicians and Surgeons, wrote: "at the very moment that Americans began to pride themselves on the openness of their society, when the boundless frontier became the symbol of opportunity and equality, an idea developed: those convicted of crimes would be confined behind walls, in single cells, and would follow rigid and unyielding routines."[15] In 1817, New York constructed a state prison in Auburn, 250 miles northwest of New York City in central New York. In 1821, the Auburn State Penitentiary warden pioneered a "congregate system": inmates were isolated at night but worked with fellow inmates by day. Despite working and eating together (which was not permitted at Eastern State Penitentiary), prisoners were forbidden to speak to one another when working and during meals. In an attempt to implement a disciplinary regime at the prison, Auburn's warden, Captain Elam Lynds, a veteran of the War of 1812, required the inmates to walk in lock-step and wear uniforms with prison stripes so escaped prisoners would be immediately recognizable. Instead of using prisoner's names, Lynds instituted prison numbers.

Auburn also pioneered the practice of using inmates for cheap labor. The state of New York negotiated contracts with manufacturers, and inmates—many of whom were imprisoned at Auburn—produced shoes, carpets, tools, clothing, and furniture. This convict labor helped fund the institution. Auburn inmates also played an instrumental role in building the Sing Sing prison upstate in Mount Pleasant-on-the-Hudson. In 1825, Lynds chose one hundred inmates who he relocated to build the prison. In 1910, Lynds "led them to the spot and camped on the bank of the Hudson without a place to receive or walls to secure his dangerous companions. He made everyone a mason, carpenter or other useful laborer with no other power than the firmness of his character and the energy of his will and thus for several years the convicts were engaged in building their own prison."[16] Lynds became the warden at Sing Sing when the prison opened its doors in 1828.

Before Alexis de Tocqueville wrote *Democracy in America*, he and his friend attorney Gustave de Beaumont traveled to the United States under a commission from King Louis-Phillipe to inspect American prison systems for the French government. They began their study in Newport, Rhode Island, in the spring of 1831 and visited a great many American prisons, including Sing Sing in New York and the Eastern State Penitentiary in Pennsylvania. The United States represented principles of individualism and equality, and after the French Revolution Europeans often traveled to America to observe how the government operated. After visiting prisons from New England, to New Orleans, and even Michigan, Tocqueville and Beaumont returned to France in 1832. In the *Penitentiary System in the United States and Its Application in France*, they wrote: "To sum up the whole on this point, it must be acknowledged that the penitentiary system in America is severe. While society in the United States gives the example of the most extended liberty, the prisons of the same country offer the spectacle of the most complete despotism. The citizens subject to the law are protected by it; they only cease to be free when they become wicked."[17]

Throughout most of the 1800s federal prisoners were housed in state prisons. The U.S. government paid the state prisons boarding fees to compensate them for housing the inmates and allowed them to use federal inmates to work at the facilities in prison labor jobs.[18] This practice received a major blow in 1887 when Congress passed legislation eliminating the contracting of federal inmates to private employers. Without the ability to use federal inmates for labor, these prisoners were not as attractive to state penitentiaries. The Federal Prison System was established in 1891, and the first federal prison was under construction at Leavenworth, Kansas, in 1897.[19] The second federal prison was built in Atlanta, Georgia, in 1902, and the first federal women's prison was erected in Alderson, West Virginia, in 1928. In a move to ensure better control over the various federal prisons throughout the nation, the Bureau of Prisons was created in 1929.

Crime Politics

Although prisons gained a foothold in the early 1800s, it was a century and a half later before they became central to crime and punishment. In the early part of the twentieth century, the dominant theory of corrections was a philosophy of rehabilitation. This is evident by certain changes to corrections: the implementation of indeterminate sentencing (which added discretion to release an inmate early if he or she indicated an ability to "rehabilitate" while behind bars), parole (which promoted early release policies), and the creation of a separate juvenile justice system. Throughout the first half of the 1900s, correctional administrators and legislators championed programming focused on improving the circumstances of those behind bars. In 1929, Congress authorized the federal Bureau of Prisons to "develop institutions that would ensure the proper classification, care, and treatment of offenders." The 1950s became known as the "Era of Treatment" in corrections, with California serving as a model state in rehabilitative programming, offering psychotherapy and group therapy to its inmates.[20]

The U.S. prison buildup can be traced to the mid-1960s, when there was a dramatic shift away from the rehabilitative view of punishment. Around 1960 new investigations into the efficacy of rehabilitation led sociologist Robert Martinson to argue that "nothing works" in treatment programs intended to prevent recidivism.[21] Martinson surveyed 231 studies on offender rehabilitation in his research and summarized his finding with this statement: "The present array of correctional treatments has no appreciable effect—positive or negative—on rates of recidivism of convicted offenders."[22] Martinson's research was widely read, and he appeared on *60 Minutes* in 1975. Most criminologists emphasized a new retributive justice, a sort of "just desserts."[23] Policy makers and legislators modified sentencing schemes to de-emphasize rehabilitation. Martinson later reversed his conclusion on programming not having rehabilitative value, but his original works received far more attention. In the winter of 1980, Martinson committed suicide by jumping out of a ninth floor window of his Manhattan apartment.[24] Martinson's "nothing works" article remains "among the most cited of criminological writings."[25]

One reason the philosophy shifted away from treatment lies with the rise in crime that began in the early 1960s. The nation was in the throes of the Vietnam War, and protestors took to the streets. The so-called long, hot summers of 1964 and 1965 saw urban uprisings in Harlem and Los Angeles, which were sparked largely by the treatment of black Americans by white police officers. In the summer of 1965, a hostile encounter between police officers and an African American family set off six days of protests in South Central Los Angeles in what would become known as the Watts Riot. Thirty-four people died and almost 4,000 were arrested. The multiple-day riot caused more than $40 million in property damage.

In March 1965, President Lyndon B. Johnson called for a "War on Crime" in a speech to Congress: "I hope that 1965 will be regarded as the year when this country began in earnest a thorough, intelligent, and effective war against crime."[26] He established a Commission on Law Enforcement and Administration of Justice to study the U.S. criminal justice system, and followed that with the Omnibus Crime Control and Safe Streets Act of 1968, which authorized more than $400 million in federal grants to law enforcement. These efforts funded an investment in police and opened the door for generations of policy makers to fund anticrime initiatives and to campaign for harsher prison sentences.

University of Michigan Historian Heather Ann Thompson was one of the first academics to write about the link between liberal policy makers and mass incarceration. Thompson argues that liberals and Democrats at all levels of government "fueled" their constituents' concerns about safety, and points out that President Lyndon B. Johnson's administration established the "largest crime-fighting bureaucracy the nation had ever seen" through a series of laws and reports: passing the Law Enforcement Assistant Act (LEAA), creating a national crime commission, endorsing the District of Columbia Crime Bill, issuing a "voluminous" report titled "The Challenge of Crime in a Free Society," and passing the Omnibus Crime Control and Safe Streets Act of 1968.[27] Ultimately, Thompson asserts, "postwar liberals had been high-ranking generals in the nation's new war on crime, not its unhappy conscripts."[28]

Harvard Historian Elizabeth Hinton also traces the roots of mass incarceration to Johnson, the same president who championed the Civil Rights Act and oversaw the greatest expansion of social services since the New Deal. Most historians point to President Ronald Reagan's War on Crime as the catalyst for today's current levels of incarceration. Hinton, however, argues that President Johnson's Great Society policies—aimed at improving conditions for the most impoverished Americans—laid the foundation for mass incarceration and its attendant racial injustices. Reagan's policies, she writes, were merely "the fulfillment of federal crime control priorities that stemmed initially from one of the most idealistic enterprises in American history during the era of civil rights."[29]

Other scholarly accounts trace the roots of mass incarceration to liberal policy makers who paved the way for this country's unprecedented prison buildup and sizable racial disparities in the justice system. Naomi Murakawa, Princeton political scientist and associate professor of African American Studies, points to federal legislation written by liberal policy makers to reduce discretion in sentencing and parole. Although their aim was to avoid racially disparate punishment, judges generally used their discretion in ways that hurt racial minorities. Time has shown that reducing judicial discretion resulted in more racial disparities, and African Americans ended up spending more time in prison as a result.[30] Today, African Americans are incarcerated at nearly six times the rate of whites; African Americans are approximately 13 percent of the U.S. population but represent 37 percent of the nation's prisoners.[31] Marc Mauer, executive director of the Sentencing Project and author of *Race to Incarcerate*, which details how sentencing policies led to the explosive expansion of the U.S. prison population, believes there is some merit to these arguments. He agrees that the law enforcement apparatus created at the federal level infused funding for police hardware and ramped up the enforcement of crimes. But Mauer points out that although "these policies did create some of the structure for how mass incarceration could take off, they don't get all the blame."[32] Politicians across the nation, whether progressive or conservative, competed for the heavyweight title "toughest on crime."

In 1968, President Richard Nixon campaigned as the law-and-order president against a backdrop of urban riots and burning cities. He ran this television spot in his deep, guttural voice overlaid with images of ordinary Americans: "In recent years, crime in this country has grown nine times as fast as the population. At the current rate, the crimes of violence in America will double by 1972. We cannot accept that kind of future for America." In 1971, President Nixon declared, "America's Public Enemy Number One is drug abuse." Fordham Law Professor John Pfaff points out that despite Nixon's rhetoric "his actual policies tended to favor public health responses over punitive ones."[33] Since 1971, more than 40 million arrests have been recorded for drug crimes.[34]

In 1970, Congress passed the Comprehensive Drug Abuse Prevention and Control Act, which authorized police to conduct "no-knock" searches but emphasized treatment and rehabilitation. Three years later, however, Nixon signed an executive order to create the Drug Enforcement Administration (DEA) to establish a single unified command to combat "an all-out global war on the drug menace."[35] This superagency merged the Bureau of Narcotics and Dangerous Drugs (BNDD), the Office of Drug Abuse Law Enforcement (ODALE), more than 500 special agents of the Bureau of Customs, and additional federal officials. This agency would become Nixon's drug war legacy. At its inception, the new agency had 1,470 special agents and a budget of less than $75 million. Today the DEA boasts nearly 5,000 special agents and a budget of over $2 billion.[36] The four decades from the 1960s to the 1990s marked a punitive turn in criminal justice that the nation had never before seen. State and federal policy marched toward more and longer punishment for those who violated the criminal code.

Following in Nixon's footsteps, in 1980 Ronald Reagan ran for president on the promise that he would crack down on street crime. Under

Reagan's watch, Congress passed the Sentencing Reform Act of 1984, establishing the U.S. Sentencing Commission and abolishing federal parole. In September 1986, with the nation preoccupied with the danger of drugs, first lady Nancy Reagan took to the television airways and kicked off her "Just Say No" campaign to warn Americans about the dangers of drugs, including a then new drug called crack cocaine. Mrs. Reagan told the nation, "Today there's a drug and alcohol abuse epidemic in this country, and no one is safe from it—not you, not me, and certainly not our children, because this epidemic has their names written on it."[37] With the country focused on the dangers of drugs and crime, Congress passed the Anti-Drug Abuse Act of 1986, the first significant reform of federal drug policy and a key piece of legislation in the War on Drugs. The law reinstated mandatory minimums for drug possession, but even more significantly, it established federal grants to fund drug enforcement in states with similar policies.

Marie Gottschalk, University of Pennsylvania professor of political science, offers a new lens with which to understand the history leading to today's high incarceration rates. She contends that the causes of mass incarceration are deeply bipartisan, pointing out that fear of crack cocaine introduced into urban drug markets created support from some key liberal groups, including the majority of the Congressional Black Caucus who supported the Anti-Drug Abuse Act of 1986. That law notoriously, and controversially, punished crack cocaine use (a crime African Americans are more likely to be convicted of) one hundred times more harshly than powder cocaine use (which skews more white).[38]

Scholar Michelle Alexander believes the war on drugs targeted black men, creating a contemporary form of social control. Funds for law enforcement began to soar to combat the drug war, and "almost immediately after crack appeared, the Reagan administration leaped at the opportunity to publicize crack cocaine in an effort to build support for its drug war."[39] Crack cocaine did devastate communities, especially in New York City, but when Reagan officially announced his War on Drugs in 1982, "less than 2 percent of the American public viewed drugs as the most important issue facing the nation."[40] Alexander points out, crack cocaine emerged in inner cities in 1985, three years after Reagan announced his War on Drugs.

With the rhetoric of the drug war overtaking the nation, there was no room for soft-on-crime talk in American politics. In 1988, Vice

President George H. W. Bush ran against Massachusetts Governor Michael Dukakis, who had clinched the Democratic Party nomination. Today Bush's campaign is remembered for an attack ad called "Weekend Passes," which was funded by the Americans for Bush arm of the National Security Political Action Committee (NSPAC). The ad likely cost Dukakis the election. The commercial accused Governor Dukakis of furloughing convicted criminal Willie Horton, who committed assault, armed robbery, and rape on leave from prison on a weekend furlough program, which he qualified for even though serving a life sentence for murder without the possibility of parole.

Covering the New York City mayoral election in 1989, the *New York Times* pointed out that liberal had become a dirty word. "Not long ago, law and order was one critical test that divided liberals from conservatives. Today, with crime the top issue on voters' minds, there is no candidate who will not promise to get tough with criminals."[41]

President George H. W. Bush would go on to perpetuate President Regan's harsh stance on drugs and a perceived lawlessness in the streets, seizing on American's fear of crime. In a September 1989 televised speech he gave on drug policy, President Bush held up a plastic bag filled with a thick white substance and announced, "This is crack cocaine" that was "seized a few days ago in a park across the street from the White House. . . . It could easily have been heroin or PCP."[42] The prop was orchestrated by Bush and his speechwriters to show the country how rampant America's drug problem had become. What the nation did not know was that DEA agents drove the drug dealer to the park across the street from the White House to make the sale. According to a *Washington Post* story published a few months after the speech, the drug dealer asked an undercover DEA Agent, "Where the [expletive] is the White House?" This statement was preserved as part of a conversation secretly tape-recorded by the DEA.[43]

Republicans were not the only ones who stood to gain from a punitive stance on crime. Having learned a lesson from the 1988 presidential election, presidential candidate Arkansas Governor Bill Clinton flew home to oversee the execution of Ricky Ray Rector, who was convicted of killing a police officer. This was a significant moment for the presidential hopeful, cementing his tough-on-crime public image.

In the last quarter of the twentieth century, state and federal sentencing laws grew more draconian. These included mandatory minimums, truth-in-sentencing, and "three strikes and you're out" laws; federal funding for prison construction; and sentencing regimes that sent more people to prison longer and exploded the prison population.[44]

States developed sentencing guidelines, enacted mandatory minimum sentences, and adopted reforms to increase time served and toughen penalties for certain offenses, especially drug charges. The first truth-in-sentencing laws were signed in Washington in 1984, and a domino effect ensued. These laws typically required inmates to serve a substantial portion of their prison sentence, usually 85 percent. By 1994, more than twenty states had enacted similar legislation. California enacted the first three-strikes law in 1994, which also had the intent to keep people in prison longer. If a defendant was convicted of any new felony after having one prior conviction for a serious felony, the defendant was sentenced to state prison for twice the term otherwise provided for the crime. If the defendant was convicted of any felony with two or more prior strikes, the law mandated a state prison term of twenty-five years to life.

Crime politics played out in every branch of government. In one illustrative example, during the 1998 Missouri U.S. Senate race between former governor Republican Christopher "Kit" Bond and the state's Democratic Attorney General Jay Nixon, the *St. Louis Post-Dispatch* pointed out that the two candidates could be running for the office of police chief instead of for the U.S. Senate.[45] Nixon criticized Bond for commuting the sentences of murderers, rapists, and other violent criminals, including allowing paroled inmates to get jobs as correction officers. Bond vilified Nixon for his office's inability to convict a man at trial who allegedly shot and killed a sheriff. The paper pointed out that the debate over "who is tougher on crime has virtually killed debate over their other key issues: health care, tobacco, education, Social Security and civil rights," and astutely pointed out: "So why are Nixon and Bond so obsessed with crime? Because the public is obsessed with crime, too."[46]

The 1994 Crime Bill and the Private Prison Industry

In 1994, Congress passed the Violent Crime Control and Law Enforcement Act, authorizing almost $8 billion (about $12.7 billion in 2017 dollars) in state construction grants for prisons and boot camps.

The legislation marked four decades of federal dollars being spent to support more arrests and more incarceration. The original 1994 act does not mention private prisons, but President Clinton's budget proposal for 1996 claimed it would "cut costs through privatization."

> While the Bureau of Prisons widely uses private facilities to house juvenile offenders and prisoners near the end of their sentences, the Administration plans to privatize the management and operations of most future Federal facilities under construction. Candidates include most future pretrial detention and minimum- and low security facilities now under construction. The Administration will privatize three of five minimum- and low-security prisons and one detention facility scheduled to open in 1996.[47]

The Appropriations Act of 1996, which amended the entire text of Subtitle A of the 1994 Crime Act, does explicitly mention the industry: "A State may use funds received under this subtitle for the privatization of facilities to carry out the purposes of section 20102."[48]

This new mention of private prisons may be attributable to well-timed testimony on Capitol Hill by the chairman of a company called Wackenhut, today known as the GEO Group. On July 27, 1995, Wackenhut Chairman Timothy Cole testified in front of Congress supporting specific amendments to the 1994 crime bill, including making clear that prison grants would "help pay for the entire range of correctional services states can provide in-house or under contract."[49] Cole testified, "Our proposed amendment . . . would help to assure that these grants will help the states incarcerate more violent criminals and not make the state governments more dependent on federal tax dollars in the long term."[50] He spoke about the "urgent need" for more cells in secure facilities and said, "current law encourages billions to be spent on new or retrofitted facilities that are not large enough, secure enough or efficient enough to keep the maximum number of violent criminals in prison for the least cost."[51]

By August 1994, Corrections Corporation of America (CCA) was hard at work building four new prisons to add to the fleet of seventeen the corporation owned or operated. Stock in CCA rose 11 percent during the crime bill debate, and at the time Wackenhut Corrections Corporation CEO George Zoley commented, "I always thought it was inevitable Congress would have to pass some sort of crime bill because crime is the public's top concern."[52] The week the crime bill passed, an analyst with Prudential Securities gave Wackenhut a "buy rating" and said that "private prisons are an idea whose time has come and whose use is accelerating rapidly."[53]

Twenty-eight states and the District of Columbia received truth-in-sentencing grants between 1996 and 1999.[54] In 1996 and 1997, Connecticut, Florida, Oregon, and Arizona were among the states to receive millions of dollars each in grant funding from the crime bill for enacting draconian laws that lengthened time behind bars. Before receiving this money, these four states passed legislation allowing or expanding the use of private contracts for correctional facilities.[55]

A few months after President Clinton signed the 1994 crime bill, which incentivized states to build more prisons and toughen sentences, White House Counsel and Advisor to the President Abner Mikva delivered a speech to Ohio law students: "In addition to the cost, there is a national shame factor. We now have more people in jail in relation to our population than any other country in the world. Are we really the most lawless nation around?"[56] When the White House counsel spoke to these students, incarceration had steadily increased from the mid-1970s to 1994 and reached a rate of 389 per 100,000 Americans. Unaccustomed to such high rates, Mikva and the rest of the country, were unaware that incarceration rates would keep rising.

When President Clinton left office in 2001, federal and state prison populations had risen under his watch more than under any other president, including under presidents George H. W. Bush and Ronald Reagan combined.[57] In fact, federal and state prison populations rose by 673,000 inmates during Clinton's eight-year tenure as president.[58]

Incarceration Grows

Did these punitive measures set the nation on a trajectory toward mass incarceration? The phrase "mass imprisonment" was coined by sociologist David Garland in 2000 for the rapid increase of imprisonment between 1975 and the late 1990s. Incarceration rates remained relatively steady for most of the twentieth century, but the 1980s and 1990s saw exponential increases. Between 1990 and 1995, the nation built 213 state and federal prisons (163 state and 45 federal) to house the rapidly growing prison population.[59] Despite this vast infusion of prison capacity, the Department of Justice reported in August of 1997 that as of the 1995 census about one in four state correctional facilities was under a court order or consent decree to limit its inmate population or address a specific condition of confinement.[60]

Prison construction continued at breakneck speed. The number of state and federal adult correction facilities had risen from 1,277 in 1990 to 1,821 by 2005—a whopping 43 percent increase.[61] The price of incarceration has been dramatic and far-reaching, both socially and economically. Today criminal justice spending totals more than $260 billion.[62]

Perhaps these statistics would not be so striking if it had always been this way. The Department of Justice's Bureau of Justice Statistics (BJS) has reported the annual imprisonment rate for state and federal prisons since 1926.[63] The imprisonment rate quadrupled between 1978 and 2014. Since 2009, due to reforms enacted by state legislatures, the prison population has declined marginally, by 3 percent,[64]

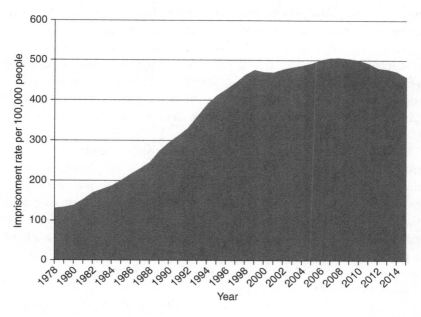

Figure 1.1 U.S. imprisonment rate, 1970–2015 *Source*: Bureau of Justice Statistics, various years.

and much of the decline is attributed to California. Partly because of a court order to reduce its state prison population and a ballot initiative that reclassified lower-level property and drug crimes as misdemeanors, California reduced its prison population by 20 percent, which accounts for 65 percent of the nationwide decrease.[65] Yet the decline is incremental.

The United States incarcerates more than 2.1 million people.[66] Nearly one out of every hundred adults is behind bars. Even more alarming, more than 70 million Americans (one in three people) have a criminal record.[67]

This incarceration rate is extraordinary considering that today's national crime rate is about half of what it was at its height in 1991. Violent crime has fallen by 51 percent and property crime by 43 percent. In 2013, the violent crime rate was the lowest since 1970. Despite dramatically safer streets, Americans remain petrified of crime and convinced it is rampant. For more than a decade, Gallup polling has found that the majority of Americans believe crime is up despite the fact that crime rates have plummeted in almost every small and large city since the 1990s. In fact, according to a 2016 Gallup poll, a majority of Americans worry "a great deal" about crime, and American's level of concern about crime and violence is at its highest point in fifteen years.[68]

A 2014 National Research Council report confirms what many researchers, criminal justice experts, and advocates have argued for years: incarceration rates have dramatically increased without yielding large crime-reduction benefits for the country, and high rates came about not because of an increase in crime but because of policy choices.[69]

Incapacitation is the dominant form of punishment today. Incapacitation refers to the goal of averting future crimes by physically isolating convicted individuals and removing them from society during the period of their incarceration. Many of these people are serving sentences hundreds or thousands of miles away from their families and communities. Seventy-four million children in the United States have a parent in prison. The nation is warehousing so many of its parents behind bars that just a few years ago *Sesame Street* introduced Alex, a Muppet whose father is in prison.

Almost two centuries after Tocqueville's visit, America's prisons still represent "the spectacle of complete despotism" he wrote about in the early 1800s. Sentences in this country are harsh, prisons are dangerously overcrowded, rates of sexual abuse are increasing, and rehabilitation programs in prisons are scarce or nonexistent.[70] The nation has participated in an imprisonment binge that it cannot afford, spending $80 billion on corrections annually. One out of nine state workers is employed in a prison, and, disconcertingly, many states spend more on incarceration than they do on education. In fact, eleven states spent more of their general funds on corrections than on higher education in 2013.[71]

The private prison industry emerged against this backdrop of increased incarceration rates, ultimately resulting in unprecedented growth in prison populations. The pressure of increased incarceration rates and runaway correctional costs paved the way for private companies to operate correctional facilities in the United States.

Privatization Takes Hold in the Criminal Justice System

Privatizing government services is not new. Private police and security guards have long kept Americans safe. Private judges and arbitrators hear cases when parties agree to forgo traditional court proceedings, and private military contractors have sometimes outnumbered ground troops during wartime. Today corrections is a multi-billion-dollar industry encompassing food services, telephone and video visitation services, email, health care, transportation, education, rehabilitation, and even specially made niche items such as rubber pencils that can't be used to stab someone. Private industry is enmeshed in the very fabric of "public" corrections. As Harvard Business School Professor Herman Leonard wrote, "No state agency makes its own chain link fence or steel reinforcing rods."[72]

The 1980s gave birth to a new form of correctional privatization: corporations that owned and managed prisons. *Barron's* noted, "There's a whole new industry developing . . . from the unlikely meeting of pinstripes and prison stripes."[73] In 1984, the United States spent $10 billion on corrections. With most correctional facilities filled to the brim with inmates, conditions were ripe for a prison boom.

Currently, eighteen states and the federal Bureau of Prisons are operating prisons above their largest maximum design capacity. Prison facilities in Illinois are holding so many inmates that they have far exceeded the state's design capacity and are housing inmates at 165 percent of the state's design capacity. Other jurisdictions with more inmates than the maximum number of beds include Nebraska (125 percent), Massachusetts (123 percent), and Delaware (117 percent). In total, Bureau of Prisons facilities could house 134,500 inmates in 2015, but instead housed 161,000 prisoners—120 percent of the maximum capacity.[74]

Newspapers show pictures of inmates double- and triple-bunked in prison gymnasiums. Suicide and sexual abuse is prevalent behind bars. Some argue that this is enough to justify relying on private corporations to ease the burden of governments that simply can't keep up with the demand for prison cells.

Hiding in plain sight is America's massive private prison industry. Although the prison boom of the 1980s and 1990s has slowed, most new prison construction has been funded by private corporations. Almost all new prisons that opened their doors from 2000 to 2005 were private; the number of private facilities increased from 16 percent (264) to 23 percent (415) of all institutions during those years.[75]

The *privatization of prisons* refers to the takeover of existing government prisons by private corporations and to the building and operation of new prisons by for-profit firms. Private prisons can hold inmates from any state if the state is not legislatively barred from doing so. North Dakota and Oregon are the only states that specifically bar exporting prisoners out of state for profits.[76] Some private prisons contain inmates in the state where the facility is located, and others house inmates from several states who are transported to private facilities across the country to reduce costs and overcrowding.

The Department of Justice began tracking the number of prisoners in private facilities annually through the National Prisoner Statistics (NPS) in 1999. As noted in figure 1.2, the prison population housed in private prisons has grown 77 percent since 1999, from 71,208 prisoners in 1999 to 126,272 in 2015 (a little more than 8 percent of the total U.S. prison population).[77] The overall prison population grew only 11.9 percent (from 1,363,686 to 1,526,792 prisoners) during the same time.[78]

Private prison use was at its maximum in 2012, when 137,200 inmates (almost 9 percent of the total U.S. prison population) were housed in private facilities.[79] There are now at least 190 private prisons and detention centers in the United States.[80]

Since the private prison industry was born in the mid-1980s, private prisons have exploded into a $5 billion industry. Revenue for the nation's two largest private prisons corporations, GEO Group and CoreCivic, has climbed more than 86 percent since 2006.[81]

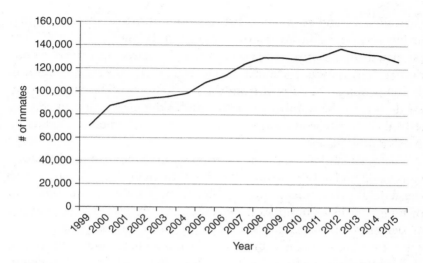

Figure 1.2 Number of Federal and State Inmates Held in Private Prisons, 1999–2015 *Sources*: "Prisoners Series, 1999–2015," Bureau of Justice Statistics, and Ann E. Carson and Elizabeth Anderson, "Prisoners in 2015," Bureau of Justice Statistics Bulletin NCJ 250229, December 2016.

These companies—both publicly traded on the stock exchange—earned a combined $4.3 billion, with $382 million in profits in 2016 alone (see figure 1.3).[82] This is more than Airbnb, Snapchat, Pandora, and the Dallas Cowboys combined.[83]

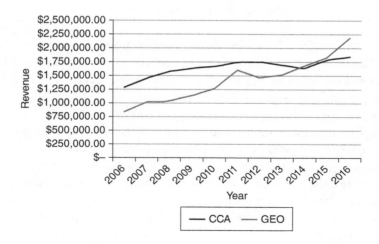

Figure 1.3 CCA and GEO Group Annual Revenue, 2006–2016 *Sources*: Annual reports of GEO Group and Correction Corporation of America, 2006–2016.

Academics and researchers express optimism that the nation may finally reverse its incarceration binge, but change is sluggish. The estimated total number of prisoners held by state and federal correction authorities was 1,526,800 on December 31, 2015, a reduction of 35,500 people, or 2 percent from the previous year. This was the largest decline in the number of people under the jurisdiction of state or federal correctional authorities since 1978.[84] Yet a 2 percent reduction is still a modest one.

The state and federal prison population is not the entire story. CoreCivic and GEO Group owe much of their financial success to the federal government's willingness to turn over the management of huge swaths of immigrant detainees. <u>Private prisons house about 65 percent of Immigration and Customs Enforcement (ICE) detainees</u>.[85] In total, CoreCivic and GEO Group each currently run twelve ICE contracted facilities. In fact, nine of the ten largest ICE detention centers are private, and nearly a fifth of GEO Group's business comes from ICE contracts.[86] With the inauguration of Donald Trump as the nation's forty-fifth president—a man who called for the removal of people who have only been charged with a crime, including those whose only crime may simply be being in the country illegally—the country is poised for an increase in the number of private detention facilities.

Should We Privatize Prisons?

Should the United States privatize its corrections? Supporters advocate that they are an innovative, cost-effective way to build and run prisons. They point to the benefits of using private capital to bear the costs of building correctional facilities.

Critics argue that private prisons are profitable because they cut corners to save on costs, prioritizing profits above all else. Detractors don't believe in punishment for profit and contend that our criminal justice system is a function of the state. They point to inherent conflicts of interest when the private sector operates prisons. Other criticisms against private prisons focus on high staff turnover rates (staffing costs account for about 80 percent of operational expenses for prisons), higher rates of violence, lack of public accountability, and little evidence that private prisons save taxpayer money after all.

One of the biggest criticisms levied against these corporations is their business model. Opponents of the industry worry that the profit motive is deeply at odds with the goal of corrections, which is to treat and rehabilitate individuals in an attempt to keep them from returning to prison. Higher recidivism rates (one's likelihood of returning to prison) are financially lucrative for the private prison industry. At the heart of this debate are disagreements about the ways companies can maximize profits by housing as many inmates as possible at the lowest cost, with little oversight and limited accountability. Many feel there is a basic ideological conflict between reducing the sheer number of people behind bars with the financial incentives of private prison operators to incarcerate as many people as they can.

Private prison companies are paid on a per capita basis to house inmates, and reforms to criminal justice that reduce incarceration are a threat to their business. In its 2016 annual report, CoreCivic—a company that owns almost 60 percent of all private prison beds in the United States—lists risk factors that would decrease the demand for their facilities: "the relaxation of enforcement efforts, leniency in conviction or parole standards and sentencing practices or through the decriminalization of certain activities that are currently proscribed by criminal laws. For instance, any changes with respect to drugs and controlled substances or illegal immigration could affect the number of persons arrested, convicted, and sentenced, thereby potentially reducing demand for correctional facilities to house them."[87] Many private prison contracts are structured on predetermined occupancy rates, regardless of whether beds are full. Some contracts require 100 percent inmate occupancy, forcing states to keep their prisons filled to capacity or pay for unused beds. The nation's largest for-profit prison companies have consolidated over the last three decades and now wield incredible influence in how many prisons are built, where inmates are housed, and what towns are made or devastated by the unpredictability of new prison construction.

A central question emerges: "Does contracting out private correctional services significantly change how we punish such that it compromises our democratic values?" Some argue that private prisons have become a symbolic statement of the nation's morals. Jeremy Travis, former director of the National Institute of Justice, argues that the United States has exceeded the point where the number of people in prison can be justified by social benefits; instead, it produces injustice and social harm.[88] Changes in sentencing policy, prison policy, and social policy to reduce the nation's incarceration footprint are all recommended. "I think there is a deep need on the part of Americans to identify evil forces," said Travis. "There is no research indicating that the way we provide detention services is a cause of the rise in incarceration. The human mind needs to wrap its head around a single cause or theory."[89]

If improving the criminal justice system is our ultimate goal, is the movement to eliminate private prisons a distraction from improving the lives of those who cycle into and out of our nation's prisons? I focus on this question in the chapters that follow.

As state and prison populations have stabilized, for-profit prison corporations are reading the tea leaves and diversifying their business model. The ACLU wrote that CoreCivic plans to become the "Wal-Mart of reentry."[90] In 2013, CoreCivic purchased Correctional Alternatives, which focuses on reentry programs and home confinement. GEO Group saw the value in investing in reentry services before its biggest competitor did and positioned itself as a government partner. In 2009 GEO Group purchased Just Care, a medical and mental health service provider, and two years later it bought Behavioral Interventions, which bills itself as the world's largest producer of monitoring equipment for those awaiting trial or serving probation or parole sentences. In the spring of 2017, GEO Group purchased Community Education Centers, a national provider of rehabilitative services in reentry services with beds in more than thirty government-operated facilities.

Private prison corporations are hedging their bets by expanding their business model in light of significant sentencing reform sweeping the nation. Although arguably a more humane business endeavor than warehousing hundreds of thousands of inmates behind metal bars, many criminal justice experts such as sociologist Michael Jacobson, who formerly ran New York City's Department of Corrections, worry about introducing private capital into the world of reentry and community corrections. "You don't want to mess with the fabulous job parole is doing now," Jacobson said (sarcastically), "But you can actually do worse."[91]

For Jacobson and many others, the line is clearly drawn. They worry about the financial incentives of for-profit corporations who build their companies on warehousing Americans. The entry of for-profit corporations into this new world of community corrections ought to be monitored to ensure that the financial incentives are structured appropriately, perhaps based on recidivism rates and employment success. As the nation's criminal justice landscape changes, the for-profit prison industry will either sustain mass incarceration or inspire reform of the necessary reentry and job training services for the 700,000 people who are released from prison each year.

Who opened the window for private prisons? To understand where they come from, chapter 2 looks at the privatization of government services that started in the early 1800s.

CHAPTER TWO

How the Government
Privatized

Privatization follows in the great tradition of free enterprise
and private ownership of property that has long been
a part of American history.

PRESIDENT RONALD REAGAN, STATEMENT ON THE PRESIDENT'S
COMMISSION ON PRIVATIZATION, SEPTEMBER 3, 1987

THE U.S. GOVERNMENT has contracted out or sold its services to
private business for more than two centuries. As early as the 1800s,
privately operated bridges, toll roads, fire departments, and street lights
were common.[1] Proponents of privatization say reducing the role of
big, bureaucratic government provides opportunities for businesses to
compete in the open market, and private industry can provide services
more efficiently—or at least cheaper—than the government. State and
local governments today frequently contract out fire services, paramed-
ics, ambulance services, road construction and maintenance, garbage
collection, police, and even jails and prisons.[2]

1950s to 1970s

St. Louis, Missouri, provides a case study for how essential government services have been privatized. Crime rates in the city had mark-
edly increased in the 1950s, and some middle-class residents petitioned
the city for the deed to their streets, taking ownership of their own

neighborhoods with the idea that they could improve public safety.[3] A mother of two who lived on a private street in St. Louis told journalist Theodore Gage, "One night about eleven o'clock, I was walking the dog and she got away, I called out, and the lights in about five houses went on and a couple of people stuck their heads out their doors. It's the kind of thing that makes you feel pretty secure."[4]

With the deed, the residents became responsible for maintaining their streets, sewers, streetlights, garbage collection, and security services except fire and police, which were provided by the city.[5] Title to the streets was deeded to the property owners and "vested in an incorporated street association to which all property owners must belong and pay dues."[6] These property owners restricted the vehicles that could enter the street to their own vehicles and those of their visitors—and they meant business. If a neighbor failed to follow the regulations of the street association, residents could ask the court for an order for compliance.[7]

This practice fell out of favor in St. Louis in the 1960s but became popular again in the 1970s. One study comparing crime rates in private and public streets in the city found that the crime rate for adjacent public streets was 108 percent higher than the rate for private streets.[8]

Rising crime rates were a financial boon for the private security industry. In addition to privatizing streets, in the 1960s and 1970s homeowners increased their private means of security, buying alarm systems, window bars, and safes.[9] A 1971 Rand Corporation study found that private security services generated substantially more employment and money than did local, state, and federal law enforcement services combined.[10]

President Reagan's Privatization Push

In the 1980s, the idea of privatization provided an outlet for those frustrated by the rising cost and perceived ineffectiveness of government. President Ronald Reagan championed the privatization of government services and created two commissions to study this.

When air traffic controllers went on strike in 1981 as part of a labor dispute about working conditions and salaries, President Reagan claimed the strike violated the federal no-strike law and ordered the air traffic controllers to return to their jobs or face termination of their employment. When they did not return to work, President Reagan fired all 11,345 participating air traffic controllers belonging to the Professional Air Traffic Controllers Organization (PATCO).

Although many saw this as a union-busting move, it is difficult to decouple Reagan's actions from his push for privatization. By drawing attention to the strike and increasing the publicity of the walkout and his across-the-board firing, Reagan drew attention to the inconvenience and safety problems public sector unions could wreak on critical services.

In June 1982, Reagan created the President's Private Sector Survey on Cost Control, referred to as the "Grace Commission," whose chairman was J. Peter Grace, CEO of W. R. Grace & Company.[11] The commission included more than 150 top executives from the nation's largest companies and financial institutions. Its mandate was to "conduct a private sector survey on cost control in the Federal Government" and advise the president "with respect to improving management and reducing costs."[12] More succinctly, Reagan told the commission to "work like tireless bloodhounds" in its search for waste and inefficiency in the federal government.[13]

Grace shared Reagan's unease about the federal government's inefficient spending and said in a 1983 interview: "I have 9 children, 12 grandchildren, and I'm concerned about their freedom. . . . We've got to get this growth rate and the outlays down. It can't go on this way. If this deficit goes to $1 trillion a year, our freedoms are gone."[14]

A vast undertaking, the commission consisted of thirty-five separate task forces that examined ways to improve the efficiency of federal agencies. The task forces themselves relied on the work of roughly a thousand experts from companies across the nation. The commission's "Report on Privatization" urged adoption of nearly 2,500 recommendations to eliminate waste in government that could save $424.4 billion over three years. Speaking about the commission's findings in January 1983, Grace did not mince words: "The government is run horribly."[15] One of the commission's most notable findings proposed that the federal government turn over the dams and power stations in the Pacific Northwest to private enterprise, for a three-year savings of $20 billion, or raise electricity rates to market levels for $4.5 billion in new revenues.

The Grace Commission's eighteen-month inquiry caused Democrats in Congress to point fingers at the commission's inherent conflict of interest: relying on corporate executives to root out government waste and propose policies that would benefit their bottom lines. But even so, the largest commission ever created to study the privatization of government services and elimination of government waste made waves. State and local governments followed suit and created their own privatization commissions. Citizens Against Government Waste was established and provided a toll-free hotline for citizens to report government waste.[16]

A mere four years later, the President's Commission on Privatization was created. Reagan appointed University of Illinois economist and professor David F. Linowes to chair the twelve-member commission. Reagan stated that the "Commission will propose how we can return appropriate Federal activities to the private sector through the safe government operations and assets, the use of private enterprise to provide services for government agencies, or the use of vouchers to provide services to the public through the private sector."[17]

Established to study the breadth of activities that could be transferred to the private sector and to explore the transition across multiple government agencies, the commission studied everything from low-income housing, to air traffic control, to contracting out military and correctional services. A year later the commission detailed their recommendations for "increased private sector participation" in the delivery of almost every government service they studied, from low-income housing, to the postal service, to selling off Amtrak.

The report recommended that some of the Federal Aviation Administration (FAA) air traffic controller jobs were ripe for privatization because the "private sector can be more flexible in personnel requirements than the public sector."[18] The report also devoted a chapter to the privatization of prisons, recommending that local, state, and federal prisons be privatized because the private sector provides significant flexibility in assisting the government in recalibrating the size of its prison system more quickly and at lower cost.

The report pointed out the overcrowded conditions in the country's prisons and jails, finding that "41 states and the District of Columbia were either under court order to improve conditions or subject to litigation challenging their operations."[19] The voluminous report also found that the government's ability to contract out prisons to private companies "gives public officials a method to meet their responsibilities to provide facilities to accommodate prisoners while avoiding some of the constraints imposed by spending limitations and local resistance to prison siting decisions."[20] The commission found that prisons were not only overcrowded but also out-of-date: "the average prison cell is 40 years old, and 10 percent of convicts are placed in prisons built before 1875."[21]

The report recommended that the Department of Justice prioritize research on private sector involvement in corrections and supported the exploration of how to privatize more prisons. Foreshadowing the enormous reliance the federal government would develop with the private sector to house immigrant detainees, the report also recommended that Immigration and Naturalization Services (INS) ["be encouraged to continue to experiment and to evaluate the cost and effectiveness of contracting its detention facilities."[22]]

President Reagan supported the broader notion of privatization, but his administration didn't sell very many assets. One exception is Conrail, a freight railroad privatized in 1987 for $1.65 billion. The sale of Conrail was a high-water mark for the Reagan administration: the administration's first successful privatization initiative and the largest public stock offering in U.S. history. Elizabeth H. Dole, Secretary of Transportation, said, "We have succeeded in the largest privatization in U.S. history, and this success should break ground for more privatizations to come."[23]

Although Reagan tried to privatize many government services, his administration can only point to Conrail as a successful endeavor in this arena. Nevertheless, Reagan's privatization commission paved the way for subsequent administrations. His friend, British Prime Minister Margaret Thatcher, began the privatization trend in the United Kingdom that led to the British government selling more than a trillion dollars' worth of state-owned services to investors in the 1980s and 1990s.[24]

Paradoxically, President Bill Clinton made more headway than President Reagan with his selloff of the El Hills Naval Petroleum Reserves for $3.6 billion, the U.S. Enrichment Corporation for $3.1 billion, and selling billions of dollars of electromagnetic spectrum.[25] Clinton also began competitive contracting for more than a hundred airport control towers and select military base functions.

Privatization Today

Today the breadth of U.S. privatization of government services is remarkable. A 2011 survey on local government contracting, privatization, and outsourcing practices found that the most commonly outsourced government services are solid waste, road and bridge construction, and pension fund services.[26] In 1995, the top ten most privatized services in the largest U.S. cities were ambulance services, building security, drug and alcohol treatment, employment and training, legal services, printing services, solid waste collection, streets and signals, street repair, and vehicle towing.[27] In 2001, the average city provided almost forty different services, and of these, 20 percent were privatized.[28]

Sandy Spring, Georgia, with a little over 100,000 people, has taken this philosophy to an extreme. It has privatized every part of the government (except fire and police services) and outsourced it all to a single company, which purchased a commercial building to serve as the seat of City Hall. The city runs surpluses every year and has no unfunded liabilities.[29]

The waste management industry leads the pack in U.S. privatized government services, reflected in its $55 billion in revenues. In fact, private firms claim a 78 percent market share of the industry while government controls the remaining 22 percent.[30]

Firefighting also has its roots in the private sphere. In the early 1800s, private fire brigades competed with one another to arrive first at the scene once insurance companies began to pay the brigades bonuses for extinguishing fires. The competition was so intense that some fire companies hired criminals to help them compete to put out fires. In 1853, Cincinnati introduced the first paid municipal fire department, partly to professionalize the industry and reduce the violence and chaos that competition had produced.[31] In recent years, Scottsdale, Arizona, reported cost savings as high as 50 percent for private fire services.[32]

Criminal justice legal services are no exception to the privatization movement. Public defense often is contracted out to nonprofits or to individual defense counsels where a conflict of interest arises, which is common in multiple defendant cases. Some cities even contract out the role of the prosecutor. Officials in Albany, Oregon, recently paid a private law firm an annual fee of more than $200,000 for prosecution and other legal services.[33] Governments have contracted out the use of private prosecutors in handgun, lead paint, tobacco, and antitrust litigation, and even retained "a Wall Street firm to serve as a legal advisor to the Treasury Department on the implementation of the 2008 financial bailout."[34]

The Internal Revenue Service (IRS) also contracts out some of its legal work. In 2013, the IRS paid the white shoe litigation shop Quinn Emanuel to help conduct the examination of Microsoft Corporation's tax returns, specifically its audit of Microsoft's cost-sharing arrangements with affiliates in Puerto Rico and Asia. Some criticized the decision to allow a private law firm to examine Microsoft's tax returns as a delegation of a core government function.[35]

Judicial services frequently are contracted out in ways that don't appear private because they are seamlessly woven into the court system. At least 75 percent of commercial disputes are settled through private arbitration or mediation, which are essentially out-of-court solutions to dispute resolution.[36]

In California, private judges, affectionately referred to as "rent-a-judges," are officially part of the state court system. In 1976, two California lawyers discovered an 1872 law authorizing individuals in a dispute to have a court hearing before "any referee they choose."[37] At the time, California had a substantial case backlog with a median pretrial delay of a little over four years.[38] These enterprising attorneys— who wanted a complex case settled with speed—located a retired judge who had the necessary knowledge in the specifics of the conflict at issue. They paid the former judge attorney's fee rates, and in the process ultimately saved their clients a good deal of money.[39]

At first blush, the judge looks and smells like any other judge, except for the method of payment. The parties split the cost of the private judge's time. These costs are usually considerably less than the costs of protracted litigation and save litigants time in backlogged court systems where they would have to wait months, if not years, for their cases to be heard and resolved. [The practice has been criticized for creating a two-tiered legal system: one for the wealthy who can afford to rent a judge at prices sometimes upward of $1,000 a day, and one for the poor who have to wait years for access to the courts.[40]]

The U.S. government has contracted out military services since its earliest days as a nation. Contractors were hired as wagon drivers and suppliers of beef, clothing, weapons, and engineering services during the Revolutionary War.[41] In recent decades, the United States has become increasingly dependent on military contractors for operations overseas. During the Bush administration's growing dependence on private firms to protect the country, this new civilian workforce was described as a "shadow army": "When U.S. tanks rolled into Baghdad in March 2003, they brought with them the largest army of private contractors ever deployed in modern war."[42]

By the fall of 2012, approximately 137,000 contractors were working for the Pentagon in Iraq, Afghanistan, and eighteen other countries.[43] Of that total, 40,110 were U.S. citizens, 50,560 were local hires, and 46,231 were from neither the United States nor the country in which they were working.[44] In fact, there were more military contractors in Iraq and Afghanistan than the number of U.S. ground troops in both countries.[45] With the significant withdrawal of troops from Iraq and Afghanistan, substantially fewer military contractors were used by 2016. U.S. Central Command reported approximately 45,550 contractor personnel in early 2017.[46]

Military contracts extend well beyond boots on the ground. The United States relies heavily on private businesses to produce military equipment and ammunition. In 2015, Lockheed Martin, the country's largest defense contractor, derived 78 percent of its $46.1 billion in net sales from the U.S. government, and 58 percent of that was from the Department of Defense.[47]

The United States also relies on private contractors to provide military training and security in combat zones. Private military corporations (PMCs) reduce the stress and burden on troops operating in hostile areas by providing support and security services. Blackwater, now called Academi, is notorious for its controversial tactics. Blackwater's founder Erik Prince infamously stated, "We are trying to do for the national security apparatus what FedEx did for the Postal Service."[48]

These quasi-government relationships often are plagued by complicated issues around the government delegating core public responsibilities. In the fall of 2007, Blackwater military contractors were accused of killing seventeen Iraqi civilians in Nisour Square, Baghdad, when the private guards—who were working for the U.S. State Department at the time—fired machine guns and grenades from their armored vehicles under the mistaken idea that they were under attack. The episode marked a horrific moment in the Iraq War and highlighted how dependent the United States had become on military contractors such as Blackwater—which was awarded more than $1 billion in government contracts—to maintain security in combat zones around the world.[49]

Currently, the private military industry grosses several hundred billion dollars annually and operates in more than one hundred countries on six continents.[50] PMCs also provide cover for the U.S. government.

For example, deaths of PMC members are not counted in official military death toll statistics.

Like military contracts, policing is rooted in private activity. "The policing of homicides in ancient Athens was primarily a family matter."[51] Although government-run police forces emerged in the United States in the mid-1800s, private police forces predate public policing in America.[52] In colonial times, communities paid sheriffs and constables on a fee-for-service basis, with payment dependent upon the number of arrests made, subpoenas served, or tax dollars collected.[53] These constables and sheriffs delegated responsibilities to other workers that they hired at their own discretion.[54]

It was not until the early 1800s that policing became a serious public function both in England and in the United States. As more people moved from rural areas into urban London during the eighteenth and nineteenth centuries, a dire need to maintain law and order emerged. Sir Robert Peel, Secretary of the Home Office, established the first modern urban police department with the passage of the Metropolitan Police Act, which authorized the creation of the London Metropolitan Police Department. The officers later became known as "bobbies" in a tribute to Peel.[55]

Across the Atlantic, in 1838, the city of Boston modeled its police agency after the London Metropolitan Police Department. One year later New York followed suit. As the U.S. population more than doubled from the 1860s to the early 1900s, the population of police officers more than tripled.[56] Soon the nineteenth-century police forces were unable to handle the population in the cities, and corruption among law enforcement became rampant. As a result, wealthy families paid for their own private protection and "citizens took policing into their own hands."[57]

Even as police departments took root in the United States, law enforcement struggled with inadequate funding. Dwindling budgets and increasing personnel costs have made it difficult for police agencies to remain fully staffed and to police effectively. This paved the way for increased paid private security (store detectives, security guards) and for the civilianization of police organizations. Civilian employees now perform many of the duties historically provided by sworn officers—911 dispatchers, crime analysts, evidence management specialists, and public information officers—which saves police department's significant money, especially because civilians are not unionized and are easier to fire. St. Petersburg, Florida, and other cities have contracted with private firms in lieu of hiring more police officers.

Today private police officers outnumber their publicly funded counterparts roughly three to one nationwide.[58] In the early 1950s, the city of Kalamazoo, Michigan, was the first to hire an all-private police force, granting a private firm responsibility for street patrols and arresting traffic offenders.[59] Critics of privatization claim that the practice shifts financial burdens from government budgets to the end users, allowing private firms to collect compensation from those they serve. As the privatization watchdog group In the Public Interest points out, "public services ranging from tax collection to probation have been impacted by this 'user-funded' dynamic."[60]

An increasing number of governments have signed contracts with private, for-profit companies that offer misdemeanor probation services at no cost to the government in exchange for the right to collect fees from the probationers they supervise. In this arrangement, people who cannot pay their fine in full at the time of sentencing are given probation because they need more time to make their payment. In Georgia, 80 percent of those who receive probation as punishment for misdemeanor offenses—including offenses as minor as traffic infractions—are supervised by private contractors. Because so many courts and state agencies lack the resources to supervise misdemeanor defendants, a growing number are contracting out supervision services to private companies. More than a thousand court systems across at least ten states use these private probation services.

"Pay only probation" discriminates against the poor because they are charged significant fees because they cannot afford the fine up front. In some cases, these fees reach thousands of dollars, and delinquency on the fee or the fines can lead to imprisonment. In Georgia, where thirty or more companies supervise more than 140,000 probationers, the Georgia Department of Audits found a high frequency of case management problems, including failure to impose general supervision standards, failure to respond to probationers who missed reporting dates, and cases in which people were required to continue paying probation fees after their probation terms expired.

With President Trump in the White House, Reagan's push for privatization has come full circle. Trump created the White House Office of American Innovation, which plans to incorporate the ideas of private sector leaders to improve how the federal government does business.

Shortly after the office was created, the *Washington Post* reported that "the office could direct that government functions be privatized, or that existing contracts be awarded to new bidders."[61]

Given the sheer breadth of privatized government services, the privatization of corrections doesn't seem like such an outlier. As long as this country has had prisoners, they have come with a price tag. Inmates have been valued for their labor, for the money to be made off the beds they sleep in each night, and for their potential to buy products they need behind bars. The privatization of corrections takes many forms.

CHAPTER THREE

Prisoners as Commodities

I would never apply the word *commodity* to human beings.
I would say that they are becoming some kind of economic unit
that represents a cost and, to the receiving facility or region,
represents an economic benefit.

JAMES R. ROBERTS, VICE PRESIDENT OF DOMINION[1]

THE EMERGENCE OF private prisons in the late twentieth century does not mark the first time private industry has profited from U.S. prisoners. Indeed, whether through slavery or incarceration, the United States has a long history of using captive labor for economic purposes, separate and apart from the moral or ethical questions that these practices present. Incarcerated people, much like slaves, were first and foremost a cheap and disenfranchised form of labor.

Early Prison Profiteers

Before the Revolutionary War, the British government sent thousands of convicted individuals to the Colonies to serve their prison sentences. The practice of "transportation" was deemed beneficial to Britain because it provided a way to remove the criminal element from society. The British government also avoided paying to house and feed these individuals in their jails by paying British merchant shippers the cost of the journey to transport these individuals to the Colonies. Those lucky enough to survive the long journey at sea, which was filled with outbreaks of typhoid and cholera, would become indentured servants. Once the boats arrived, merchants made money by auctioning off the convicted individuals, mostly to plantation owners, who bought the prisoners for their labor. After the war, as the number of slaves grew, especially in southern states, the practice of transporting convicted individuals was replaced with the slave trade.

One early example of how private prisons emerged comes from Kentucky, where prison privatization first took hold in 1825.[2] The state leased the eighty-five-inmate Kentucky State Penitentiary at Frankfurt to Joel Scott, a businessman and textile manufacturer who pledged to return half of the net prison labor profits to the state.[3] The contract authorized Scott to employ the inmates in "hard labor" and gave him the power to "inflict such punishment, either by solitary confinement or otherwise, as may be reasonable and best calculated" to meet the employment and manufacturing objectives described.[4] The incarcerated men constructed chairs, shoes, wagons, sleighs, and engaged in weaving. Two-thirds of the inmates were engaged making rope from hemp. This privatized leasing model continued in Kentucky for fifty-five years.[5]

Many trace the origins of privatization in corrections to the emergence of the 'convict lease system', which became prevalent after the Civil War during Reconstruction. The Thirteenth Amendment—most famous for abolishing slavery—simultaneously abolished "involuntary servitude, except as a punishment for crime whereof the party shall have been duly convicted." After slaves were released from their owners' captivity, they were frequently labeled "trespassers," "vagrants," and "loiterers" on their former owners' plantations.[6] In 1876, the Mississippi legislature passed the "Pig Law," which redefined grand larceny as "the theft of a farm animal or any property valued at ten dollars or more." Violation of Mississippi's Pig Law resulted in up to five years in prison.[7] Once incarcerated for these petty crimes, former slaves found themselves leased to private companies and forced to rebuild after the destruction of the Civil War. The convict lease system emerged as a new form of slavery, with the Thirteenth Amendment's "conviction" exception functionally imposing a de facto form of slavery that it ostensibly legally abolished.

Convict leasing attempted to solve the labor shortage facing the southern economy and provided southern states with revenue after the Civil War. In practice, a private company would pay a fee to the government for the lease of its convicts, and the private vendor would house, feed, and even discipline the convicted individuals. The convict lease system put these inmates—almost all of whom were former slaves—to work mining coal, logging, creating turpentine, laying railroad track, and working farms and plantations.[8] Leasing out convicts allowed industries to pay significantly lower wages than would be paid to workers who were not imprisoned. In 1868, Georgia issued a convict lease for prisoners to businessman William Fort for work on the Georgia and Alabama Railroad. The contract specified "one hundred able bodied and healthy Negro convicts" in return for a fee to the state of $2,500.[9]

These inmates, almost all black, worked long hours in unsafe conditions and often were treated worse than they had been as slaves. One account notes that those who died as part of these construction projects had their bodies tossed into the excavations where they became part of the levees they were building.[10] In South Carolina, for example, the death rate of inmates leased to the railroad industry was 45 percent in the late 1870s.[11] Although record keeping was not very meticulous, between 1885 and 1920 "ten thousand to twenty thousand debtors, convicts, and prisoners toiled under these circumstances on an average day, the great majority of them African-American."[12]

The convict lease system ended at the close of the nineteenth century, mostly due to the deteriorating economic conditions sweeping the nation. In Tennessee, for example, the economic depression of the 1890s depleted the profitability of the mining industry, which had taken advantage of most of the inmate labor.[13] Around this time, a handful of states delegated the management of their prisons to wealthy entrepreneurs. By 1885, thirteen states contracted out their incarcerated populations to private contractors.[14]

In Louisiana, Samuel James, a Confederate major, was awarded a lease in 1869 to run the Louisiana State Penitentiary.[15] Eleven years later, Major James bought Angola, an 8,000-acre plantation where he kept prisoners who were otherwise occupied building levees on the Mississippi River. His son took over the lease after James died in 1894, but media accounts of inhumane conditions inflicted on the prisoners forced the state of Louisiana to retake control of the state penitentiary system in 1901.

California's San Quentin Prison also traces its roots to private management. Famous today for housing the largest death row in the country, San Quentin was one of the country's first private prisons. In 1851, California leased San Quentin for ten years to two private entrepreneurs, James E. Estell and Mariano Guadalupe. Although there were only thirty-five state prisoners when the two businessmen signed the contract, a decade later the state prison population had grown to more than 600 inmates.[16] According to accounts from the time, inmates slept on a ship offshore at night and built the prison by day, completing it in 1854.[17] The prison eventually became notorious for its political corruption and budget woes. The guards mingled and drank with the men incarcerated at the prison, escapes were frequent, and it was rumored that the owners sold pardons for $200.[18] Estell allegedly forced prisoners to make bricks and even refused to construct a wall to keep the inmates inside the prison grounds, forcing the state of California to build a wall at the prison. Before the state reluctantly erected the wall, almost fifty inmates escaped every year.[19]

In 1857, Governor John B. Weller, who disliked Estell and coincidentally happened to be running for the U.S. Senate, took the political opportunity to seize control of the prison in the presence of reporters. Although effective for publicity, the move was eventually ruled illegal by the Supreme Court of California because the lease was still active. San Quentin was returned to Estell, but he soon died and John F. McCauley and Lloyd Tevis became the owners of the prison contract.

McCauley, like his predecessors, turned a blind eye to conditions at San Quentin and was known to ignore prison inspectors and keep "prisoners barefoot and half-clothed."[20] None too pleased by this treatment of state prisoners, the California legislature voided the lease with McCauley, and Governor Weller took back the prison in the spring of 1858. McCauley sued the state and the governor for restitution of the seized property and prevailed in court. The judge ordered the state to return the prison to McCauley with an additional $12,229 plus court costs. On April 14, 1860, McCauley sailed to San Quentin on a chartered boat with a brass band.[21] After a short-lived return, McCauley accepted the state's offer of $275,000 and returned the operation of the prison to the state of California. The state has owned and operated San Quentin ever since.

Foreshadowing the 2016 sudden curtailment by the Department of Justice of relying on private prisons, in 1887 Congress passed a law forbidding contracting for any inmates in the federal prison system.

A domino effect ensued; New York banned private prison contractors in 1897, with Massachusetts and Pennsylvania quickly passing their own legislation to eliminate private prisons in their states. Newspaper accounts of appalling conditions, malnourishment, whippings, and overcrowding ultimately motivated states to terminate leases on privately run state prisons in the early 1900s.

This history provides some context for examining modern privatization in corrections. In fact, the privatization of inmates in the United States is inexorably intertwined with how jails and prisons emerged and were formed. Although important lessons can be learned from America's early dabbling in private corrections, today's mega corporations operate within a set of norms, rules, and regulations that simply did not exist in the nineteenth century. As UCLA law professor Sharon Dolovich has written: "Today, there is also a stricter standard of political accountability, an extensive public bureaucracy with the capacity to regulate and administer complex institutions, and the default expectation that the state bears the burden of financing the prison system."[22]

Despite modern regulations and laws restricting how private corporations operate in corrections, the legacy of slavery morphing into convict leasing casts a pall on modern-day incarceration. African Americans are incarcerated in state prisons at a rate six times that of whites, and in five states (Iowa, Minnesota, New Jersey, Vermont, and Wisconsin) the ratio is more than ten to one.[23] The nation's policies created these disparities, but the legacy of profiting off of human suffering still haunts the privatization of corrections today.

Much of the first half of the twentieth century was marked by legislation limiting the privatization of corrections. Between 1929 and 1940, Congress enacted three separate laws aimed at protecting workers who faced stiff competition from the low-wage prison labor supply during the Great Depression. The Hawes-Cooper Act was enacted in 1929 and required that goods produced by out-of-state prison labor be subject to the laws of the importing state.[24] As a result, states with laws on the books prohibiting in-state prison goods could restrict the sale of goods produced by out-of-state prisoners. Six years later, in 1935, Congress passed the Ashurst-Sumners Act, strengthening the Hawes-Cooper Act by making it a federal offense to ship prisoner-made goods to a state in which state law prohibited the receipt, possession, sale, or use of such goods.[25] In 1940,

Congress went one step further and enacted the Sumners-Ashurst Act, which made it a federal crime to knowingly transport prisoner-made items in interstate commerce for private use, regardless of existing laws in the states.[26] Since then, goods made by inmates, such as license plates and soap, have been sold to other state agencies and not exported to other states. As unemployment decreased across the nation in 1978, Congress repealed the Hawes-Cooper Act.[27] The next year Congress passed the Justice System Improvement Act, which lifted the Sumners-Ashurst Act's ban on interstate trade of prison labor products and paved the way once again for inmate labor.

Although the next wave of privatization of adult correctional facilities did not emerge until the 1980s, private companies have owned and operated juvenile correctional facilities since the early 1900s. In the early 1970s, it was a common practice for nonprofits and private companies to run juvenile institutions. The Weaversville Intensive Treatment Unit for Juvenile Delinquents was one of the first privately owned high-security institutions operated under contract to the state by RCA Services.[28] In 1982, Florida contracted out the operation of the Okeechobee School for Boys to the Eckerd Foundation, a non-profit organization endowed with $100 million from Jack Eckerd's fortune from his drugs store chain. In 1983, nearly two-thirds of the 3,000 juvenile detention and correctional institutions in the United States were privately operated.[29]

Overcrowded Facilities and the Birth of Modern Private Prison Firms

Today, almost weekly, media stories focus on overcrowded conditions in jails and prisons. In 2016, Alabama made headlines with news that it packed more than 24,000 inmates into a system designed to house about half that number. In California, one state prison squished 650 inmates into a makeshift dormitory inside the prison gymnasium, placing bunk beds side by side with almost no room to walk. A few years ago some California prisons were so crowded that inmates slept in triple bunk beds lining the walls of prison gymnasiums. In one of these so-called dormitories, an inmate was beaten to death, and correction officers neglected to notice the incident for several hours. In 2011, the U.S. Supreme Court forced California to reduce its prison population because its facilities were so overcrowded and unhygienic that they constituted "cruel and unusual punishment."[30]

Prison overcrowding first became apparent four decades ago. Between 1972 and 1985 the nation's prison population more than doubled to 440,000 inmates, which played a major role in prison riots across the nation. The most notorious was the 1971 Attica uprising, in which inmates took control of a maximum security prison near Buffalo, New York, seizing hostages and issuing demands in front of a national television audience. The five-day riot resulted in the deaths of twenty-nine prisoners and ten hostages, and an additional 118 people had been shot. The 1972 New York Special Commission on Attica called the incident "the bloodiest encounter between Americans since the Civil War." In Texas, the state prison system was filled to 200 percent capacity, and inmates slept on hallway floors and outside in tents. One Texas prison had to serve meals constantly from 2:00 AM to 11:00 PM to ensure that everyone was fed.[31] In the mid-1970s, inmates in states across the country filed litigation challenging conditions of confinement.

Some legal relief occurred in 1980 when a federal judge in Texas ruled in *Ruiz v. Estelle* that the state prison system violated the Eighth Amendment's protection against cruel and unusual punishment. The federal court found that conditions in the Texas Department of Corrections were deplorable, noting that inmates were "crowded two or three to a cell or in closely packed dormitories, inmates sleep with the knowledge that they may be molested or assaulted by their fellows at any time. Their incremental exposure to disease and infection from other inmates in such narrow confinement cannot be avoided. They must urinate and defecate, unscreened, in the presence of others. Inmates in cells must live and sleep inches away from toilets; many in dormitories face the same situation."[32] The Texas prison system was immediately placed under court supervision, and this tipped the first domino.

Prisoners across the nation began to win their lawsuits, and by 1985 prisons in two-thirds of the states were under court order to improve conditions that violated the Constitution.[33] Caps on how many inmates could be housed in prisons were set, and some states released prisoners early to relieve overcrowding. Three years later the prison systems in thirty-nine states, the District of Columbia, Puerto Rico, and the Virgin Islands were under federal court orders to remedy conditions of confinement that violated constitutional standards.[34]

In 1983, 500 Michigan prisoners joined approximately 14,000 other formerly incarcerated individuals nationwide whose sentences had been shortened since 1980 because of prisons bursting at their seams.[35] Even the federal prison population operated between 27 percent and 59 percent over capacity.[36]

Not all prisoners could be released early, so the larger effect of overcrowding was a demand for more cells and new prisons. The nation's willingness to build itself out of overcrowding is perhaps the pivotal moment in the history of private prisons. Policy makers could have invested in treatment and diversion programs, reversing the tide of bodies triple- and quadruple-bunked in U.S. prisons. Instead they gorged on an unprecedented prison spending spree. Taxpayers invested in an expansion of metal and bars resulting in an unparalleled investment in corrections, from slightly under $7 billion in 1980 to $40 billion by 1995.

State after state faced a massive crisis to reduce its prison populations or build additional, expensive facilities, and policy makers had to choose. Taxpayers were soon unwilling to foot the bill to pay for more prisons, but legislators would lose reelection if they appeared to be soft on crime. Any "discussion of alternatives to incarceration was the kiss of death."[37]

In 1982 the national unemployment rate topped 10 percent, and more Americans were unemployed than at any time since the Great Depression. Taxpayers voted down bond issue after bond issue to fund state prison expansion. Hypocritically, they continued to call for tougher sentencing laws and more imprisonment to improve public safety. This hypocrisy doubled the nation's prison population between 1972 and 1984. In 1984 the Department of Justice stated that "prison administrators and staff continued to grapple with a shortage of available housing capacity to accommodate the 1983 population."[38]

Modern Private Prisons Emerge

By the mid-1980s, a great many states faced significant budget shortfalls traceable to the increased costs associated with operating their growing prisons systems.[39] While correctional agencies raced to comply with court orders to reduce overcrowding, a group of astute businessmen pored over inmate projection reports and analyzed a new growth industry—the privatization of prisons.

(*Privatization* is a contract process that shifts public functions, responsibilities, and capital assets, in whole or in part, from the government to the private sector) Specific services can be contracted out, which requires a competitive bidding process, and most jails and prisons privatize a whole host of services: medical, mental health, educational programming, food services, maintenance, and administrative office security.[40] Under this model, the correctional agency continues to run the facility and the day-to-day operations. In another form of privatization—the one most people think about—the government transfers complete ownership of assets and management duties to a corporation. In this model, a private company owns and operates the prison.

The privatization trend emerged as three realities coalesced: (1) the rising belief in the potential of the free market, (2) the skyrocketing number of prisoners, and (3) the price tag of mass incarceration.[41] Consistent with President Reagan's philosophy, this trend stemmed from the growing costs of imprisonment and a desire to reduce the size and scope of the government.

Leaseback Agreements

For a few years in the early 1980s, a 1981 change in the federal tax law encouraged private investment in correctional facilities. This was a precursor to the private corporations of today owning and operating jails and prisons: a "quasi-public body" had the legal authority to sell shares to investors to finance the building of prisons. State and local governments contracted with private companies to build facilities and lease them back to the government. At the time, government agencies saw this as a boon because they were not forced to raise taxpayer dollars to build jails and prisons. Instead, they could invest in businesses that would repay their investment plus interest over the life of the lease. In most cases, the contract provided that the government agency would own the facility at the end of the lease term. In addition, the bonds were tax exempt for investors, and policy makers could sidestep the onerous process of gaining voter approval and authorization for capital expenditures.

E. F. Hutton traced the leaseback structure to a plan they developed for Jefferson County, Colorado, which was under federal court order to relieve overcrowding of an outdated prison facility. Voters twice rejected a proposal to raise the sales tax to finance a new jail.[42] The leaseback worked like this: a Los Angeles corporation supplied a little more than $30 million to build a jail for 382 inmates; the county leased the facility until 1992, at which time it was expected to have repaid the $30 million; the county paid investors 8.75 percent interest, and the county would own the facility by 1992.[43]

By 1985, E. F. Hutton had created a $300 million prison leaseback plan for the state of California in addition to a $65 million jail lease-back for the city of Philadelphia. That same year, Shearson Lehman Brothers announced that it brokered a $32 million prison leaseback for Kentucky, an $18 million jail for Los Angeles, and a $15 million jail for Portland, Oregon.[44]

Three major Wall Street players—E. F. Hutton, Merrill Lynch, and Shearson Lehman—had high hopes for the future of the lease-back agreements, but "despite some initial ballyhoo, they never swept the nation."[45] The waning interest among investors can be traced to another change to the 1986 federal tax code, which limited the availability of tax-exempt financing for private industry.[46] Although not often mentioned in discussions of the history of correctional privatization, tax reforms paved the way for private corporations to profit from the national prison boom.

New York also toyed with tax credits for private prison construction in reaction to what was seen as an out-of-control drug problem in New York City in the 1960s and 1970s, and likely because of presidential aspirations of Governor Nelson D. Rockefeller. The governor signed legislation in 1973 enacting the harshest drug laws in the nation. The penalty for selling 2 ounces or more of heroin, morphine, opium, cocaine, or marijuana, or of possessing 4 ounces or more of the same substances, was a minimum fifteen-year sentence and a maximum of twenty-five years to life in prison, similar to a sentence for second-degree murder.

The prison population skyrocketed as drug offenders in New York's correctional facilities surged from 11 percent in 1973 to a peak of 35 percent in 1994. Despite the political backing for tougher drug sentences, not all taxpayers agreed. In 1981, a statewide coalition of church and criminal justice groups organized to strike down Governor Carey's proposed $475 million bond issue to expand state and local prisons.[47] New York voters rejected the bond issue that November by a slim margin of 13,000 votes.[48] To find a solution to New York's conundrum, New York Senator Alfonse D'Amato sponsored the Prison Construction Privatization Act of 1984 to sway private industry to invest in prisons by permitting investment tax credits and accelerated depreciation for these investments.[49] This solution played out in states across the country because the citizenry demanded public safety, less crime, and more people in jail but didn't want to foot incarceration's expensive bill.

Private Prison Corporations Unveiled

The 1980s saw a great deal of activity around innovative ways to lock up prisoners. A 1982 congressional proposal to build a federal prison for serious offenders in the Arctic failed.[50] However, the decade also gave birth to the modern private prison, an experiment that has flourished.

The biggest players in the game in the early 1980s—and those poised to notice the tremendous financial potential of America's penchant for metal bars—were the founders of Corrections Corporation of America (CCA). It was formed in 1983 by Thomas Beasley, formerly head of the Republican Party of Tennessee; Robert Crants, a businessman with connections to Sodexho-Marriot Services; and T. Don Hutto, who served as the president of the American Correctional Association and as the director of corrections in Virginia and Arkansas. Hutto was no stranger to the profit motive when it comes to corrections; in 1978 the U.S. Supreme Court found that Arkansas "evidently tried to operate their prisons at a profit" as inmates were ordered to work on prison farms ten hours a day, six days a week, without appropriate clothing and footwear.[51]

CCA was originally funded with $10 million raised primarily by a Nashville venture capital firm, Massey Burch Investment Group,[52] the financiers of Kentucky Fried Chicken and the Hospital Corporation of America (HCA).[53] The Massey Burch Group was headed by Jack Massey, a close friend of Governor Lamar Alexander. Born with political connections and venture capital backing, CCA had the right stuff to convince policy makers to entrust them with the care of America's inmates.

Beasley told a reporter in 1983 that "CCA will be to jails and prisons that are owned and managed by local, state, and federal governments what Hospital Corporation of America has become to medical facilities nationwide."[54] Founded in the late 1960s, HCA acquired hundreds of nonprofit hospitals claiming that it could run them better and more efficiently. It has achieved some successes, such as "economies of scale and purchasing power," but HCA's record has also been spotty. Practices such as reducing staff and accusations of "cherry-picking" patients to "garner profitable admissions" have been criticized.[55]

The Department of Justice launched a ten-year investigation into the charging practices of HCA, looking into claims that it defrauded the government by exaggerating the seriousness of the illnesses they were treating when it billed Medicare and Medicaid programs.[56] In late 2002, HCA settled the complaint and agreed to pay the U.S. government $631 million, plus interest. Although plagued by scandals—filing false cost reports, fraudulently billing Medicare for home health care workers, and paying kickbacks in the sale of home health agencies and to doctors to refer patients—the company remains profitable today.[57] In March 2011, HCA sold 126.2 million shares for $30 each, raising about $3.79 billion, making it the largest private-equity-backed IPO in U.S. history.[58]

Beasley and the other cofounders of CCA held up HCA as a model for how the private sector could more efficiently run facilities. The challenge to CCA's business model was that the corrections industry is an expensive proposition. Departments of corrections are responsible for the food, clothing, and housing of thousands of inmates, and the largest expense is labor. Prison guards are expensive, almost always unionized, and require benefits beyond salaries such as pensions, health insurance, education, and training.

For the government to turn a profit on any private venture, the contract price must be lower than what the state would pay to operate the facility itself. This puts private operators in a bit of a Catch-22. To save money, private corporations need to run their prisons at a lower cost but ensure that the facility complies with the contract and state and federal regulations. Because the bulk of prison costs stem from labor (65 to 70 percent of operational costs are for staff salaries, benefits, and overtime), private companies tend to rely on cheaper nonunion labor.[59] Private correction officers are generally not members of a union, and in 2015 they earned salaries about $7,000 lower than that of the average public corrections officer.[60]

CCA entered the correctional scene in October 1984 when it signed a contract to manage the Silverdale Detention Center in Hamilton

County, Tennessee. This marked the first time that government at any level in the United States contracted out the entire operation of a jail, and the county hoped for a substantial savings. The milestone was noteworthy for another reason; the county learned that it was on the hook to pay $200,000 more than budgeted. Some county officials spoke up that it was a mistake to hand over control of the institution to CCA because the county would have spent less money without the deal.[61]

CCA contracted to operate the jail for a per diem fee of $21 a prisoner, which was $3 less than the county paid to house the inmates. The deal seemed to make sense at the time, in part due to strict enforcement of the state's driving while under the influence laws.[62] But the inmate population soon exploded, and Hamilton County had not planned for this contingency. The county would have paid only an extra $5 a day to house the overflow prisoners, but CCA's contract guaranteed a per diem payment of $24 per person when the jail reached a specific capacity. This was an enormous boon for CCA, which eventually double-bunked the inmates. The Hamilton County contract was a harbinger of things to come in thousands of jurisdictions across the country.

Because so many of the costs of maintaining and running correctional facilities are fixed, the total costs are not greatly affected by each additional prisoner. For example, approximately the same number of staff members (guards, kitchen staff, janitors, medical staff) are needed whether the facility is running at capacity or 25 percent below capacity. It costs the same amount to operate a facility at 60 or 70 percent capacity as it does to operate a facility that is full. Similar to the business model for hotels, once cleaning staff, front desk personnel, bellmen, and managers are paid, it is far more remunerative to keep the hotel at its highest occupancy rate. So when a private prison company is paid per inmate, it is almost always more financially profitable to operate at capacity. In Hamilton County, CCA earned massive profits by keeping the facility full.

In November 1984, Thomas Beasley appeared on *60 Minutes* to promote CCA's venture into private prisons. Before turning to Beasley, Morley Safer said, "Just a few years ago, the very idea of prison for profit would have seemed ludicrous, given the escalating costs and problems of running prisons, given that it's an area of public service that only brings blame and rarely praise. Yet, here they are, companies like CCA."[63] After pointing out that prisons are a "growth industry,"

Beasley told Safer, "the prison population in this country has never gone down but twice—during World War I and World War II—and those operations are self-explanatory, I think."[64]

CCA Attempts to Take Over Entire Tennessee Prison System

Prison conditions worsened in the decade between 1975 and 1985. In 1985, Tennessee's prisons were operating under court supervision for prison overcrowding, and a federal court ordered it to reduce the number of inmates because of overcrowding, unhygienic, and unsafe prison conditions. Tennessee's prisons were under scrutiny for hundreds of assaults, dozens of killings and riots, and a slew of inmate escapes.[65] U.S. District Judge Thomas Higgins ordered the state to refrain from adding additional inmates as long as the state prison system remained overcrowded.

By the summer of 1985, Tennessee inmates had reached their breaking point. Furious over new prison uniforms with horizontal stripes, inmates at four Tennessee prisons burned buildings and took guards hostage. The four prisons were the Turney Center in Only, the State Penitentiary in Nashville, the Morgan County Regional Correctional Facility at Wartburg, and the Southeastern Regional Correctional Facility in Bledsoe County. At the state prison in Nashville, inmates refused to release the guards until they had a chance to talk about their conditions during a televised news conference. On live television, one inmate stated, "The stripes, I think, were the main concern. Stripes don't hold people, bars do." The inmates also expressed frustration about bad food, overcrowded facilities, and a lack of programming.[66]

A group of criminal justice experts started working with the Tennessee Department of Corrections and legislators to safely reduce the state's prison population. Peggy McGarry, from the Center for Effective Public Policy's National Prison Overcrowding Project, was asked to advise them on how to effectively meet the judge's mandate while ensuring safe communities. As McGarry sat outside Governor Lamar Alexander's office in the fall of 1985, a retired Appeals Court judge who chaired the task force of state and local criminal justice experts who were studying the overcrowding issue came out of the governor's office shaking his head. The judge said that he "had just heard the most amazing thing. Private prisons have offered to take over the entire state!" McGarry said that the "CCA went directly to the governor. They certainly did not work through the task force. We didn't know about their offer until they told the governor."[67]

To McGarry's dismay, this news was more than mere rumor. CCA lobbyists were seen traversing the halls of the state capitol, and the offer soon splashed across newspapers.[68] CCA had offered to take over Tennessee's entire prison system for $250 million, along with a ninety-nine-year lease. Responding to the unconstitutional conditions of the state's prisons, CCA President Thomas Beasley told reporters, "If I was the state, I couldn't do it fast enough."[69]

It is not surprising that CCA bypassed the task force and made their bold offer directly to Alexander. The governor had close (familial) ties to CCA. His wife, Honey Alexander, was an early investor in the company, as was Tennessee's Speaker of the House, Ned Ray McWherter. Considering CCA's offer, the governor told reporters, "We don't need to be afraid in America of people who want to make a profit. . . . This state's taxpayers would boot us clear into Kentucky if we turned our backs on a plan that would save us $250 million."[70]

On the day CCA offered to take over Tennessee's prison system, the fledgling for-profit corporation had already secured seven contracts to run correctional facilities: two to operate facilities for illegal immigrants in Houston and Laredo, Texas; a federal prerelease treatment center in Fayetteville, North Carolina; two juvenile facilities in Memphis, Tennessee; the Hamilton County Jail, in Chattanooga Tennessee; and a work camp in Panama City, Florida.[71] A prescient description of CCA's aggressive entrance into Tennessee corrections honed in on the core of what would become a debate over private prisons for the next four decades: "There was considerable disagreement as to whether Corrections Corp. of America's lobbyists, roaming the Capitol halls last week, were cavalry coming to the rescue or profiteers coming to exploit."[72]

Despite the severe pressure state officials faced from the federal courts to get their prisons under control by January 1, 1986, some in Tennessee's government were less than smitten with this business proposition. One of those with grave concerns was state Attorney General W. J. Michael Cody, a President Jimmy Carter appointee in the Tennessee U.S. Attorneys' office. Cody was concerned about hiring private guards for a "quasi-judicial function" and said, "they are going to impose punishments. They are going to advise parole boards.

All of that is very different from private businesses providing government with transportation and food services."[73] In the end, Tennessee did not accept CCA's proposition, but Governor Alexander proposed a compromise that still would benefit CCA. He recommended that private prison corporations build, own, and possibly even operate two new prisons with room for 500 inmates each. CCA had claimed that it could build the two new maximum security prisons in two years, twice as quickly as the state.

In another nod to the private prison industry, Tennessee passed the Private Prison Act of 1986, which paved the way for private prisons to operate in the state. The legislation granted the Tennessee Department of Corrections the authority "to contract with private concerns on a limited basis to afford an opportunity to determine if savings and efficiencies can be effected for the operation of correctional facilities."[74] CCA also received tremendous free publicity and national attention with the *New York Times* headline: "Company Offers to Run Tennessee Prisons."[75] Hutto stated that "it forced everyone to take us seriously. The offer ran on a full front page of the afternoon paper. We were a national story."[76]

The private prison industry's moment had arrived. By 1988, private correctional companies were running twenty-four correctional facilities and five detention centers under contract with the U.S. Immigration and Naturalization Service (INS).[77]

Growth of the Private Prison Industry

Remarkably, with almost no track record measuring the effectiveness of their activity, CCA grew quickly. CCA's first federal contract was awarded by INS, which authorized CCA to build and manage an immigration detention center in Houston. It opened in 1984. The first state contract was awarded to CCA in 1986 to operate a prison in Marion, Kentucky. In 1987, CCA signed contracts for the construction and management of a regional juvenile facility in east Tennessee and two minimum security, prerelease facilities in Texas. In acknowledgment of the profit opportunity the next few decades would bring, CCA's 1994 Annual Report to shareholders stated, "there are powerful market forces driving our industry, and its potential has barely been touched."

Although CCA was the biggest private prison firm, it was not the only game in town. The demands on state governments to address crowded prisons encouraged a slew of companies to join the nascent industry. Security services leader Wackenhut Corporation (now the GEO Group) and other companies bid on the management and operation of prisons across the nation. By 1984, Ted Nissen, founder of Behavioral Systems Southwest, held $5 million in contracts with California, Arizona, and the federal Bureau of Prisons to manage halfway houses, and held two contracts with INS to manage immigrant detention facilities.[78] Two brothers, Charles and Joseph Fenton, founded Buckingham Security Ltd., which constructed a $20 million, 715-cell maximum security prison north of Pittsburgh in 1985. At the time, the brothers anticipated that they would house prisoners from several states.[79]

Private prisons began to gain a grip in the corrections field. Because government-run facilities failed to meet minimum constitutional requirements for a safe and humane environment, a market for private prisons emerged. Vendors began to move beyond their traditional role of running halfway houses and juvenile facilities and made proposal after proposal to build or operate jails and prisons.

Private Prisons Get Their First Congressional Hearings

The emergence of the for-profit prison industry in the early 1980s generated a great deal of interest from policy makers on Capitol Hill who had watched from afar. From November 1985 to March 1986, the House Judiciary Committee held its first ever congressional hearings on private prisons. Legislators hoped the hearings would provide insight into certain questions about this budding industry: whether privatization would save money, whether conditions of confinement would be improved in private prisons, and whether the government is even legally authorized to delegate this power to private companies. Ira Robbins, a law professor at the American University Law School, alluded to the feeling among many that "the government has been doing a dismal job in its administration of correctional institutions" and that prisoners are often "kept in conditions that shock the conscience, if not the stomach."[80]

The subject matter was so novel that a staff attorney for the American Civil Liberties Union (ACLU)—an organization that advocates to eliminate private prisons today—testified that the "ACLU probably will not take a position with respect to the public policy aspects of privatization."[81] However, the ACLU warned that privatization "must be examined closely" before the government invests substantial resources into the private sector to run prisons and jails.

Some organizations expressed unease early on. The American Federation of Government Employees (AFGE) warned of impending doom. David Kelly, president of the Council of Prison Locals for the AFGE, said private prison "profit is directly linked to a constant and increasing supply of incarcerated prisoners. For the first time, it is in someone's self-interest to foster and encourage incarceration."[82]

The occasion provided CCA with its first opportunity to testify on Capitol Hill. Richard Crane, vice president of legal affairs for CCA, made the case for the government's need to save money: "Yes, there are indeed con-artists in this world. But, if we are going to attribute that attitude to everyone then the government better get in the business of running everything from used car lots to taco stands."[83]

So novel was the industry at the time that Kentucky Congressman Ron Mazzoli asked Crane, "What do your people wear? Do they wear uniforms?" Crane answered, "Uniforms." To which Congressman Mazzoli asked, "The same uniform that would be standard, blue trousers and so on?" Crane responded, "No, brown is our color, light and dark brown."[84]

Professor Robbins testified about the constitutionality of it all. "Government liability cannot be reduced or eliminated by delegating the governmental function to a private entity."[85] At the close of the November hearings, Judiciary Chair Kastenmeier thanked the witnesses for testifying: "It is something which in year 2000 we may look at in terms of failure or it may have disappeared from the scene or, indeed, it may have become something very significant in terms of this country."[86] The subcommittee met again to discuss this topic in March. The only two witnesses who testified were the director of the Bureau of Prisons and the president of the Council of Prison Locals, American Federation of Government Employees.

Excitement swirled around the idea of expanding the use of private prisons. Government officials and taxpayers alike clung to notions that private industry would raise the initial capital to build facilities more cheaply and efficiently than government. How? Corporations could circumvent years of government studies, bids, and approval by voters to issue government bonds to finance prison construction. Private prison corporations benefited from the political challenges state policy makers faced when fund-raising to build new prisons, and to build them fast enough to meet demand. As Crane testified during the congressional hearings: "We can do it less expensively. We know, for example, that our construction costs are about 80 percent of what the Government pays for construction."[87]

CCA Emerges on Wall Street

The congressional hearings and CCA's offer to take over Tennessee's entire prison system gave CCA and the emerging private prison industry incredible publicity. Completing the trifecta, in October 1986 CCA went public on the stock exchange with 2 million shares and a total valuation of $18 million. In its prospectus CCA noted that "the corrections system, in whole or in part, of thirty-four states were under court order to improve conditions."[88] The prospectus also pointed out that "the privatization of the prisons and corrections industry offers federal, state and local governmental agencies an alternative in their efforts to comply with federal and state court orders on a cost-efficient basis."[89] The day after CCA emerged as a public company it was reported that the "average contract with the company provides for $31 a day per inmate and it costs CCA $6 a day per inmate, a profit of $25 a day per inmate."[90] In 1991, CCA's revenues were barely over $50 million. A few years later, law professor and criminologist Norval Morris wrote that "it is unclear whether private prisons are the wave of the future of corrections . . . there is mixed evidence as to whether they are fulfilling their initial promise of less-expensive, more efficient service."[91]

In 1994, Wackenhut Corrections Corporation's initial stock offering was valued at almost $20 million. On the day of the offering, the corporation managed nearly 8,000 prison beds. By 1997, CCA's revenues had increased nearly tenfold to $462 million, with a profit margin of over $50 million. At the same time, the number of prison beds CCA managed jumped from about 5,000 to more than 38,000, giving it a U.S. market share of over 50 percent.[92]

As figure 3.1 indicates, prison construction took off in the late 1980s and continued growing until the late 2000s. As figure 3.2 indicates, between 1995 and 2000, there were more than 150 new private prisons

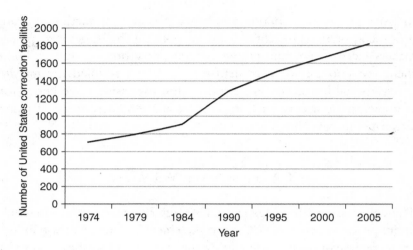

Figure 3.1 Growth in Number of U.S. Correctional Facilities *Source*: Bureau of Justice Statistics, "Census of State and Federal Correctional Facilities," Series 1974–2005.

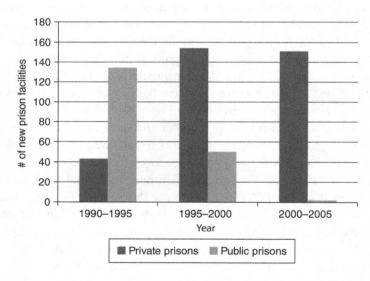

Figure 3.2 Rate of Growth in Private and Public Prisons, 1995–2005 *Source*: Bureau of Justice Statistics, "Census of State and Federal Correctional Facilities," Series 1974–2005.

built across the country compared to about 50 public prisons. And, between 2000 and 2005, this trend continued with only two new public prisons constructed versus 151 private correction facilities, which drove almost all of the increase in the number of prisons built.[93]

If the private prison industry had a pivotal moment, it was in the mid-1980s. The nation, and the world, started to pay attention to the private industry as it wove its way into the fabric of the U.S. correctional system. No longer bearing the names of state departments of corrections and county jails, correction officers' uniforms suddenly bore corporate logos. In 2011 it was reported that "over time, most states signed contracts, one of the largest transfers of state functions to private industry."[94]

Many prison facilities were under emergency court orders to reduce the number of inmates they housed, so state and federal policy makers were reluctant to explore alternatives. Dealing with lagging budgets and barely making court ordered deadlines, most states turned their backs on conversations focusing on safely reducing incarceration, improving sentencing, and reducing recidivism.

It's difficult to make the case that private industry created mass incarceration, but the very existence of private prisons let policy makers off the hook for recalibrating our nation's system of punishment. The emergence of private prisons was a diversion from the real discussion about incarceration. They provided much-needed relief to inhumane and overstuffed prison cells, but these corporations promised to quickly build prison after prison, preventing a necessary examination of whether incarceration was the appropriate sanction for so many Americans who violated the criminal code.

Selman and Leighton pointed out that "the debate over private prisons included no discussion of alternatives to incarceration; nor did the congressional hearings or the commission's final report include the word 'rehabilitation.'"[95] Where were the inspiring debates about the proper role of incarceration and punishment? Why were these conversations so rare? Policy makers missed a valuable opportunity to engage in an examination of whether too many people were in prison or whether there were more effective methods for addressing the underlying issues that caused their incarceration. In the next decades, corporations would seize the opportunity to make money off of almost every aspect of incarceration.

CHAPTER FOUR

The Prison Industrial Complex

> The prison-industrial complex is not only a set of interest groups
> and institutions. It is also a state of mind. The lure of big money
> is corrupting the nation's criminal-justice system, replacing
> notions of public service with a drive for higher profits.
>
> ERIC SCHLOSSER, "THE PRISON-INDUSTRIAL COMPLEX,"
> *THE ATLANTIC*, DECEMBER 1998

WHETHER PUBLIC OR private, all prisons, jails, and detention
centers need to feed, clothe, house, transport, and guard the inmates
who live in their facilities. These facilities are responsible for providing
health care, programming, video visitation, telephone, and sometimes
even email services to those housed behind bars. Most facilities also
operate a commissary that sells food and personal items. Widening the
lens to the 4.65 million people under some sort of correctional control outside of brick-and-mortar institutions, private probation companies, electronic monitoring companies, and even drug and mental
health treatment companies turn a profit from those enmeshed in the
criminal justice system. There are innumerable opportunities to profit
from the incarcerated in the United States. Private prisons are just one
part of this multi-billion-dollar business.

Twice a year the American Correctional Association (ACA) hosts
a conference for its 5,000 members, an opportunity for corrections
officials, academics, and other experts in the field to attend pan-
els, workshops, and make their way through the largest correctional
trade show in the country. These industries have a financial stake in

keeping prisons filled and in serving people enmeshed in the criminal justice system.

I attended the ACA conference in Louisiana in January 2016. The massive convention hall was filled with products from more than 180 companies and provides a glimpse into the extensive network of private companies that support the nation's $80 billion incarceration industry. In the convention hall, Aramark, one of the nation's largest providers of food services to governments (serving 380 million meals to correctional facilities across the country each year) handed out bags of cookies and pretzels.

Founded in 1870 as the National Prison Association, ACA is the oldest correctional association in the nation. Shane Bauer wrote that the ACA functions as "the closest thing [the United States has] to a national regulatory body for prisons."[1] The ACA is the accrediting body for the nation's public and private jails and prisons. The national accreditation process was developed in 1978 in response to the need for national standards for U.S. prisons and jails. With a federal system, fifty different state systems, and thousands of local jails and detention facilities, ACA accreditation ensures consistent standards in detention.

From specially made "laundry loops" that make it easier to carry laundry and ensure nothing is hidden in the clothing to inmate restraint seats, corporations advertise their products and services to the nation's correction facilities, spending $2,000 to $8,600 for a booth. Dedrone, founded in 2014 to develop technology to protect against civilian drones, advertised that the twenty-first century has brought new challenges to correction officials, in this case, drones that might carry drugs or weapons to inmates in the yard.

In 1995, a trade magazine for marketers featured a "little-known field with great marketing potential that has grown dramatically in the last decade, [which] is expected to grow even larger, and is recession proof. That field is prisons."[2] One hundred and fifty state and federal prisons were expected to be built that year, and 177 facilities were set for expansion. Profits were available from laundry services to food services to long-distance phone systems. Between 1984 and 2005 a new prison opened every eight and a half days.[3]

President Dwight Eisenhower, who served as the supreme commander of the allied forces in World War II, addressed the nation on January 17, 1961. He devoted his farewell speech to warning about the military industrial complex. Three days before John F. Kennedy became the thirty-fifth president of the United States, Eisenhower pleaded with the country to remain vigilant regarding the vast industry associated with the military:

> This conjunction of an immense military establishment and a large arms industry is new in the American experience. The total influence—economic, political, even spiritual—is felt in every city, every State house, every office of the Federal government. We recognize the imperative need for this development. Yet we must not fail to comprehend its grave implications. Our toil, resources and livelihood are all involved; so is the very structure of our society. In the councils of government, we must guard against the acquisition of unwarranted influence, whether sought or unsought, by the military-industrial complex. The potential for the disastrous rise of misplaced power exists and will persist.[4]

Eisenhower saw the defense industry mount a campaign to convince policy makers of a significant "missile gap" between the United States and the Soviet Union, a narrative that the defense industry perpetuated despite little evidence. From his unique perch in the Oval Office, he could clearly see the defense industry's dubious scheme to generate fear in U.S. citizens.[5]

In 1998, Eric Schlosser coined the phrase *prison industrial complex.* "Three decades after the war on crime began," he wrote, "the United States has developed a prison-industrial complex—a set of bureaucratic, political, and economic interests that encourage increased spending on imprisonment, regardless of the actual need."[6] The prison industrial complex, according to Schlosser, included architecture and construction firms, Wall Street investment banks, private prisons, plumbing supply companies, food service, and even health care companies.

The criticism levied against these businesses by those working to reduce the nation's reliance on incarceration has to do with incentives. The industry surrounding corrections is dependent on the very existence of the carceral state to make money. For example, a marked shift toward decarceration could prove financially disastrous to the companies that rely on a captive inmate population for their revenue. Although it is estimated that today corrections is an $80 billion business (this includes jails, prisons, probation, and parole), the nation spends much more because many of the costs are invisible or difficult to estimate.[7]

The ACA convention hall showcases just a small slice of that business. For example, the bed-brokering business emerged a few years ago as another corrections moneymaker that treats prisoners as commodities. Imagine that a busload of tourists stormed into a hotel with no vacancy and asked for rooms. The concierge would call around to see if any neighboring hotels have extra capacity. Instead of a hotel concierge, in the bed-brokering business an independent businessperson works with jail and prison administrators to find empty beds in other correctional facilities—for a fee. JailBedSpace.com works to "put the buyers and sellers of 'County jail bed space' in touch with each other. Buyers of bed space may be other jail administrators, the U.S. Marshal's service, and the Immigration and Naturalization Service to name just a few."[8]

Bed brokers were at their peak in the 1990s. Oklahoma-based Dominion Management filled 8,000 beds in eight states and Puerto Rico between 1993 and 1997. The motto of bed-brokerage company Inmate Placement Services was "a bed for every inmate and an inmate for every bed."[9] In an entrepreneurially savvy move, the company created a monthly newsletter to send to corrections wardens, sheriffs, and private prison operators, aptly named the "Bed Space Locator." The newsletter contained listings of available jail and prison space in correctional terms:

120 beds. Male and female. Minimum security. Four-person rooms. No history of violent or sex offenses. (Exceptions on a case-by-case basis.) Constructed in 1988. Renovated in 1995. Per Diem negotiable.[10]

The brokers were awarded a flat fee for each bed they rented. Some facilities were even encouraged to send inmates out of town to another prison to free space so they could rent their own beds at a higher rate than what they paid to house their inmates elsewhere.

When the late twentieth and early twenty-first centuries are judged on their great public works, prison building will stand as one of the nation's largest infrastructure projects. By 1991, prison spending on construction, renovations, and major repairs of institutions reached a peak of $4.6 billion.[11] The nation's prison boom has rattled the architectural profession. In 2004, almost a thousand architects and designers signed a petition calling for a boycott of the design, construction, or renovation of a jail or prison in their practice.[12] In early 2015, the

American Institute of Architects rejected a petition to censure members who design solitary-confinement cells and death chambers.

Michael Sorkin, the architect critic of *The Nation*, reported that the mission of the country's leading prison design firm, DLR Group, is to "elevate the human experience through design."[13] Sorkin writes that the DLR Group earned more than "$3.5 billion from work in the field and created the first federal supermax prison, the Florence Administrative Maximum Facility (ADX) in Colorado," also affectionately known as the "Alcatraz of the Rockies."[14]

Six transportation companies dominate the prison industry, led by TransCor America, which generated more than $4 million annually in 2014 and 2015.[15] Owned by CCA, TransCor claims to have "safely transported more than one million prisoners or detainees."[16] Private prisoner transportation services operate pursuant to the Extradition Clause of the U.S. Constitution and the Extradition Act, and these companies have the same authority as government agencies when transporting prisoners.[17] The companies have settled many inmate lawsuits over the years for alleged cases of abuse, neglect, and deaths of inmates.[18]

The bus trips are often the most disturbing aspects of confinement for inmates transferred between prisons. In 2008, thirty-nine-year-old Colin was sentenced in the state of Vermont to a minimum of five years and a maximum of thirty-five years for possessing child pornography.[19] In October 2013, Vermont prisons ran out of space, and the Department of Corrections shipped Colin to a private prison in Kentucky owned and operated by CCA. When we spoke about his experiences, Colin told me that "this is done so often that it actually has a name: Diesel Therapy."

> They'll put you on a bus and send you thirty hours down to Kentucky. That's the part of my experience that approaches Guantanamo. You're shackled. You have a belly chain. You've got handcuffs on, attached to the belly chain, and your legs are shackled. You're attached to the person sitting next to you in the bus. It's a hard plastic bench seat, which for the first thirty minutes is fine, and for the next 39 hours is the most uncomfortable and painful thing I've ever experienced. The bathroom facilities are a joke.[20]

Colin relayed that he doesn't remember any Vermont correctional officials riding with them. The Vermont Department of Corrections guards escorted the inmates onto the bus, and staff working for the private transport company checked their names off on a clipboard: "once you are on the bus, you're in the hands of the private contractor that is transporting you."[21]

The prison industrial complex remains alive and well today, providing video visitation systems, uniform supplies, and even prison pens. A New York City correction officer suffered permanent hearing loss after an inmate in a Queens jail grabbed a doctor's pen during a medical examination and stabbed him. The Bend-Ez prison pen is flexible, safe for staff and inmates, and nonconductive. Bend-Ez pens are constructed with a clear barrel to expose contraband and are the number-one selling prison pen in the country.

According to its packaging, the Ecosecurity Utensil (ESU) provides the "safest eating utensil available for correctional, psychiatric, and security facilities." Their paper spoons look more like a paper airplane than cutlery. Made from paperboard similar to that used for milk cartons, in one fold they become a scoop for solid food. These paper utensils cannot be used as weapons and are advertised to reduce self-harm and prevent costly lockdowns.

Other companies specifically cater to the economy of prisoners. Crossbar sells law-enforcement-designed e-cigarettes specifically for use in prisons. Crossbar markets to correctional facilities because "almost every inmate in a correctional facility arrives with an addiction to nicotine." Crossbar's marketing to prisons reads:

> Is your correctional facility searching for an additional revenue generator? The sale of crossbar is your solution. Crossbar products will help generate revenue and increase profit margins necessary to help support your correctional facility in its efforts to continue the operation of various inmate programs.

Spending on corrections has skyrocketed in the last three decades. Between 1986 and 2013, adjusted for inflation, state support for K–12 education grew by 69 percent whereas corrections spending grew by 141 percent.[22]

The prison telecommunications business is booming. Inmates can only make calls through the provider that has an exclusive contract with the prison, and telephone companies make enormous profits from prison phone calls, earning $1.6 billion a year.[23] By 1995, MCI had installed its telephones throughout the California prison system at no charge and offered the California Department of Corrections a 32 percent share of revenues from inmates' phone calls.[24] In 1999, MCI provided long-distance service at thirty-three California state prisons, and GTE provided pay-phone service at four. The state received $16 million that year from these contracts. Today phone calls from prison can cost up to $15.00.

Three companies dominate the prison communications industry: Securus, Telmate, and Global Tel Link. The Federal Communications Commission (FCC) has tried to implement rate caps for prison telephone calls. After decades of price gouging, in 2015 the FCC voted to cap national rates for out-of-state calls at 21 cents per minute for debit or prepaid calls, 25 cents per minute for collect calls, and 11 cents per minute for in-state calls from state and federal prisons. The companies have sued, and litigation is currently ongoing.

Inmates are often shuffled from prison to prison far from home, making it difficult to stay in contact with their loved ones. I spoke to Elizabeth Cree, whose fiancé, Charlie, has bounced around between different Arizona prisons, both public and private. She told me how hard it is to communicate with Charlie, who was then held at the CCA-owned and -operated Red Rock Correctional Facility in Eloy, Arizona. She started a support group on Facebook with six other women who had loved ones at Red Rock. Cree said they share information, talk about their visits, and even pass messages to their loved ones through the other women. Cree, like many of the other families of inmates, lives far from the private prison. She drives four hours each way to Eloy for a visit that lasts about two and a half hours. Cree calls Charlie when she can. She isn't sure if the prison is set up for video visitation, but even if it was, she would still only call him on the phone because video chats are too expensive. The Eloy prison does not have video visitation, but more than 600 prisons in forty-six states do offer video visitation, which can cost upward of $30 for a thirty-minute session.[25] Both public and private prisons have come under fire in recent years for eliminating in-person visits because of the new technology. Phone calls, by contrast, are about $5.00. The phone calls, care packages, and commissary services all are provided by subsidiaries of the Keefe Corporation, which Cree told me has monopolized the prison care system in Arizona. "So no matter what, we are paying Keefe in some way."[26]

Keefe Corporation earns $1 billion annually, but it got its start in the corrections market by creating packaged drink mixes. Because some of the items (bottles and cans, particularly) could be used as weapons, the company developed pouches for commissary food items. Today the company has contracts with more than 800 public and private prisons; the bulk of its business is in commissaries. Keefe also provides telephone and email services. Its phone division has more than 200 facility service contracts around the nation. Common to most of these contracts, the county or the state receives a commission from the contracts. For example, a contract with the St. Louis County Jail allows the company to charge a $6.95 fee for funds deposited into a prepaid account, and Keefe pays almost 75 percent of its commission to the county.[27]

As new technology emerges, corporations are quick to provide it to inmates and their families—at above-market prices. In research for this book, I used JPay,—a technology company some have called the Apple of the prison system. I spent 40 cents per email through JPay to correspond with inmates currently incarcerated in government-operated and private prisons. If the inmates wrote back, they had to spend 40 cents on a stamp unless I prepaid for them. JPay's website advertises: "Send money to your loved one in state prison. Email your cousin in county jail. Chat with a friend using video visitation or give the gift of music with the JPay Player."

The company profits from its services, for example, charging $4.95 to transfer $20.00 to an inmate in the Dwight Correctional Center in Illinois. A thirty-minute or less video visitation session with an inmate at the Northern State Correctional Facility in Newport, Vermont, costs inmates $9.95. JPay recently began selling prison-safe electronic tablets, which inmates can use to listen to music, compose and send emails, and play games. The most recent gadget introduced on the prison market is the JP5Mini, a $70 tablet with wireless capabilities and an app store.

Correctional agencies are incentivized through profit-sharing arrangements to contract these services. JPay makes it hard for correctional agencies to pass up these lucrative contracts. The Washington Department of Corrections, for example, earns 5 percent of gross revenue from all email services.[28] In twelve years, JPay has grown to provide services at 1,200 facilities in twenty-four states. In 2014 alone, inmates at jails and prisons across the country sent more than 14 million emails and 650,000 mobile payments through JPay.[29]

Capitalizing on the lucrative market of probationers and parolees, JPay now partners with many states to process supervision fee payments, which are fees parolees are required to pay to their supervision officer. These monthly fees help defray the government's cost of supervising individuals in the community. In Tennessee, parolees can make supervision payments through a JPay kiosk or online. JPay collects a fee for each transaction, and in Tennessee they collect up to $10.40 for a payment over $200 if the probationer or parolee pays by phone.

Providing health care to prisons and jails is also a lucrative business. Today, fourteen states provide their own correctional health care, and thirty-six states contract at least some health care responsibilities to an outside vendor.[30] Corizon Health, the nation's largest private correctional health care provider, currently works in more than 110 correctional facilities, serving 345,000 jail and prison inmates in at least twenty-seven states. The company earned $1.4 billion in revenue in 2014 and $1.55 billion in 2015.[31] Corizon also relies on a registered lobbyist who splits his time working for them and CCA, which often bids for contracts naming Corizon as its health care provider.[32]

Corizon has recently come under scrutiny for the quality of the health care services it provides to inmates and has lost contracts with several states, most recently Florida, New Mexico, and the Riker's Island jail in New York City. More than 1,300 lawsuits were filed against Corizon between 2010 and 2015.[33] Right around the time Corizon lost its lucrative contract with the state of New Mexico, the health care conglomerate paid more than $4.5 million to settle lawsuits brought by New Mexico inmates from 2007 through May of 2016.[34] Woodrow Meyers, the company's CEO, drilled home that Corizon is a business. When asked why the company is often less than transparent about its activities, Myers said, "The Ford Motor Company doesn't go around and show its plans for a Taurus to GM. GM doesn't show its plan for its new Chevy Volt upgrade to Ford. It's that kind of a business issue that we face in our business as well."[35]

Reggie Wilkinson, the former head of the Ohio Department of Corrections, now sits on the board of directors for the private prison corporation Management and Training Corporation (MTC). MTC is the nation's third largest provider of secure adult correctional facilities with yearly revenue streams of over $500 million. When I spoke to Wilkinson, he drove home the extent to which the private industry has infiltrated U.S. prisons. "Privatization, generally looked at, does not only include outsourcing and the operations of an entire prison; we have medical and food services. You name it; it can be and will be outsourced through private operators." Wilkinson paused. "So I think there becomes an issue when the entire prison is outsourced to a for-profit company, versus outsourcing a lot of other services, which are significant. And by the way, none of this is new for corrections throughout the system, and throughout the history of my involvement. Something has always been outsourced to a private concern."[36]

Private industry has always benefited from incarceration, from the convict lease programs of the early 1800s to the food services industries providing thousands of meals a year to inmates today. But the contemporary prison industrial complex is far larger than anyone could have imagined. Today companies are selling prisons clear typewriters, uniforms, firearms, and even tools for quickly finding escapees. ENSCO's MicroSearch security inspection system uses advanced technology to determine whether human beings are hiding in vehicles or containers by detecting the vibrations caused by the person's heartbeat. In addition, lobbyists from Greenberg Traurig, received $350,000 from CCA over the last three years to "monitor issues pertaining to the construction and management of privately-operated prisons and detention facilities."[37]

Journalist Mark Dyer once called the prison industrial complex "a collection of interests whose financial well-being rises and falls with the size of the prison population."[38] The prison industrial complex is vast, far greater than the private corporations that profit from the nation's inmates. It is an entrenched economic system built by unions, perverse incentives, and capitalism. Today, the United States employs more than 469,000 correction officers and jailers[39]—that is more correction officers than pediatricians, judges, court reporters, and firefighters combined. If you include probation officers and correctional treatment specialists, well over half a million people are employed in corrections. Employment is trending positive for those interested in a career in corrections. The Department of Labor estimates that correction officer jobs are projected to grow by 4 percent through 2024.[40]

But the most publicly recognizable segment of the prison industrial complex is private prisons. The fledgling industry that Wisconsin Congressman Robert Kastenmeier said "in year 2000 we may look at in terms of failure" now has 8 percent of the nation's total prison population.[41] At the ACA convention in January, GEO Group sponsored the badges all attendees wore, and even outside of the convention GEO Group, CCA, and other private prison firms regularly sponsor dinners and other gatherings for ACA and state correctional officials.

I spoke with Eric Schlosser recently, and I asked whether he was surprised at the deep entanglement of our policies and pocketbooks that have resulted in the tremendous growth of this prison industrial complex. Schlosser said he was mostly amazed by how long it has taken the country to engage in discussions about the vastness of this industry. "It benefits certain vested interests," Schlosser said, "but it so harms the country at large that I really have been surprised at how long it's taken to have this national dialogue." Encouraged by some of the state and federal reforms, Schlosser stated that "social change takes a long time when there are powerful bureaucracies and powerful interests that resist it."[42]

This web of complex economic incentives—from prison telephone charges to architectural fees to correctional unions to private prisons—runs deep. The nation's prison industrial complex relies on a vast infrastructure of financial incentives that create significant hurdles to dismantling a mass incarceration system on which the nation has come to rely.

The next chapter examines the financial incentives for investing in the corrections industry; these incentives are attractive for small, often economically depressed towns.

CHAPTER FIVE

Private Prisons and the American Heartland

We first had trouble getting contracts when we were ready to open. The only people who were interested in talking to us were newspaper reporters who were interested in doing a story on a prison that was built and never opened. The *LA Times* and the *New York Times* did a story, as well as many regional newspapers. But it was good, interesting reading, I suppose, for some small, little town in rural Minnesota that took it upon themselves and no one came. I think that's kind of the headline of the story: "They built it, and no one came."

BOB THOMPSON, FORMER CITY COORDINATOR
FOR APPLETON, MINNESOTA[1]

IN THE SPRING of 1990, Bob Thompson, a thin man now in his early seventies who has the polite reserve of a long-time Minnesotan, had an idea. He was the city coordinator of Appleton, Minnesota, a rural town of 1,500 people far west of St. Paul. It was just a two-square-mile town where almost every street is named after a military veteran who died in combat, and it was losing people and money. The recession had hit Appleton hard, and the agricultural industry it depended on was its first victim.

After attempting to woo a casino and a furniture manufacturing plant, neither of which expressed enthusiasm for setting up shop in Appleton, Thompson settled on another idea—a prison. "I had done a substantial amount of reading about what was going on with prisons in the United States, and there definitely was overpopulation of inmates and shortages of beds," said Thompson. "And there were some private prisons being built in southern USA, and one day I called a financial consultant for the city of Appleton, located in Minneapolis, and I said, 'Steve, I've got a project for you.'" He said, "'Yeah, what's that?'

And I said, 'I'd like to build a prison in Appleton.' And there was one of those long pauses, and then he said, 'Are you serious?' And I said, 'I am. I would like to pursue it, and see if it's possible.' And after some thought, he said he would get back to me."[2]

Steve did get back to Thompson, and after many phone calls between them, they presented their plan to the Appleton Chamber of Commerce. At the packed meeting, Thompson told the residents what a prison in their town would mean for infrastructure, jobs, and economic viability. The Chamber of Commerce told him to "run with it" and see what he could do. He delivered letters to the seven board members of the Appleton Business Development Corporation, introducing the project. At first they responded with shock: "You want to build . . . a prison?" one said to him. But eventually, according to Thompson, "One gentleman at the business chamber meeting said, 'What have we got to lose? It's a downhill slide right now. Let's try it.'"

They ran into legal hurdles almost immediately, and Thompson found himself in meetings with lawyers from white-shoe Twin Cities firms searching for the money and legal authority to break ground on a new prison. The lawyers drew up the paperwork for the Appleton Economic Development Association (AEDA), a subsidiary of the city of Appleton, to create a 501(c)(3) that issued revenue bonds to 900 investors. The AEDA eventually adopted the name Appleton Prison Corporation. The transaction essentially removed the city of Appleton from any liability and gave the Appleton Prison Corporation responsibility for building, marketing, and managing the finances of the facility.

Thompson's idea became reality more quickly than he could have imagined. It took only two years to build; they broke ground in November 1990 and two years later, on a mild September day, the Appleton Prison Corporation opened the Prairie Correctional Facility, a $28-million 500-bed prison facility in the middle of a soybean field. The prison in Appleton was just one of fifty-seven privately managed prisons in operation in the country at the time.[3]

The town seemed to be onto something. The state and federal prison population had increased about 168 percent in the last decade, and "the 1992 increase translate[d] into a nationwide need for approximately 1,143 prison bed spaces per week, compared to the nearly 981 prison beds spaces per week needed in 1991."[4] The residents of Appleton hoped their 500 inmate beds came at precisely the right time to dramatically change their economy, and there was already cause for hope. A Super 8 motel had just opened with the prospect of incoming prison staff and families of those incarcerated at the new facility visiting Appleton. The town even began renovations to its small airport.

The 1990s Prison Boom

The 1990s was a time of economic prosperity, and the GDP rose continuously for almost a decade. But rural America was often excluded from that prosperity as bigger cities benefited from the rapid increase in the service market, a hugely expanding labor market, and rising stock prices. Farming communities suffered. The advent of advanced equipment and rising land prices contracted the agricultural sector, and family farms were crowded out of land and equipment. Rural populations fled to the cities and the suburbs. In 1950, about 44 percent of Americans lived on farms and in small towns, but by 1990 that number had declined to about 23 percent.

The allure of prisons as a tool of economic development in rural America grew as prison spending skyrocketed. Sociologist Michael Jacobson found that "prisons tend to create secondary and tertiary support systems that also create jobs and sustain development. Once prisons are operating, they require, for instance, outside health care systems to provide medical care to inmates and transportation businesses and hotels to bring and house people visiting prisoners."[5]

The 1990s were the heyday for prisons. An average of twenty-five new rural prisons opened each year, a marked increase from sixteen prisons per year in the 1980s and just four per year in the 1970s. The United States built 245 new facilities across 212 of its 2,290 rural counties.[6] In 1996, the nation spent $22 billion on prisons, $1.3 billion (6 percent) on constructing new facilities. Expenditures on state correctional activities rose 115 percent from $12.7 billion in 1985 to $27.3 billion in 1996.[7] New York State alone spent $716 million on prison construction projects in 1999 and 2000.[8] In the 1990s, a prison was built somewhere in rural America every fifteen days.[9]

And rural towns bent over backward to entice public and private prisons with perks: housing subsidies for prison employees, donated land, and substantial tax breaks to corporations willing to build in small towns. Rural communities that host inmates benefit from federal antipoverty funds. With a captive population behind bars earning no income but counting as residents, impoverished towns across the United States qualify for more government money based on their "low-income population." For example, the two prisons in Coxsackie, New York, made up almost 28 percent of its 1990 population in the census, which reduced its median income and made it eligible to receive more federal funds from the Department of Housing and Urban Development.[10] Some of the largest federal assistance programs—Temporary Aid for Needy Families (TANF), public education, and Section 8 public housing—depend on census data to distribute benefits across the nation.

Appleton Struggles to Attract Inmates

Despite the demand for inmate beds, the medium security prison built next to the Swift County Fairgrounds in Appleton sat empty for almost nine months; its white building blending into the perpetually snowy backdrop of the small Minnesota town. The unoccupied prison missed its first principal and interest payments to bondholders in February 1993.[11] Thompson was losing weight and sleep waiting for inmates to breathe life into the prison. He was hopeful that the Appleton Prison Corporation would sign a contract with Alaska. He was on twenty-four-hour alert and kept his bags packed in case he received a call to meet with their Department of Corrections. The deal fell through after Alaska's corrections union got wind of the potential contract. "That's when the newspapers and TV stations started coming out and saying, 'You smart people, you spent $27 million and you don't have anything to show for it,'" said Thompson.[12] Articles ran in the *New York Times* and the *Los Angeles Times*, and Michael Moore covered the story on his show *TV Nation*. State policy makers introduced legislation allowing the state to buy or lease the prison, which was on the verge of default.

Early on, once construction was completed, Appleton hosted an open house at the Prairie Correctional Facility. Thompson hired buses to bring people to the facility, where they took guided tours. They invited residents of neighboring towns, who were concerned about "prisoners getting out and ravaging through the surrounding countryside." But Thompson said these concerns were relieved after the tours. "These weren't inmates who were classified as violent, even if they had been classified as violent in the past," Thompson said. "And besides that, they aren't getting out. It's constructed like a high-security prison, razor wire and all."[13]

Thompson vowed to quit smoking once a contract to house inmates was signed.[14] He met with the Minnesota corrections secretary, and the meeting led to a surprising phone call from the state's head of corrections: "'Bob, I just got off the phone with Puerto Rico. They are looking for at least 500 beds. I gave them your name."[15] Thompson wasted no time. He flew to Puerto Rico to meet with their corrections officials and negotiated a contract to house 500 men at the prison. On his return to Appleton, Thompson met a rejoicing 185 employees who were now assured of job security. It was April 1993, and the Prairie Correctional Facility was about to welcome its first prisoners—350 Puerto Rican men. Thompson said that the Minnesota corrections secretary had warned him that the Puerto Rican inmates may be difficult. "You know, you're not professionally trained in corrections," Thompson recalled the corrections head telling him. "I know you've been around and you've seen a lot of different prisons and met with a lot of different sentencing jurisdictions, but I'm just going to warn you that there could be a problem with Puerto Rican inmates. They are not easy to handle."[16] The corrections staff brushed up on their Spanish and prepared for the men who would soon be housed behind bars at their facility.

The commonwealth of Puerto Rico officially began renting cells in May 1993, paying an estimated $50 a day per prisoner. But eventually Appleton started sending inmates back to Puerto Rico as the territory opened a new prison and individuals reached their parole dates. The Federal Bureau of Investigation opened an investigation into allegations that guards assaulted the prisoners, and in March 1995 Minnesota sent back the remaining thirty-seven Puerto Rican inmates. A spokesperson for the Prairie Correctional Facility reported that the "inmates were taken to an undisclosed airport and flown back to Puerto Rico under guard aboard a chartered passenger jet."[17] In July 1996, the FBI closed its investigation, citing insufficient evidence to support allegations by former prison employees that prison guards had beaten inmates and locked them in unheated cells during the winter.[18]

In 1994, Appleton signed a contract to house Colorado inmates. By the summer of 1995, approximately 1,000 inmates were shipped out of Colorado and sent to correctional facilities in Minnesota and Texas, and 514 of them were behind bars at the Prairie Correctional Facility.

A 1996 article noted that "the prison-building boom of the past decade has failed to keep up with lengthier sentences and tougher parole requirements, leaving the DOC with roughly eight beds for every ten prisoners."[19] Thompson's hard work appeared to pay off. The residents were cautious but soon saw hundreds of people driving out to the prison to go to work. Even former Mayor Ron Ronning worked at the facility for many years, managing correctional staff. "It's a senior citizen community, so they seemed more concerned about the far-fetched concepts," said Ronning. "What's an inmate like? Could he escape? What will happen?"[20]

Assured that the prison could potentially bring in over $10 million in revenue a year, residents soon warmed to the idea of the town's new architecture. The lights were on at night, the grocery store profited from the traffic, and the gas stations made more revenue than ever before. Thompson estimates that the prison provided about $1 million of business to the hospital each year. Thompson said they sold the prison idea on the premise that the people running it were small-town, rural people with values. Thompson recalls that soon after welcoming its first inmates, the Evangelical Lutheran Church of America founded a Lutheran congregation inside the prison called Prisoners of Hope. It had incarcerated individuals on its council.[21]

The news that Appleton had built a prison and successfully started to fill it caught the attention of small towns across the country. Thompson recalls, "A lot of towns became interested and [said], 'Why can't we have a prison, too?' If I had a dollar for every phone call that I got with someone asking that question." Prairie Correctional was built to capitalize on the overcrowding of other state facilities by housing inmates from Colorado, Idaho, and Minnesota. The supply of incarcerated individuals fluctuated, but by 1996 the prison was once again in default on the prison bonds with a $26.7 million principal debt and $9.7 million in unpaid interest.[22]

CCA Bails Out Appleton

In the fall of 1996, CCA offered to refinance and manage the Prairie Correctional Facility. They offered $22.5 million to buy the bonds, repaying the initial investors their principal plus roughly a 1 percent return. As an added bonus, the nation's largest private prison company invested $25 million to expand the facility. The terms of the deal ensured that CCA's investment would be repaid over a twenty-year term at 9.25 percent interest, and the private prison corporation would own the facility outright.

By October 1997, CCA had constructed 774 new beds for inmates, expanding the prison's capacity to more than 1,000 medium security beds. CCA became the largest payer of taxes in Swift County. For more than a decade, CCA managed the facility, housing inmates from Iowa, Colorado, Idaho, North Dakota, Wisconsin, Hawaii, Washington, and Minnesota. At its peak, the prison paid $600,000 a year in utilities and hundreds of thousands of dollars in property taxes. They donated funds to Toys for Tots, supported the town's rotary club, and assisted with upgrades to the local public golf course.

Idaho housed inmates at the Prairie Correctional Facility in Appleton because Idaho had run out of space. Its prison population nearly doubled between the mid-1990s and the mid-2000s, to just fewer than 7,000 inmates.[23] A big driver of Idaho's prison population was people sentenced for felony substance abuse offenses, which increased from 957 in 1996 to 1,807 in 2005.[24]

A 1997 article framed CCA's prison in Appleton as a success story: a "$28 million private prison built by the town of Appleton, Minnesota (population 1,300) signed a contract with Puerto Rico to house 350 inmates. Colorado and Idaho later sent prisoners. Business is now so good that the prison, which was bought last year by the CCA, is doubling its capacity to 1,076 beds."[25] Buoyant with the success of the prison, Thompson told a reporter, "It appears that the way things are going in this country, the market's never going to dry up."[26]

By October, the prison boasted a staff of 400 and an annual payroll of $8 million. Its incarcerated population mostly came from Colorado, but it also housed individuals from Idaho, Minnesota, and North Dakota.[27] By 1997, Colorado shipped nearly 1,700 inmates out of state because they ran out of prison cells in Colorado, and 1,000 of them were housed in Appleton by the summer of 1998.

There are Appletons everywhere. In 1990, city leaders in Hinton, Oklahoma, built a prison with $38 billion in bond money at a 9.23 percent interest rate. Eight years later the town's economic development board auctioned off its 812-bed Great Plains Correctional Facility. Cornell Corrections (acquired by the GEO Group in 2010) paid $43 million for the prison, adding $18 million in profit to the town of Hinton. The town used $2 million to build an eighteen-hole golf course and country club, including one hundred lots for new homes, $700,000 to build its new fire station, more than $900,000 to improve the local high school—including a 1,000-seat metal grandstand for the football stadium—and $800,000 to build a two-story terminal at its airport.[28] Ironically, Cornell Corporation deeded the prison back to the city in December 1999, which allowed Cornell to manage the prison but permitted the town to receive a share of profits if it could convince the federal government to send inmates to the prison. Although seemingly a success story, when Arizona ended its contract with the prison in 2010, it sat empty until early 2014 when the Department of Justice finally shipped inmates there. The GEO Group is under contract with the federal Bureau of Prisons to house inmates at the facility from 2017 through 2020.

Although the 1990s and early 2000s saw huge increases in the nation's prison population, growth slowed in the late 2000s. The economic downturn, partly attributed to the subprime mortgage crisis and the collapse of the housing bubble, opened huge shortfalls in state budgets. States tightened their belts and slashed their expensive corrections budgets. These expenditures were already coming under scrutiny in states as lawmakers reconsidered whether incarcerating so many people for so long actually protected public safety. For the first time in decades, prison reform became a subject of significant public discussion in Texas, South Carolina, and Louisiana.

Existing as a ready-made facility with extra prison beds was the key to the Prairie Correctional Facility's early success. But both Colorado and North Dakota hoped the Appleton solution was not a long-term one. In 1999, the Colorado prisoners who were housed at Prairie were sent home when Colorado had built enough cells.[29] North Dakota had relied on the Appleton prison for years to relieve overcrowding, but it eventually built its capacity even as the state's prison population continued to grow. North Dakota built new cells in county jails, opened a treatment center in September 2006, and expanded other facilities.[30]

Appleton soon found itself delicately balancing out of state contracts with a need to house Minnesota inmates to ensure long-term profits. Making a business calculation that reserving cells for its own state inmates would pay off, in the summer of 2006 Idaho transferred 270 of its inmates out of Appleton to a correctional facility in Texas so the Prairie Correctional Facility could house incarcerated individuals from Minnesota. After the transfer, only 31 Idaho inmates remained.[31] Despite the end of the Colorado and North Dakota contracts, and the exodus of the Idaho inmates, in early 2009 the Prairie Correctional Facility was almost at capacity, with 542 inmates from Minnesota and another 525 from Washington. Things would look different in Appleton by Christmas.

By the end of 2009, the Prairie Correctional Facility had lost its contract with Washington. Steve Conry, vice president at CCA, commenting about the loss of so many incarcerated individuals said that the company was seeing demand to house inmates in the deep South and the far West. According to Conry, Appleton's location in the Midwest proved a disadvantage because of the distance inmates would have to travel to Appleton.[32]

CCA increasingly found it difficult to sign contracts with states that struggled with decimated budgets. Many of these states reduced their prison populations to save money or double-bunked incarcerated individuals in lieu of sending them out of state.[33] Compounding CCA's troubles, two Minnesota state-owned correctional facilities underwent expansions. At one time Minnesota had housed more than 1,000 incarcerated individuals at Appleton, but by 2009 they no longer needed the private facility. Minnesota had opened four new housing units at a medium security prison in Faribault and added new beds at the correctional center in Moose Lake.[34] Prairie Correctional Facility staff pinned their hopes on a bid to the Alaska Department of Corrections to hold its prisoners being housed outside of the state, but the Alaska Department of Corrections announced it would sign a contract with Cornell Corporation to house up to 1,000 inmates at their new facility in Hudson, Colorado.[35] They couldn't fill the cells in Appleton.

In the late fall of 2009, the Prairie Correctional Facility competed against Kansas, Michigan, Nevada, Oklahoma, and Virginia to house 2,000 medium security individuals from Pennsylvania. With the support of the Minnesota Department of Corrections, the state sent a proposal to Pennsylvania, offering to relieve their overcrowded state prisons. By January 2010, Pennsylvania's prison population stood at more than 51,000 inmates housed in twenty-seven facilities intended to hold 43,222 inmates.[36] Ronning, who was Appleton's mayor at the time, said that the Pennsylvania inmates would be a "dream come true."[37]

In January 2010, Pennsylvania's Secretary of Corrections Jeffrey Beard announced that they would send the incarcerated men to state-run prisons in Michigan and Virginia. Prairie had lost the bid. Once again Appleton found itself unable to offer an attractive alternative. CCA closed the prison in February, and nearly 450 employees lost their jobs. Tim Wengler, the prison's warden, told Minnesota Public Radio, "The Department of Corrections did their job the right way and we're a victim of that."[38]

At the prison's closing, CCA's CEO Damon Hininger said, "We are disappointed to make the decision to close the Prairie Correctional Facility. Unfortunately, without an inmate population large enough to significantly utilize the facility, maintaining operations at the Prairie facility isn't economically viable. I would like to thank our outstanding and dedicated staff who have done an exceptional job, and we look forward to resuming operations at the facility at some point in the future."[39]

Appleton's economy crashed. The $1.1 million the facility provided to Appleton annually made up almost 60 percent of the city's budget. The closure reduced revenues for public utilities, and the county's solid waste fund ran at a $75,000 deficit because the prison's trash and recyclable goods were no longer part of the sewage system.[40] CCA and Swift County negotiated a tax agreement including a reduction in the 2009 valuation from $42.9 million to $32 million for the 2010 taxes, which meant a loss of $50,000 in tax revenue to the county. The city of Appleton received $250,000 less in revenue and the Lac Qui Parle Valley School District saw a decrease of $40,000 because of the lowered value of the prison.[41] Property taxes jumped 30 percent for residents the year after the facility closed in an attempt to close the deficit.[42]

The prison closure forced pizza parlors and restaurants to close, unemployment soared, and younger families moved away. Driving around the town of 1,200 residents on a 20-degree day in December 2015, I felt the desolation. The prison has been closed since early 2010, despite rumors over the years of a contract for federal inmates or that the facility would house incarcerated individuals from California. Roads were potholed, only a few restaurants remained, and the town's one gas station seemed to be the central hub of activity.

I stopped at one of Appleton's only restaurants, JJ's, known for its hamburgers and milkshakes. I ordered a coffee and sat at a booth by a window. The only other diners were a woman in a blue Walmart fleece who sat in a booth with her husband, a heavyset man on disability. She used to work at the Prairie Correctional Facility, but today she works for Casey's General Store. If the prison receives inmates again, she said she hopes Casey's will finally open twenty-four hours a day. "No store in this town is open past eleven at night," she told me. The prison reopening would be a godsend to the town. "Everything is dying now," she said.

The former correction officer said she had no previous correctional experience and CCA provided her with two weeks of training, paying her $11 an hour as a prison guard. For overtime, she collected time and a half. She had no love of working at the prison and mentioned she would never take another job there. Her husband, despite collecting disability checks, said that he would like to get a job in the towers if the prison reopens—he was an excellent marksman, he said.

Appleton Learns A Tough Lesson

It was less than a mile from the civic center to the parking lot of the Prairie Correctional Facility. A thin layer of snow covered the grass in front of the razor-wire gate, a layer of it resting on the CCA sign in front of the prison. In the near distance, the town's water tower stood head-and-shoulders over the tree-lined streets. It read "APPLETON" in proud red letters. The empty parking lot was plowed, and I parked and walked up to what appeared to be an operational prison. The door was unlocked, so I let myself in. The entrance to the prison was empty but for a drained aquarium, a plaid couch that looked twenty years old, a cactus, a dead plant, and ACA accreditation certificates on the walls. One wall was bare except for a poster of CCA's logo and vision, mission, and values statements. A metal detector stood pushed into a corner, and an open door exposed metal bars blocking off the rest of the prison.

CCA has maintained the facility since its closure, including its ACA accreditation status and a $750,000 project to upgrade its roof in 2015. Six people were employed full-time at the facility, ensuring that it stayed up to code in hopes the facility would one day reopen. One employee must flush the prison's 800 toilets each week so the pipes don't freeze.[43] Upon learning that CCA would close the facility in 2009, Minnesota State Congressman Andrew Falk wrote an op-ed in a local paper: "There is no responsibility I take more seriously than the need to create and protect local jobs. I still haven't given up hope the situation with Prairie can be resolved, and I look forward to working with everyone involved to reach a solution."[44]

In 2012, CCA proposed something surprising. As state budgets struggled with considerable deficits, CCA sent letters to forty-eight states offering to buy their prisons. In return, CCA proposed a twenty-year contract to manage the prisons with a guarantee that the prisons would remain 90 percent occupied.[45] The letter was signed by CCA's Chief Corrections Officer Harley Lappin, a former director of the federal Bureau of Prisons. The letter read, "In short, CCA is earmarking $250 million for purchasing and managing government-owned corrections facilities. The program is a new opportunity for federal, state or local governments that are considering the benefits of partnership corrections."[46] The previous year, Ohio closed a deal with CCA to sell its Lake Erie Correctional Facility to the corporation in exchange for $72.7 million, a way to reduce its budget shortfalls. CCA's self-proclaimed "corrections investment initiative" made headlines, but no state took them up on Lappin's offer.

Building Prisons "On Spec"

Many private prison companies bear the risk of building jails and prisons without any guarantee that departments of corrections will send them individuals to house. The Prairie Correctional Facility in Appleton, Minnesota, was built on speculation ("spec"), a term referring to the construction of a building that is financed and built without a contract for occupants (in the real estate market) or incarcerated individuals (in corrections). The strategy has come under scrutiny by those who worry about mass incarceration in the United States, but it was a growth strategy for private prisons in the 1990s and early 2000s. Constructing prisons before a contract is in place can be financially remunerative, as it allows the contractor to circumvent government procurement laws and presents a ready-made facility when state corrections find their own prisons overcrowded.

One of the most persuasive reasons for corrections administrators to use private prisons is the speed with which prisoners can be transferred to them.[47] Using private prisons also provides the state with flexibility; they can easily shed capacity when prison populations drop. Relying on corporations to house inmates when governments don't have enough prison beds allows departments of corrections to pivot without long-term obligations to employees for pensions or the upkeep of empty facilities.

In 1998, CCA was desperate to gain a foothold in the California prison boom and invested $216 million to build three medium to high security prisons on "spec" with just over 4,000 beds. "If you build it in the right place, the prisoners will come. . . . Clearly the need is here," David Myers, CCA's West Coast regional president, told the *Wall Street Journal.* Myers added that California has "a prison crisis. They have tough (anticrime) legislation, and they're going to need prison beds. The private sector can step up to the plate and provide them."[48] In 2000, Susan Hart, vice president of communications for CCA, justified the practice of building spec prisons: "We are anticipating their needs without costing government or taxpayers any capital."[49]

But reformers criticize how much control spec prisons give corporations over where and when prisons are built, how large they are, and how they are designed. Instead of a well-planned strategic discussion between the department of corrections and other state agencies about the need for more prison beds, where in the state those beds are located, and how the prison is constructed for the most efficient use of state resources, private companies and developers hold all the cards. Private developers do not need to apply for any authorization or license from a state corrections agency to build and operate facilities. In fact, many spec prisons—as the Appleton story shows—don't even hold prisoners from their own state.

The practice is so controversial that in 2001 Wisconsin's joint budget committee recommended banning all future speculative prison construction in the state. Despite criticism that building spec prisons encourages higher incarceration rates because the prison beds exist, private companies capitalized on the venture. Between 1990 and 1999, private prisons expanded their design capacity—meaning they could house more inmates—from just over 15,000 to an astonishing 119,000.[50] Although a tremendous growth strategy in the nineties, private prison companies have started to put the brakes on spec prisons. "They basically had overbuilt," Anton Hie said, an analyst at Jefferies and Co. who covered CCA and the GEO Group. "There was a lot of promise of new inmates that never came . . . it kind of all came crashing in."[51]

CCA's 2015 Annual Report noted, "In the long-term, we would like to see continued and meaningful utilization of our remaining capacity and better visibility from our customers before we add any additional capacity on a speculative basis."[52] GEO Group's 2015 Annual Report was more optimistic: "In addition to pursuing organic growth through the RFP process, we will from time to time selectively consider the financing and construction of new facilities or expansions to existing facilities on a speculative basis without having a signed contract with a known customer."[53]

For rural communities facing skyrocketing unemployment rates—usually from the decline in agricultural and manufacturing jobs—even the news of spec prisons sitting barren across the nation does little to deter building them or welcoming a private prison conglomerate into their towns.

The Case of Hardin, Montana

A little more than a decade after the Prairie Correctional Facility housed its first inmates, officials in Hardin, Montana, more than 600 miles west of Appleton, had the same idea. They wanted to create new jobs, increase tax revenue, and reap the economic benefits a prison can bring to a small town. James Parkey, a Texas-based prison developer and architect, approached officials in Hardin, offering to build a prison on speculation and bring revenue to the impoverished town, whose unemployment rate was closing in on 10 percent. His team—a construction firm to build the prison, dedicated staff to find prisoners and manage the facility, and underwriters to sell the bonds and conduct an economic feasibility study—would take care of everything. Parkey promised to generate 150 jobs and at least $100,000 in annual per-prisoner fees.[54]

In 2004, officials made a deal with Parkey to build a 464-bed prison in Hardin, a town of 3,600 residents in southeast Montana. The city would own the prison through the tax-supported Two Rivers Trade Port Authority (TRA). The county would finance the prison, a private prison company would manage the facility and receive a portion of the profits, and the state and federal government would send the inmates.[55] Three years later, the Two Rivers Detention Facility was poised to open its doors, but, like Appleton, the town could not find individuals to fill its beds. For seven years the $27-million facility sat vacant. The state department of corrections never sent inmates there, and the Montana Attorney General's office issued an opinion stating that the facility could not legally house out-of-state inmates. Three years later, the city overturned that opinion.

Despite the Montana Attorney General's opinion, it is common practice for states to ship inmates out of state to serve their prison sentence in a private facility hundreds or thousands of miles away from their home. A prisoner's sentence remains the same whether housed in a state or private facility, in or out of the prisoner's home state. The sentences for prisoners housed out-of-state are governed by the law of the state their conviction stems from, and that state's rules and regulations apply to the those shipped away to private prisons out of state.

Hardin continued to look for people to house behind bars in its prison. In 2009, the Hardin City Council supported a proposal to house prisoners from the U.S. military prison at Guantanamo Bay in Cuba, passing a resolution noting their capacity to provide "a safe and secure environment, pending trial and/or deportation." The facility was not equipped to house maximum security prisoners, so the plan fell through.[56]

Desperate to find inmates, in the fall of 2009 the city announced a ten-year contract with the American Private Police Force Organization (APPF), which claimed to be a paramilitary, security, and investigative services company. It was later revealed by news organizations that the company's public face, California resident Michael Hilton, had a criminal past, including a long history of civil fraud.[57]

The prison grew to become an embarrassment to the town. In 2014, Louisiana-based private prison corporation Emerald Correctional Management took over the operational reins. They procured a contract with the federal Bureau of Indian Affairs to pay the company $75 a day per inmate, all of whom came from American Indian reservations in Montana, North Dakota, and Wyoming. Despite the contract, the average inmate population hovered around 150, not nearly enough to break even.[58] The facility was $40 million in debt, and worse, the Bureau of Indian Affairs canceled its contract in November 2015. Hardin's unemployment rate had reached 10 percent, and the lack of inmates proved a grave disappointment to its residents. By January 2016, the 92,000 square foot facility reported housing zero inmates. Warden Ken Keller and his program manager, Hope Keller (his wife), were the detention center's only two employees: "There's two of us here," Warden Keller told the *Billings Gazette*, "We're keeping the lights on and chugging away."[59]

In November hopes were high again when the federal government posted help-wanted ads for cooks and correctional officers to work at the facility. More concrete news emerged in February that the Bureau of Indian Affairs was negotiating another contract to operate the Two Rivers Detention Facility, which might be signed as early as April.[60]

These spec prisons "run the risk of becoming half-empty white elephants marooned on the American landscape."[61] It is no accident that so many U.S. prisons are in rural areas where the land is cheaper and more plentiful, and where inmates who mostly hail from the cities are housed hundreds of miles from their family.

Do Prisons Really Help the Rural Economy?

The research on whether there are long-term positive economic gains associated with prison development is decidedly mixed. Sociologist John Eason's research of the prison boom on rural towns across decades indicates a slight net positive for towns that attract prisons. His analysis indicates that "on average, towns that adopted a prison in the first period of the prison boom (1969–1978) experienced an increase in median home value and median family income, and a reduction in poverty."[62] However, Eason acknowledges that prisons provided only "a short-term economic boon in some periods for rural communities that built prisons. While prison-building increases median home value, reduces unemployment, and eases poverty, these effects are not lasting."[63]

Other research suggests that prisons do not produce the economic growth rural towns once expected. Even if a prison is built in a rural community, many of its jobs are not doled out to residents. Although correction officers do not typically need advanced degrees, they need a certain level of education that is not a given in all rural communities. As was the case in Appleton, a good many correction officers came from other cities and counties. Most did not uproot their families and homes and move to Appleton; instead they commuted. Despite the Super 8 and a few restaurants, the town did not have the infrastructure that neighboring towns offered. In addition, correction officer turnover is dramatically high—41 percent in private prisons and just 15 percent in public prisons.[64] Correction officers and jailers have one of the highest rates of injuries and illnesses, often due to confrontations with inmates.[65] One study analyzed death certificate data from twenty-one states and determined that correction officers' risk of suicide was 39 percent higher than that of all other professions combined.[66]

Inmate labor may displace workers who live in rural communities because inmates are paid poorly, usually well below the minimum wage.[67] Prisoners typically earn less than 50 cents an hour, making it quite profitable for industries—and even community-based retailers— to use prison labor. Inmates in Colorado are paid between 74 cents and $4 per day for working in prison. The Haystack Mountain Goat Dairy contracted with the Colorado Department of Corrections for labor and paid inmates to work at a dairy processing cheese products the company sold to retailers such as Whole Foods. The dairy claimed that, "depending on their schedule, inmates can earn anywhere from $1,000 per year to over $2,500 per year."[68] Although inmates working in the dairy learned job skills that could translate into employment after their release, the idea that prisoners made less than minimum wage to make goat cheese for eventual sale at Whole Foods caused a public outcry. In this case, advocates protested, concerned that inmate labor was being exploited. But often communities are upset because they feel that inmates are competing for their jobs.

The median wage for state inmates is 20 cents an hour and for federal prisoners about 31 cents an hour.[69] Those housed behind bars are paid pennies on the dollar because prison jobs do not fall under the Federal Labor Standards Act (FLSA), which sets minimum legal standards for wages and working conditions.

Although inmate labor may worry local workers, local leadership may find the prospect of cheap labor appealing. Consider the 2016 announcement of planned closures of inmate work centers in Oklahoma after a deal to rent a private prison from CCA. To cut costs, the Oklahoma Department of Corrections consolidated fifteen Department of Corrections Work Centers, transferring 1,000 inmates to one prison in Granite, Oklahoma, and shuffling the inmates from the Granite prison to a private facility owned by CCA in Sayre, Oklahoma. City administrators from across the state who benefited from inmate labor from the work centers protested the decision at a Board of Corrections meeting that summer. A city administrator for the town of Marlow voiced concern that the loss of these inmates "would severely cripple our ability to continue to serve our community with mowing, street repair, maintenance, and other services." Seminole's city manager echoed this: "We got the call like everyone else this morning, and panic set in quickly."[70]

A 2003 report by the Sentencing Project studying the effect of rural prison towns in New York found that over twenty-five years there was "no significant difference or discernible pattern of economic trends between the seven rural counties in New York that hosted a prison and the seven rural counties that did not host a prison."[71] Another study noted that manufacturing industries and some others tend to generate "clusters of linked industries," something prisons do not produce.[72]

How Are Prisoners Counted?

Once a decade, the U.S. Census Bureau counts individuals that make up the population. Under the traditional "usual residence" rule, people are counted where they live and sleep. But "usual" residence might not reflect "actual" or "legal" residence. Where a person lives, sleeps, or works can differ from where he or she permanently resides or is registered to vote. So how are inmates counted? Incarcerated adults are "counted at the facility" in which they are housed, even if that facility is hundreds (or even thousands) of miles away from their actual residence.[73]

Under the bureau's usual residency rule, more than 2 million adults were and will continue to be "counted as residents of their prison cells for the entire decade following the [2010] census."[74] The census provides the data needed to apportion House seats and determine state legislative district boundaries. It also serves a critical economic purpose: it affects the annual allotment of more than $400 billion in federal and state funding to state and local governments.[75] State legislative districts are redrawn every decade after the census, and counting inmates as residents of the town where their prison or jail sits has significant political repercussions.

Residents of rural areas that house prisons benefit; their district appears much more populated than it is. Ironically, inmates can't vote in forty-eight states while they are prisoners (Maine and Vermont are the exceptions). This prison-based gerrymandering also disproportionately boosts political power to rural, often Republican, districts. Political science professor Marie Gottschalk notes that this practice also affects urban centers, which lose huge voting blocs because so many of their residents are locked away in rural America. In Pennsylvania, almost 40 percent of the state's inmates come from Philadelphia, which doesn't have a state prison. Most of these inmates are black and Latino and are considered to be residents of the counties where they're incarcerated.[76]

After the 2010 census, more than 185 counties and other small towns changed how they drew their districts and did not include prison populations.[77] These efforts even extend to Congress. U.S. House Representative Hakeem Jeffries (D-N.Y.) and twenty-three other representatives introduced a bill to the Committee on Oversight and Government Reform in 2015. The Fairness in Incarcerated Representation Act would require the secretary to count inmates at their last place of residence before incarceration. The committee has not yet reported the bill to the House floor.[78]

Advocates are attempting to change how inmates are counted through administrative challenges to the "counting-at-facility" rule. On May 30, 2015, the bureau submitted its 2010 Census Residence Rule and Residence Situations for public comment. Of the 262 comments received, "156 suggested that prisoners should be counted at their home or pre-incarceration address."[79] After reviewing the comments, the bureau rejected the proposed change. Counting inmates at a location other than their respective facilities, it concluded, "would violate the concept of usual residence, since the majority of people in prisons live and sleep most of the time at the prison."[80]

The "counting-at-facility" rule remains unchanged, and in June 2016 the bureau submitted its Proposed 2020 Census Rules for public comment. Civil rights groups were especially vocal about the hypocrisy of the bureau's proposal that deployed service members should be counted at their home address (usual residence) in the United States even if they *live and sleep elsewhere for most of the time* at the time the census is conducted.[81]

Minnesota Confronts Prison Overcrowding

In the fall of 2015, Appleton, and all of Minnesota for that matter, found themselves in the news again. The state's prison population was projected to increase. Where would they house these inmates? Ought the state change its criminal justice tactics to reduce its prison population? Corrections officials and state legislators confronted a tough decision: whether or not to send the inmates to Appleton, where CCA had ensured the prison was updated and ready to open its doors.

Since 2010 when the Prairie Correctional Facility doors closed for lack of inmates, the state's prison population had climbed. In fact, the prison population was on the rise even when the facility closed. Despite seeing the crime rate cut by more than 30 percent in the last decade, Minnesota's incarceration rate had almost doubled between 2000 and 2015. An increase in mandatory minimum sentences for certain crimes and new crimes on the books greatly increased the number of people serving felony convictions. In 2015, Minnesota claimed the fifth fastest prison growth rate in the country.[82]

Lawmakers had turned toward more draconian policies. Amid much fanfare, they enacted the state driving-while-intoxicated law in 2002. Today, 700 inmates can trace their incarceration to that law. Policy makers also focused on legislation that increased sentences for drug crimes, lowering the weight for possessing methamphetamines and heroin to the same as for cocaine, and lowering the minimum weight for high-level charges. Minnesota also cracked down on illegal guns. In 1998, state legislators increased the minimum sentence for a violent felon caught with a firearm from eighteen months to five years. This policy change, according to the Minnesota Sentencing Guidelines Commission, created a demand for about 400 more prison beds.[83]

Faced with too many inmates to house at its ten state prisons, Minnesota did something many states are forced to do—house state prisoners at county jails. County jails are not built for this; they typically don't have the resources or programming for long-term inmates. Three years after the Minnesota Department of Corrections started to send state prison inmates to county jails, nearly 400 state prisoners were housed there.[84] With the state prison population projected to grow to 10,885 by 2022, the state knew it would quickly run out of space even relying heavily on its jails to pick up the slack.

Minnesota is not alone in having increased its prison population despite dramatically lowered crime rates. Between 2006 and 2014, twenty-two states increased their prison population, and saw crime drop by an average of 20 percent.[85] The political dynamics in Minnesota are a microcosm of what states across the country face in regulating crime and punishment, private versus government run prisons, and just how large the prison population must be to ensure the public safety. In 2015, Minnesota state legislators created a task force to examine the size and scope of its prison population, hoping to pass legislation that would safely reduce the number of inmates in their prisons and jails. After debating policy solutions and hearing months of testimony from corrections officials, the sentencing commission, academics, and criminal justice experts, the task force enunciated the choice before them: they could either reduce their prison population or find new prison beds.

All Eyes on Appleton

At the center of this political and practical debate was a Department of Corrections plan to ask for $140 million in a state bonding bill to add a wing to an existing state prison rather than using the already-constructed and vacant Prairie Correctional Facility.

The politics around mass incarceration, racial disparities, criminal justice policies, and the private prison industry collided in Minnesota. CCA offered a compromise. They would lease the facility back to Minnesota for about $7 million a year. Many legislators supported the deal, and the citizens of Appleton prayed that the lights would turn on again at Prairie Correctional.

Leasing deals are not unusual. California has relied on private prisons to relieve its correctional overcrowding, sometimes leasing prison space from for-profit prison corporations but opting to manage the facilities with their own correction officers. The California City Correctional Center southwest of Death Valley National Park is operated by the California Department of Corrections and Rehabilitation, but the state leases the prison from CCA. After California extended its lease for the prison through the fall of 2020, the company's CEO stated: "Our California City Correctional Center has proven to be a great solution to provide CDCR [California Department of Corrections and Rehabilitation] with in-state prison capacity operated by the CDCR, while avoiding significant upfront capital costs associated with new construction."[86]

But many Minnesotans did not want to follow California's example of leasing the prison. Tensions ran high at the state house that day, and the legislature had to take an hour-long recess after protesters, upset about the idea of sending inmates to a private prison in their backyard, consistently interrupted the committee hearing. Black Lives Matter and other civil rights groups carried signs in the hearing room and in front of the state legislative building. One read, "We can have jobs without prisons," and another, "Funds 4 Human Needs Not More Prison Beds #STOPCCA." Some protesters yelled: "Private prisons are akin to slavery—treating prisoners as commodities." They accused the committee members of racism.[87]

African Americans make up 6 percent of Minnesota's population but 35 percent of the state's prison population.[88] A partnership of community, faith, labor, and civil rights organizations spearheaded by ISAIAH, a faith-based organization of a hundred congregations across Minnesota, publicly opposed the lease of the Prairie Correctional Facility in Appleton. ISAIAH organized candlelight vigils outside the state capital to protest the reopening. They put out a statement:

> We will vigil and pray for the thousands of incarcerated Minnesotans as well as for the community of Appleton. It is time to come together and say NO to CCA in Minnesota. No one should ever profit from the incarceration of human beings. We will also pray for the prisoners to be set free. And we will pray for the community of Appleton, MN. The people of Appleton deserves [*sic*] better than the lies and false promises being peddled by CCA and their hired gun DC lobbyists. Together, we can do better.[89]

Despite protests, the House passed the bill allowing the Minnesota Department of Corrections to manage Prairie Correctional. But the bill missed a critical deadline in the state Senate in April, forestalling the legislation.

I attended a Minnesota prison population task force meeting a few months earlier when legislators heard testimony from the state's Department of Probation about how many people were sent back to prison for technical violations of probation. A person may be sent back to prison or jail not for committing a new crime but for violating a condition of release, such as failing a drug test. The task force discussed how their prison population compared to other midwestern states and whether the sentencing guidelines should be reformed. Mayor Chad Syltie and Swift County Board of Commissioners member Gary Hendrickx sat in the audience, listening intently to the testimony about how the prison population could be reduced.

Hendrickx, who also owns a Subway Sandwich shop in Appleton, organized letters from Appleton residents to the legislature and to the Department of Corrections in support of reopening the Prairie Correctional Facility. He even helped organize a letter from local ministers stating that they would work with the inmates to rehabilitate them.

Mayor Syltie and I met in an empty room of the capital and discussed the political dynamics around the reopening of the 1,640-bed prison in his town. He told me, excitedly:

> Just take the hardware store as an example. Right now, that gentleman sees twenty people a day go through his door. He will easily see that almost double. You will see it at the café, the gas stations, the auto-repair shops. Every business will be affected. Appleton at one time had two grocery stores. Now we are down to one.[90]

For the mayor of a 1,200-person town, the discussion at the capital that day could make or break the future of his city. If the state legislature approved the lease agreement, the value of the prison would climb, meaning direct revenue for the city from CCA's annual taxes. Syltie said that before the prison closed it had a value of about $32 million. Today it is valued at approximately $14 million. "So you can see in a town of 1,200 people what it did to the value of the town. That was a devastating blow."[91]

To Mayor Syltie and the residents of Appleton, the answer was obvious. Why would the state invest in new construction when a perfectly good facility could turn its lights on tomorrow? Syltie hoped the legislature could work out its political misgivings about private prisons. He thought the lease option was a perfect compromise, allowing the state to manage and run the facility while essentially paying CCA rent and not constructing a new prison. The $140 million it would cost the state to construct new beds would equal twenty years of rent to CCA. Syltie had a valid point. The state would also limit its financial exposure if and when the prison was no longer needed by not paying bonds for two to three decades to fund a prison that may only be needed for five or ten years.

Many powerful people in the state opposed the very idea of putting money in the hands of CCA and everything the nation's largest private prison operator represented. Minnesota Corrections Commissioner Tom Roy, for one, was against the idea: "I have said very publicly, as has the governor, that the support of private prisons is not on our agenda." Roy is on record that he doesn't like the basic principle of private for-profit companies running prisons and that "it is a responsibility that falls clearly on the role of government. Incarceration . . . for corporate profit is the antithesis of America."[92]

State correction officers voiced their own frustration over any contract with the private prison in Appleton. The Minnesota chapter of the American Federation of State, County & Municipal Employees (AFSCME), which represents correction officers, opposed housing state prisoners there. Even though the facility would be run by the state, meaning that the correction officers would belong to their union, AFSCME was still opposed. In part, the opposition was speculative. AFSCME feared the political winds could shift, and the state could turn over the operation of the facility to CCA, which would make it nonunion. There also was the matter convenience. Appleton is about a three-hour drive from Minneapolis, an impossible commute for many union members. But a state lobbyist who represents CCA and other clients explained the larger underlying political forces at play for tiny Appleton. CCA had run a nonunion shop the last time the prison's doors were open, incurring the permanent opposition of AFSCME and the Department of Corrections to CCA ever again gaining a toehold in Minnesota, no matter the terms.

Unions

Private industry is not the only special interest group with a stake in keeping prisons filled. Prison guard unions emerged as a formidable force in state politics in the early 1980s.

The California Correctional Peace Officers Association (CCPOA) is arguably one of the most influential players in California politics. CCPOA began in 1957 as a small prison guards' union. Today the union represents approximately 32,000 prison guards. It rose to prominence when its president, Don Novey, a former correction officer, worked to beef up the union's footprint on California's correctional landscape in the 1980s. Novey was described as the "most important man in California politics that no one had ever heard of."[93] Novey served as president of CCPOA from 1980 until 2002, and led the union's efforts to back tough-on-crime laws. In 1994 CCPOA contributed more than $100,000 to pass Proposition 184, California's "three strikes" ballot initiative, which required lengthy mandatory prison terms for individuals who committed their third crime—it passed with more than 70 percent of the vote. Under Novey, CCPOA created a political action committee, which today is the second largest in California. During Novey's tenure California built twenty-three new prisons.[94]

In 2004, the union's PAC spent more than $1 million to defeat Proposition 66, a ballot initiative to limit the crimes eligible for a life sentence. In 2008, the PAC spent $1 million to defeat Proposition 5, a measure that would have shortened prison sentences for nonviolent drug offenses.[95] Novey negotiated a deal, which expired in 2006, that yielded an average correction officer salary of approximately $70,000 a year and potentially more than $100,000 with overtime. The union also earned members the most generous wage and benefits packages in the nation. As president, Novey negotiated pensions of up to 90 percent of salary beginning at age fifty, which is more than teachers, nurses, or firefighters receive.[96] With the state in a massive fiscal crisis, private prisons offer a way to avoid high salaries and expensive benefits packages.

The California prison union's influence has declined somewhat in the past decade, but it remains a powerful force in California state politics.[97] Since 1989, the California prison guard union has made $22 million in political campaign contributions, more than GEO Group and CCA combined.[98] Unions also butt heads with the private prison industry. California's correction officer union squared off with CCA when the corporate giant planned to open a 2,000-bed prison in California's Mojave Desert. Worried about the loss of union jobs, Novey told the *San Francisco Chronicle*, "Public safety should not be for profit. It's just kind of stupid."[99]

In 1997, around the time CCA was expanding the facility in Appleton, the company tried launching another operation in a small rural town in New York State. Wanting to expand its footprint in the Northeast, where union opposition had made it nearly impossible to increase its presence, CCA bought a tract of land in Fallsburg, a town known for its lakes, ponds, and dairy farms, and intended to build a 1,000-bed minimum security drug treatment center at the site of a former resort hotel.[100]

CCA paid $470,000 for the Olympic Hotel and Spa, a luxury resort on 185 acres, and it seemed that Fallsburg, a dying town in Sullivan County, had at last found a savior.[101] "We would rather have a Marriot or a Hilton build [*sic*] here, but they haven't called us lately," said the town's building inspector.[102] But Fallsburg and CCA ran into a wall of opposition, including Republican Governor George Pataki, the state attorney general, and the head of the corrections department. CCA planned to import prisoners from other states because of New York's ban on private prisons holding New York state prisoners. The prison guard union stood ready to fight the construction of the private prison in Sullivan County. Bob Lawson, the public relations director of the prison guard union, said that private prisons will come to New York "over my dead body."[103] New York's state attorney general vowed, "I'm not going to stand idly by while they bring in prisoners from an undisclosed jurisdiction."[104]

New York is home to one of the nation's other most powerful correctional unions, the 20,000-member New York State Correctional Officers & Police Benevolent Association (NYSCOPB). After lobbying from the union, in 2000 the New York legislature passed the Correctional Facility Moratorium Act, banning private prisons altogether. The only other state with such a ban is Illinois. CCA never built the facility in Fallsburg.

The dependence of poor, rural communities on prisons for employment confronted New York Governor Cuomo in 2011. With more than 4,500 vacant beds in state prisons, Cuomo announced he was closing seven of them, saying in his State of the State address in 2011 that "an incarceration program is not an employment program."[105] To make the plan more palatable, Cuomo promised an aid package of up to $100 million to "help communities end their reliance on incarceration as a major source of employment and economic sustainability."[106]

Typically, the corrections unions balked and trotted out their most effective public rhetoric: Any change in the status quo will harm law-abiding citizens. The president of the state prison guard union called the plan "a direct threat to the public safety of all New Yorkers," adding, "it will jeopardize the safety of inmates and the brave men and women who serve as New York's correctional officers. If enacted, the closures will make New York's tough times even tougher by damaging a prison system that is already overcrowded and understaffed."[107]

By January of 2016, Cuomo had closed thirteen state prisons. In fact, New York reduced its prison population by more than 25 percent from its peak in 1999. Even with this huge dent in its prison population, New York's corrections budget increased by nearly one-third to close to $3 billion.[108] Despite cost-savings from shuttering facilities, it costs more to run the maximum security prisons that didn't close, and New York's strong correctional guard union has ensured that the state will retain as many correction officer jobs as they can.

Texas, too, is home to a powerful prison guard union. Since 2006, Texas has desperately tried to find and retain prison guards. The state Department of Corrections has struggled to compete with high-wage job growth in the state's oil-rich private sector.[109] The Texas chapter of the American Federation of State, County, and Municipal Employees (AFSCME) has joined inmates' rights groups to advocate for improved prison conditions—arguing that prison conditions are dangerous to both employees and inmates—and called for curtailing solitary confinement for death-row prisoners who pose the lowest security risk.[110] The AFSCME Huntsville chapter called for the abolition of private prisons in the state, arguing that if these private facilities aren't closed, looming budget cuts will cost hundreds or even thousands of correction officers their jobs.[111]

Yet University of Michigan Historian Heather Ann Thompson suggests that it is misguided to focus on unions as such powerful forces motivating mass incarceration as opposed to self-interested corporations. "American prison guards organized because they were consistently paid less than workers in other institutions, such as factories and schools, while they were equally exploited on the job and endured far more on-the-job injuries. These injuries stemmed from working in overcrowded prisons where the inmate–guard ratio was dangerously high."[112] Thompson argues that prison guard unions criticize "draconian" policies that lead to mass incarceration since it is prison guards who must consequently manage more inmates than they can handle. Thompson writes that there is "scant evidence" that prison guard unions have much, if any, effect on mass incarceration, and focusing on them rather than on the role of private corporations "obscure[s]" who the "most crucial players" really are.[113]

Appleton's Future Hangs on Its State Legislature

The battle in Minnesota gets to the heart of the complexity of the debate about private prisons. Reopening Prairie Correctional exacerbates concerns about the size and scope of the criminal justice system, including the unprecedented rise of mass incarceration and reliance on the for-profit prison industry. Appleton's story is not abstract, it is concrete. The debate affects an impoverished rural town that built a prison to spur its own economy. Appleton faced years of uncertainty when the prison fought to attract inmates. Now, after years of darkened prison cells, the town can improve its financial security. The prison is owned by CCA, and even though CCA would have no role in its day-to-day operations, the town's future is embroiled in a political debate about the acceptability of private prisons. It did not matter to those opposed to reopening the prison that the state Department of Corrections would operate the facility. The state would still be providing money to a private prison vendor, thereby supporting the for-profit prison industry.

Senate Judiciary Chair Ron Latz (D–St. Louis Park), has represented constituents in his state's legislature for more than a decade. As a cochair of the Minnesota Prison Population Task Force, Latz has had a bird's-eye view into the deliberations. Latz told me that he convened the task force to explore options and possible solutions concerning the state's runaway prison population. Although aware of the unemployment in rural Minnesota, the significance of opening a prison—even if it was only one of the reasons—with economic development goals in mind was fraught. "The last thing we want to do is make criminal justice policy based on economic development." He appeared almost professorial for a moment, as he paused before continuing, "but my goal is not to have to build additional prison space."[114]

Harvard professor Herman "Dutch" Leonard, cochair of the Social Enterprise Initiative at Harvard Business School, would call the proposed relationship between CCA and the Minnesota Department of Corrections "nominal privatization," a partnership in which the private company owns the prison and another entity operates it.[115] According to Leonard, "given the authority to use the existing facility, either public or private operators can provide the services within it; who owns (tax) the title to the property is an insignificant matter."[116] In fact, Leonard believes this type of relationship can provide significant benefits such as avoiding construction delays and eliminating the need for public bond issuance.

I spoke to Latz about the possibility of reopening the Prairie Correctional Facility, and he noted that many legislators, including himself, had no appetite for the proposal. "There is no such thing as a short-term lease. Once you set up an operation like that and the local community becomes dependent on it, it is almost impossible to pull out of it." Latz looked down for a moment. "It's like pulling out of a military base."[117]

In April 2016, the editorial board of the *Star Tribune*, Minnesota's largest newspaper, published an editorial supporting a dramatic reform to the state's sentencing laws. The commission claimed their proposal was the best hope to reduce the state's prison population and eliminate overcrowding in its state prisons. The editorial conceded, however, that if the overcrowding could not be eased, "the state should reopen Appleton as a state-run facility before considering more brick-and-mortar projects to expand existing prisons."[118]

The Legacy of Rural Private Prisons

The Colorado legislature struggled with the future of its own prisons that same April. Colorado's prison population had declined by more than 1,000 people between 2014 and 2015, dramatically reducing the number of individuals housed in the CCA-owned and -operated Kit Carson prison in Burlington. The state legislature debated whether they should bail out CCA by providing $3 million to stave off closure of the prison in eastern Colorado. Policy makers who advocated for the bailout argued that the rural community of Burlington would be devastated by the prison's closure. In a town of barely 4,000 people where the median income was $33,000, the loss of the prison would destroy the community.

Through an arrangement common in private prison contracts, Colorado's contract with CCA guaranteed that the state's Department of Corrections would pay for 3,300 inmate beds no matter how many inmates the facility housed. This occupancy requirement ensured that CCA received a guaranteed revenue each month. The legislature eventually passed the budget, which included $3 million to ensure that CCA would not shutter its facility. Even so, the facility closed in July of 2016, a terrible blow to the community that had benefited from 140 jobs and $1.2 million in property taxes.[119] The Burlington facility only housed 402 inmates when it closed, even though it had the capacity to hold more than 1,400 inmates.[120] Kit Carson became the fourth private prison to close in Colorado since 2009, leaving only three in operation.[121]

Throughout the United States, the story repeats itself. Adelanto, California, a rural desert town two hours north of Los Angeles, is currently home to three correctional facilities with beds for over 3,000 individuals. Two of the facilities are privately owned and operated by GEO Group, and one by the county sheriffs' department. In 2016, the town's city council voted to construct two new privately run correctional facilities. In desperate need of jobs, the town's unemployment rate in 2011 was almost 22 percent. Today that number has dropped to 12 percent.[122]

These small towns show the tension between ensuring enough prison space exists and projecting how to profit from the people who will one day end up behind bars. As Eric Schlosser told me, mass incarceration can't simplistically be attributed to private prisons, but "there is no question that the economic motive has been a major incentive in driving mass incarceration." He pointed to efforts to shut down prisons in New York as an example of how prisons anchor rural economies. "The economic motive, both in building the prisons in the very beginning, and then in maintaining them, has been a real drive of mass incarceration, of which the private prison industry is a subset."[123]

Many argue that for-profit prisons play only a small role in the economics of mass incarceration. Former New York City Corrections Commissioner and Secretary of Corrections in Pennsylvania Martin Horn agrees with Schlosser that economics matter, but he believes the vast influence of correctional unions is more significant in the financial structure of mass incarceration. "Private prison operators aren't the only ones with an economic self-interest in the location and operation of prisons," he explained. "Public prison employees and their unions as well as the communities where public prisons operate similarly lobby hard against closing prisons, for example, look at the difficulty the State of New York had when it tried to close prisons following the falloff in population after the reform of the Rockefeller Drug Laws."[124]

Rural communities with soaring unemployment rates and dwindling economic opportunities have latched onto the idea: if you build it, they will come. Both government agencies and for-profit prison corporations are culpable for promising economic prosperity in exchange for metal and bars. But the difference, although subtle, is significant. Private prisons know what is coming: adding prison beds to an oversaturated prison landscape, often subverting taxpayer bond initiatives, and avoiding politically fraught city council meetings. Prison proposals anywhere tend to provoke vigorous debate; residents fear prison escapes and depressed property values. What incentive does government have to reduce incarceration if companies such as CCA spend millions of dollars a year to maintain prisons in perpetuity?

In April 2017, the Minnesota House of Representatives passed a bill that would allow inmates to be housed in non-publicly-owned facilities. Specifically, the bill would require Minnesota to contract with CCA to operate and purchase or lease to own the Prairie Correctional Facility to alleviate the state's own prison bed shortage. If the bill gets through the Senate, Governor Mark Dayton (who is not a supporter of opening the facility) would have to sign the legislation.[125]

A quarter of a century after Bob Thompson began his quest to build a prison, he looks back at all the challenges he and the town officials faced to keep the lights on at the prison in Appleton. The airport can't land commercial aircraft, and even the closest airports require bussing inmates a hundred miles or more once they land. He told me that, in retrospect, Appleton is not really an ideal town for a prison.

CHAPTER SIX

The Prison Divestment Movement

Yale is [an] intellectual institution and leader and should not
be investing in something that destroys entire populations and
is used to keep people down in our society. As an intellectual
institution, it is our job to promote a way of investing
that shows how humans interact with each other.
JOSEPH GAYLIN, CLASS OF 2019, YALE UNIVERSITY

DIVESTMENT IS THE practice of declining to invest in companies deemed immoral or unethical, and it has a long history as a topic of activism on college campuses. I spent an evening with the Yale Students for Prison Divestment on a cold February night and learned that they believed their university's investment policy should reflect the school's values.

> We, concerned students of Yale University, have reason to believe (prior investment history) that Yale is investing in American private prison corporations, which are engaged in highly unethical practices. Private prison corporations are perpetuating a system of modern slavery through prison labor programs that disproportionately affect black Americans. Our organization exists to further education about private prisons and their injustices, and challenge Yale to take an affirmative stance against these corrupt organizations.(Yale Students for Prison Divestment's mission statement)[1]

Six undergraduate students were huddled around a wooden table, working to ensure that their university wasn't complicit in America's mass incarceration. They were meeting to discuss the logistics of Facebook pages, social media tools, PowerPoint presentations, banners, posters, and event planning. The chair of the group, an African American upperclassman, was instructing them to keep track of volunteer lists, advising where to print materials, and suggesting well-known activists and potential speakers on criminal justice reform issues for a campus event. One student read aloud a draft email she planned to send to the university to request funding for printing materials to "inform other Yale students about private prisons."

They debated about the kind of event that would grab the attention of their classmates. One student suggested "something educational. Perhaps a presentation by some or all of us on why this cause matters, about why private prisons are a thing. Prior divestment history, and why we think this is causing considerable social harm, and maybe at the end, outlining what steps we would take to move away from that situation."

Why were these students here? One grew up with a father in prison. Another had studied mass incarceration and drug policy and was moved enough to join this group, even recruiting his roommate to the cause. One undergraduate spoke passionately about how corrections should never be for profit: "These companies, CCA and GEO Group, the guys that own these private prisons, they are subsidized by the government per head, by beds that they fill. They have cases for judges being indicted for . . . filling up beds under the influence of these corporations, so something like corrections, there should be no reason why more is better if profit is the motive. There should be no profit from corrections."

Students at Columbia University had discovered pension investments in private corrections. These Yale students worried that their school might have similar ties, and their hunch was rooted in history. In 2005 the university had invested in CCA but eventually divested. One student blurted out, "I mean, accidentally divested in that the mutual fund they were investing in just dropped that particular small investment, I think it was $1.5 million in CCA."

Unsure of how to proceed, one student explained how the students at Columbia University found out that the school invested in private prison corporations. The Columbia campaign launched after a student asked the university for its investment portfolio to inform her school research project. "That seems like a way we can't exactly use, because tricking someone in a certain way only works once," one of the students excitedly stated. "I'm sure all the other universities would have instant red flags go up if students said 'we need your financial records for a research project,' considering what happened to Columbia afterward."

Columbia University Divests from Private Prisons

In 2015, Columbia University became the first U.S. institution of higher learning to divest from the private prison industry. Columbia President Lee Bollinger announced that the university would "divest any direct stock ownership interests in companies engaged in the operation of private prisons and refrain from making subsequent investments in such companies." It was a victory remarkable not just for its results but because the campaign that convinced one of the world's foremost universities to reform its investment practices was created and directed by students.

The Columbia University divestment campaign started in 2013 with Asha Rosa, a black undergraduate student activist who was a member of Students Against Mass Incarceration, the student group that became the umbrella group for Columbia Prison Divest. Telling members of the Columbia University administration that she was conducting research for her senior thesis on urban studies, Rosa approached the associate director of finance for the Columbia University Advisory Committee on Socially Responsible Investing and asked for investment information.[2] It would be months before the university found out this was a contrived request: Rosa was working on no such thesis at the time.[3]

According to Ella Every, an undergraduate member of Prison Divest who worked with Rosa on the divestment campaign, the investment report indicated that Columbia held approximately $8 million in shares of CCA. The document also revealed that Columbia owned around $2 million in shares in G4S, the world's largest security company. With more than 600,000 employees across 110 countries, G4S owns and operates prisons globally and reported earned 296 million pounds in profit (about $370 million U.S. dollars) and 7.59 billion pounds in revenue in 2016 (almost $9.5 billion U.S. dollars).[4] Roughly a quarter of its revenue comes from North America.

When we spoke about the Columbia campaign, Every acknowledged their fortuitous circumstances: "It was honestly just a total fluke in a lot of ways. Many of these universities keep a very tight hold on their investment lists,"[5] she noted. Although Columbia University's website states that 10 percent of their investments are public, and that the public should have access to them, they don't publish those investments. Other students have tried to obtain further investment details from the university, according to Every, but the administration has proved less forthcoming since Rosa.

Rosa, Every, and a group of eight to twelve core organizers felt they had the information they needed to move forward with a full-fledged divestment campaign. The students worked over the next eighteen months, holding weekly meetings, appealing to the administration, writing letters, and planning events. They won the administration's attention when their campaign officially launched in February 2014. They marched to President Bollinger's office and read a list of demands, which included full divestment from CCA and G4S. They also demanded that the university promise that it would never again invest in CCA, G4S, and GEO Group. Although President Bollinger wasn't in his office when the group read the letter (the students read the letter to his secretary), the event served as a wake-up call for the university and for institutions of higher learning across the country.

The letter to President Bollinger was videotaped and posted on YouTube and quickly garnered attention outside the university gates, including an article in *Rolling Stone* a few months later. Nevertheless, the group faced months of stalled negotiations with the administration, who requested that the organizers work with the Advisory Committee on Socially Responsible Investing. From the students' perspective, the committee stalled negotiations and seemed to overhaul its membership routinely. The student organizers presented to the committee multiple times without progress, but they mobilized tremendous student support, which convinced the university Senate to pass a resolution that Columbia should divest from the private prison industry. The university's Board of Trustees met in June, and prison divestment was on their agenda. The student group received an email from the Advisory Committee on Socially Responsible Investing as soon as the board voted for divestment.

For decades, student activists have protested their schools' investments, from the tobacco industry to today's campaigns against fossil fuels. The widespread student protest of South African apartheid was especially effective in its calls for divestment. In the late 1970s, student activists at college campuses from California to New York began agitating for university officials and trustees to divest from industries conducting business with South Africa in protest of apartheid. In Berkeley, California, students boycotted classes and demonstrated throughout campus "to dramatize the plight of black South Africans, students built shantytowns and resisted police who removed them."[6] In 1977, Hampshire College became the first school to divest stock in all companies trading or conducting business in South Africa. Columbia University students who organized as part of the Columbia Committee Against Investment in South Africa led a successful campaign in the late 1970s with demonstrations focused on university ties to corporations engaged in business with South Africa. The antiapartheid divestment campaign proved incredibly successful. By 1988, 155 universities had at least partially divested, selling holdings in companies doing business in South Africa.[7]

Prison divestment has emerged as a modern-day civil rights issue on today's college campuses. It sits at the intersection of students' discontent with mass incarceration, racial disparities in the criminal justice system, overpolicing in black, low-income communities, income inequality, and equal access to justice. At Columbia, just west of Harlem in upper Manhattan, the Black Lives Matter movement was gaining momentum, and students were protesting violent overpolicing in communities of color. Columbia Prison Divest expressed outrage regarding the school's expansion, concerned that Columbia was destroying a low-income community with gentrification.[8]

Although Columbia probably invested in other corporations with poor human rights track records, Every explained why the students were targeting the private prison industry. "Look, we have this privilege of being in this university, and it's because of, [in] a lot of ways, this [is a] system that locks up young black and brown people in unreasonable numbers." Every went on to add: "And in the end, we profit from it financially because of the money that the school makes off of its investment in that system, but also because of opportunity. And we aren't any more deserving of being here than they are deserving of being there."[9]

A month after their initial meeting, the Yale undergraduate students wrote an open letter to the university's administration and the Yale Corporation detailing the unjust practices of the private prison industry and asking the university to divest from it. With more than 289 signatures, the letter requested that "the Yale Corporation immediately divest from the for-profit prison industry, publicly denounce the for-profit prison industry and affirmatively state that it will not invest in the for-profit prison industry in the future."[10]

The Yale Corporation oversees the university's investments, and a separate committee—the Board of Ethics and Investments—is tasked with ensuring that the university doesn't invest in companies or funds that have a role in producing "grave social injuries." Joseph Gaylin, a rising sophomore at the time of the demands, explained why he continues to fight for divestment at Yale. "Yale is an intellectual institution and leader. It should not be investing in something that destroys entire populations."[11] Almost a year later, in 2017, the group of Yale undergraduate students met with members of the University's Advisory Committee on Investor Responsibility to demand that the Yale Corporation sell any current investments in private prisons, publicly denounce the industry, and promise not to invest in private prisons in future years.

Since 1972, the Yale Corporation has considered divestment requests for nonfinancial reasons by following guidelines spelled out in *The Ethical Investor*, which specifically states: "A security will be sold where the company is committing grave social injury and where all methods of correcting these practices have failed or appear doomed to failure."[12] Since the 1970s, the Yale Corporation has relied on these guidelines to divest from twenty-four companies that engaged in business in South Africa under apartheid or conducted business in Sudan when the country was under scrutiny for allegations of genocide in 2006.

The advisory committee considered similar student demands in 2005 to divest from private prisons. At that time, it decided that investments in CCA did not constitute a grave social injury.

The Domino Effect

After the Columbia divestment victory, students from colleges across the country reached out for advice on how to launch divestment campaigns on their own campuses. The volume of emails and telephone calls was so enormous that the Columbia students had trouble keeping up. Their success was the beginning of a wave of similar demands nationwide.

Six months later, the University of California system became the first public education system to divest its holdings in private prison companies when it announced it would sell its $25 million stake in GEO Group, G4S, and CCA. Expressing concern about "pampering student whims" and the outsized power students wield to force the hands of college trustees in shaping their investment practices, a finance professor at UCLA commented that "if you start going down the list of Fortune 500 companies, I'm sure we can come up with reasons we should divest from each one."[13]

Student campaigns continued to gain momentum across the nation. In 2016, Northwestern University student members of Unshackle NU, a group focusing on the effects the prison system has on communities of color, joined forces with Fossil Free NU and Northwestern Divest. Princeton University students submitted a referendum in April 2016 calling for the Council of the Princeton University Community and the Princeton University Investment Company to divest from private prisons. In early 2017, Princeton University graduate and undergraduate students met to lobby the university to divest from corporations that profit from incarceration, drug control, and immigrant deportation policies. The graduate group Princeton Private Prison Divest stated that "private prisons perpetuate a national civil-rights crisis, one that falls disproportionately upon the most vulnerable people in our society."[14] Students at Swarthmore College continued to meet throughout 2016 and 2017 to discuss a broader divestment effort aimed to persuade their administration to divest from fossil fuels and private prisons.

Lindsay Holcomb, an undergraduate at Swarthmore, joined the prison divestment campaign on her campus as part of her efforts to encourage the college to reform its admissions policies and accept students with criminal records. "Ban the Box" campaigns have found traction with student activists who strive for more inclusive admissions at their universities. The campaign name refers to an application question that requires prospective students to check a box if they have a criminal history. The practice is common in admissions offices nationwide, and administrators claim the question provides them with a fuller picture of prospective students and ensures public safety on their campuses.

Although Holcomb's initial focus was on convincing the college to end this admissions practice, she also moved in the direction of demanding divestment. She joined other Swarthmore students in submitting a FOIA request to gain access to information about Swarthmore's endowments and secondary holdings. These investments are housed with privately managed financial institutions, so this information may prove hard to obtain.

In 2015, the campaign was still in its infancy, and the students were unsure of the extent (if any) of Swarthmore's holdings in private prisons. Holcomb was fairly certain there was a connection because Swarthmore's finances were held by Wells Fargo, which has holdings in CCA and GEO Group. "When we are invested in these people, then our education is through a long and indirect chain, sponsored by what is essentially the captivity of these humans who may be innocent, may be mothers who are going to be deported, maybe any number of situations in which private prisons and companies like GEO Group deal."[15]

Student-led prison divestment campaigns have occupied Board of Trustee agendas from California to New York the past few years, but not all college campuses are focused on cutting ties to the for-profit prison industry. In fact, one university in south Florida looked for ways to increase its visible connection with one of the nation's largest private prison corporations. In February 2013, Florida Atlantic University announced that the school's new football stadium, home of the Florida Atlantic Owls, would bear the name of the GEO Group, whose CEO, George Zoley, is an alumnus of the school and formerly served as chair of the university's Board of Trustees. For the honor of seeing the company's name on the school's football stadium, GEO Group promised Florida Atlantic University $6 million over twelve years. Student resistance was swift. They immediately stormed the president's office; some began calling the stadium Owlcatraz.[16] In April, the university canceled its contract with the GEO Group, and the president resigned shortly afterward.

Will Student Movements Make an Impact?

Ella Every admitted that the students at Columbia University made a conscious decision not to engage with the private prison companies. "We wanted to send the message that it didn't matter how these companies reform themselves, that private prisons are still wrong. So engaging with the companies was setting us down a trajectory that would suggest that these companies could be fixed in some way and made better and then they would be okay."[17]

After Columbia University and the University of California system announced complete divestiture from private prisons, CCA and GEO Group issued statements through their press offices. "While the University of California system has maintained its action was based on long-term investment goals, by appearing to bow to activist demands the decision nevertheless represents a missed opportunity for honest and thoughtful dialogue around corrections systems, the role of our industry and the distinction between rhetoric and reality," said Jonathan Burns, director of public affairs for CCA.[18] Pablo Paez, vice president of corporate relations for the GEO Group similarly wrote: "Attacks on private prisons ignore the ways our industry and our company have, for more than three decades, worked to deliver education and rehabilitation programs and post-release, reentry services to thousands of inmates, so they can reintegrate successfully into society."[19] By campaigning to break all ties with the industry, do students send the message that the for-profit prison sector can do no right?

Frank Smith, a retired seventy-eight-year-old Alaska state social worker, has spent decades helping local communities fight against private prisons and is well known in the private prison activist field. He has worked as a field organizer for the nonprofit Private Corrections Institute, which operates in a handful of states and has a budget of about $20,000 a year, mostly funded by correction officer fraternal associations rather than unions. Smith currently consults with the Private Corrections Working Group. If a community is protesting the siting of a private prison or conditions at a private prison somewhere in the United States, Smith is probably involved.

Smith tracks all the employees of private prison companies who have been indicted and keeps voluminous records regarding their activities. But even Smith acknowledged the real effect divestment campaigns will have: "If Columbia divests, it doesn't really matter. Vanguard owns an enormous amount of stock. . . . If they divested, it might make a difference in the price." Although some universities are divesting as much as $10 million in holdings from private prisons, this is a drop in the bucket for a $5 billion industry. As of late 2015, the Vanguard Group held 14 percent of CCA stock, valued at $447 million. But Smith also recognized the huge political effect images of students protesting and media coverage have on the public's opinion. "If a Columbia or NYU decides to divest, then people will look up and take notice. In terms of fiscal effect, it is close to zero. But in terms of public relations, it's big."[20]

William MacAskill, associate professor of philosophy at Oxford University, wrote about the effect of divestment campaigns and CEO compensation. Companies that are labeled unethical have earned the dubious title "sin stocks," but they often produce better returns than their ethical alternatives. MacAskill pointed out that "as soon as an ethical investor sells a share, a neutral or unethical investor will buy it."[21]

But one can't argue with the publicity these student campaigns have garnered, calling attention to the issues around private prisons and mass incarceration. When Harvard University divested from the tobacco industry in 1990, Harvard University President Derek Bok explained that Harvard did not want "to be associated with companies whose products create a substantial and unjustifiable risk of harm to other human beings."[22] When Columbia University President Lee Bollinger issued a statement supporting Columbia's divestment from private prisons, he wrote that the "issue of mass incarceration in America weighs heavily on our country, our city, and our University community."[23]

Not Just Students

In October 2009, Pershing Square Capital Management, a New York–based hedge fund run by billionaire Bill Ackman, extolled the value and growth potential of CCA. Noting that public sector corrections were operating at or beyond capacity, that inmate populations in the United States have grown regardless of economic factors, and that federal demand alone could fill CCA's inventory over the next years, the hedge fund's presentation concluded that CCA is a "high quality business at a substantial discount to intrinsic value" and noted its "strong management, role as market leader, and secular growth opportunity."[24]

In February 2011, the hedge fund sold approximately 3.4 million shares of CCA stock. At one time, the hedge fund owned 10 percent of CCA, the largest share of any single investor. Three months later, activists protested outside Ackman's Manhattan apartment building during a "day of action" in which protestors targeted Pershing

Square and other investment houses that had ties with private prisons. The event was loosely organized by Enlace, an umbrella group of community organizations in the United States and Mexico that launched a national prison divestment campaign. A few days after the protest, Ackman sold the rest of his investments in CCA. In the end, Pershing Square Capital Management sold a stake of almost $200 million in the company.

In January of 2012, the United Methodist Church Board of Pension and Health Benefits—the largest faith-based pension fund in the United States—divested almost $1 million in stocks from GEO Group and CCA. That same year, General Electric fully divested its CCA shares worth $54 million.

In one week in 2014 three corporations divested from GEO Group and CCA. After intense pressure from the civil rights nonprofit Color of Change, which persuaded more than 150 companies to divest from private prison companies, asset management company Scopia Capital Management, Netherlands-based chemical company DSM North America, and Amica Mutual Insurance sold off $60 million in investments from CCA and GEO Group.[25]

The City of Berkeley had more than $6 million invested in Wells Fargo in 2014 when Wells Fargo came under criticism by divestment advocates for its substantial holdings in CCA and GEO Group. Wells Fargo owned 1 million shares of CCA, valued at nearly $37 million. In July 2016, the Berkeley City Council adopted a resolution calling on the city to divest from private prisons and sent a letter to the city's business partners asking them to follow suit. Berkeley became the second major city to take substantial steps toward prison divestment. Earlier that year, the Socially Responsible Investment (SRI) committee voted unanimously to recommend that the City of Portland, Oregon, divest $40 million in Wells Fargo corporate bonds due to the company's financial investment in for-profit incarceration. And in September trustees of the New York City Employees' Retirement System, one of five pension funds that make up the $163.1 billion New York City Retirement Systems, voted to study divesting its $6 million stock holdings in private prison companies.[26] After months of deliberation, New York City's Comptroller announced in June of 2017 that the city's pension funds had sold its $48 million in stock and bonds from three private prison companies—GEO Group, CoreCivic, and G4S.

In announcing the divestment, New York City Comptroller Scott Stringer stated:

> As President Trump ratchets up hateful rhetoric and steps up deportations, private prison companies are going to see enormous reputational harm—and that means they'll become even riskier investments. Morally, the industry wants to turn back the clock on years of progress on criminal justice, and we can't sit idly by and watch that happen. Divesting is simply the right thing to do—financially and morally."[27]

At the time of the announcement, New York City's pension system became the only one to fully divest from the for-profit prison industry. Although the divestment amount represented a small fraction of the more than $175 billion pension fund held on behalf of New York City's police officers, fire fighters, and other civil service workers, the decision marked a symbolic victory for the private prison divestment movement.

Enlace, the small grassroots advocacy organization that coordinated the 2011 "day of action," has pressured hedge funds and mutual funds to divest from the private prison industry. They also supported university divestment campaigns at Columbia University and UCLA. Enlace, along with members of the Afrikan Black Coalition (ABC), which represents black students in the University of California system, introduced the resolution to the Berkeley City Council in June of 2016.

Enlace was founded in the late 1990s, and Director Daniel Carillo states that their mission has been "to support and build the capacity of organizations to advance a pro-worker, pro-immigrant, racial and economic justice agenda."[28] Over the years Enlace has worked with teachers, retired manufacturing workers, maquiladoras, seafood processing and chain workers, and retail employees, among others. Enlace is especially interested in working with activists at the beginning stages of a campaign.

Before launching the divestment movement at Columbia University, the student group met with Enlace representatives who provided them with a Private Prison Divestment Campaign Toolkit to get them started. Enlace's Toolkit is user friendly and can be implemented by almost any student group across the country. One section is titled

"How to Begin a Divestment Resolution," and the text suggests identifying your target (state, city, church, university) and then researching whether the institution has a direct relationship with CCA or GEO Group. It recommends strategies that include searching Yahoo Finance. The Toolkit instructs that even if the institution is not directly invested in CCA or GEO Group, a connection could exist between the institution and other top investors in the private prison industry. Finally, the guide suggests leveraging media attention by using social media outlets such as Facebook and Twitter and by writing op-eds and letters to the editor.

Enlace's private prison divestment strategy aims to break the lobbying power of organizations such as CCA and GEO Group. Although their combined more than $4 billion in revenue is small compared to a company like Apple, which earned close to $216 billion in 2016, Enlace claims that the two companies' lobbying power at the federal level played a pivotal role in increasing the government's use of immigration detention. According to Enlace, these companies vastly increased their influence by relying on lobbyists who represent some of their major investors. Specifically, Enlace points to lobbyists for Wells Fargo, General Electric, and the Financial Services Roundtable who advocated policies and appropriations that contributed to the growth of the private sector immigrant prisoner market.[29]

Private Prisons and the Banks

The American Friends Service Committee, a ninety-year-old Quaker organization that "promotes lasting peace with justice," created a database on their website that lists companies it considers "punishment profiteers." The database is the first of its kind in mapping the prison industry. It allows users to upload investment portfolios and scan them for companies that profit from the prison industry. "We hope that the research presented in this publication will help investors refrain from any investment in the prison industry, unless they intend to use it for corporate engagement and shareholder activism to help companies change their policies and transition out of this industry."[30]

The five companies the organization suggests divestment from are CoreCivic Inc. (formerly CCA), G4S, Providence Services Corporation (an international, publicly traded corporation that provides government sponsored misdemeanor probation and supervision services and other court-mandated services), Sodexo SA, and the GEO Group Inc. They also suggest divestment from publicly traded companies that provide food services to U.S. prisons: Compass Group, Aramark, and Sodexo. Most phone companies that service prisons are not publicly held, but divestment from CenturyLink, the only publicly traded major prison phone company in this sector, is recommended.

Despite a groundswell of divestment from private prisons over the last few years, Wall Street banks have largely stayed put. In fact, Bank of America, BNP Paribas, JPMorgan Chase, SunTrust, U.S. Bancorp, and Wells Fargo are heavily involved in financing the growth and expansion of CCA and GEO Group.[31] These companies rely on debt financing in credit, loans, and bonds to operate and acquire smaller companies. In practice, this means that these banks underwrote bonds and helped finance their growth through loans and hundreds of millions of dollars in revolving credit.

In the Public Interest is working to reduce the footprint of private prisons in the United States, and it makes the case that by helping these private prisons grow and by collecting interest and fees on outstanding debt, the banks are complicit with CCA and GEO Group. Critics blame these banks for profiting from mass incarceration and the criminalization of immigration. By June 2016, a syndicate of at least six banks—BNP Paribas, Bank of America, Barclays, JPMorgan Chase, SunTrust, and Wells Fargo—had loaned GEO Group $450 million through the company's revolving credit.[32]

Revolving credit ensures that CCA and GEO Group can cover their expenses under a business model that allows them to pay little in taxes. Operating as Real Estate Investment Trusts (REITs), these companies receive favorable tax benefits but are required to pass on 90 percent of taxable income to their shareholders. This leaves the companies with little cash on hand to cover the cost of day-to-day operations, such as overhead costs at prisons and staff salaries. They must rely on revolving credit from large banks to run their operations and pay their investors per the REIT requirements. To illustrate just how advantageous this tax status is, in 2015 GEO Group paid a mere $7.4 million in international, federal, and state income taxes on its $1.84 billion in revenue.

Although activists express frustration at what they see as an enormous tax advantage, there are financial downsides to restructuring as a REIT, and it's not really a fair criticism to complain that these companies are receiving an extra benefit. REIT status has its trade-offs such as forgoing the flexibility of retaining earnings and significant compliance requirements. In addition, the downside to corporations losing the ability to retain their earnings and amass a war chest of capital on their hands is huge.

In addition to the loans and bonds that large banks underwrite for private prison corporations, some of these banks also own shares of GEO Group or CCA on behalf of their clients. Private prison divestment advocates criticize this practice because banks are theoretically profiting twice over on for-profit prisons: first from interest and fees they collect from CCA and GEO Group, and again by owning or investing their clients' money in private prison firms. Bank of America, JPMorgan Chase, Wells Fargo, and U.S. Bancorp also own GEO Group and CCA stock or invest in the stock on behalf of their clients.[33]

It is unlikely that divestment campaigns will harm private prison revenue because another investor will swoop in and purchase the shares—especially if they are a sound financial investment. But this groundswell of support to eliminate ties with the private prison industry has impressed major university presidents, their boards of trustees, and some of the largest hedge funds. Just as the leading Democratic candidates saying no to private prison donations are a stain on the for-profit prison industry's reputation, the divestment campaigns provide another blow to the powerful corporations who many argue have disproportionate political influence.

More than a year after I attended the Yale Divestment from Private Prisons student meeting, the group still had few answers. They submitted a two-page memo to the Yale Corporation Committee on Investor Responsibility outlining their rationale for the university to divest from the private prison industry, wrote op-eds in the *Yale Daily News*, and organized marches on campus. Gaylin was still active in the campaign and called me right before a divestment rally on campus to provide an update on what the student divestment group had discovered. Gaylin said they know the Yale endowment is invested in Vanguard, which is invested in private prisons, but it was still a bit of a black box as to whether the university was a primary investor in private prisons. "As for what we know about the endowment, we have been operating on the assumption that Yale is invested in private prisons. Thus, if Yale is not invested in the private prison industry, we would need confirmation and a statement that they will not invest again in the future. Additionally, we know through SEC filings that Yale is invested in a number of mutual funds that are invested in the private prison industry, so there are secondary investments."[34]

Despite these successes, the efforts so far have not engaged policy makers' interest in evaluating and reforming private prison contracts, arguably the most effective way to improve their practices. Divestment campaigns are pivotal for raising awareness of the problems in the private prison industry, but they only move the needle so far. It is ultimately pressure on policy makers that will change the industry's incentives, transparency, and accountability requirements. The next chapter considers the role policy makers play with respect to the vast for-profit prison industry.

CHAPTER SEVEN

The Politics of Private Prisons

It is wrong to profit from the imprisonment of human beings and
the suffering of their families and friends. It's time to end this morally
repugnant process, and along with it, the era of mass incarceration.
BERNIE SANDERS, FOR PRESIDENT, 2016[1]

I do think we can do a lot of privatizations and private prisons.
It seems to work a lot better.
DONALD TRUMP, TOWN HALL IN GREEN BAY, WISCONSIN,
MODERATED BY MSNBC's CHRIS MATTHEWS, MARCH 30, 2016[2]

TWO DAYS AFTER the funeral of Freddie Gray, a twenty-five-year-
old African American man who died in police custody in Baltimore,
Hillary Clinton gave one of her first campaign speeches. The streets
in Baltimore were still smoldering from riots. Standing at a podium
at Columbia University she said, "It's time to end the era of mass
incarceration. We need a true national debate about how to reduce
our prison population while keeping our communities safe. I don't
know all the answers. That's why I'm here—to ask all the smart people
in Columbia and New York to start thinking this through with me."[3]

Clinton was a mainstream political candidate married to the president who proudly signed the 1994 crime bill authorizing billions for
more police and more prisons—the world took notice. She was neck
and neck with progressive candidate Bernie Sanders, who pledged to
end the private prison industry as we know it. Clinton acknowledged
that her Ready for Hillary PAC had collected more than $133,000
in donations from private prison lobbyists. The bad press over these
donations could sink her polling numbers. Clinton's campaign promised to give the private prison donations to charity. Sanders was already

on record saying that he would introduce legislation to abolish the private prison industry, and he called taking campaign contributions from prison company lobbyists "immoral."[4] By the fall of 2015, both leading democratic presidential candidates had sworn off campaign donations from private prisons. This marked the first time in U.S. history that a mainstream party turned its back on the for-profit prison industry.

Clinton's speech acknowledged how difficult it would be to chip away at the vast racial disparities plaguing the nation's justice system and its prisons. The statistics bear this out. Between 1983 and 2011, the number of black men sentenced to more than a year in prison increased 231 percent compared to a 198 percent increase for white men.

Private prisons are a political issue. Criminal justice reform and immigration were key issues in the 2016 presidential election as well as down ballot in most elections to state legislatures. Journalists and good government groups examined every connection candidates had to the industry. Some state legislatures have made changes to reduce the power and influence of private prisons, but Congress has not moved bills to curb the industry's foothold. In fact, the private prison industry is so entrenched within the framework of corrections that even the president cannot check its influence.

Conservatives and Criminal Justice

Private prisons are not such a pivotal issue among Republican voters. "More than three in four Republicans (77 percent) say the bigger priority should be to strengthen law and order through more police and greater enforcement of the laws; 17 percent say the priority should be to reduce bias against minorities. Majorities of both Democrats (60 percent) and independents (52 percent) prioritize reducing bias against minorities in the criminal justice system by reforming court and police practices. However, Republicans tilt more toward strengthening law and order than both of these groups do toward reducing bias."[5]

Criminal justice reform emerged as a bipartisan issue. Conservatives often tout the price tag of the federal prison population's growth by nearly 800 percent between 1980 and 2013, which bloated the budget of the Bureau of Prisons by almost 600 percent, from $970 million to $6.7 billion. Conservatives also increasingly embrace the "smart-on-crime" mantra—a play on words from the four decade "tough-on-crime" rhetoric. This smart-on-crime attitude is the new philosophy that accounts for decades of research on the effectiveness of evidence-based practices, alternatives to incarceration, and reentry services to ensure safe communities while also reducing prison populations. Former Attorney General Eric Holder's initiative bears the same name. As head of the U.S. Department of Justice, Attorney General Holder spearheaded a "Smart on Crime" initiative in 2013, which was intended to promote fundamental reforms to the criminal justice system to ensure the fair enforcement of federal laws, improve public safety, and reduce recidivism by successfully preparing inmates for their reentry into society.[6]

Despite his relatively low profile concerning private prisons, Donald Trump's campaign also received contributions from the private prison industry. In July, just a few months before the general election, the political action committee of GEO Group donated $45,000 to a joint fund-raising committee, the Trump Victory Fund, supporting Republican presidential nominee Trump and eleven state parties.[7] Given Trump's anti-immigration stance and promise to build a wall stretching 1,000 miles along the southern border to stem the flow of Mexican immigrants and drugs into the United States, it hardly seemed a gamble for the GEO Group to support his bid. According to Federal Election Commission (FEC) records, the GEO Group PAC made a legal $50,000 donation to Rebuilding America Now (Trump's primary PAC) August 11, 2016.[8] GEO Corrections Holdings, Inc., a subsidiary of the GEO Group, gave $100,000 to Rebuilding America Now a week later—the day after the Justice Department, under President Obama, announced it would phase out private prison contracts.[9]

Legislation Aimed at Private Prison Contracts

Policy makers have tried to reform the private prison industry for more than a decade. As early as 2001, Senator Russell Feingold (D–Wis.) and Representative Ted Strickland (D–Ohio) introduced the Public Safety Act, which would prohibit federal contracts with private prison companies and eliminate some federal grants to states that contract with private prisons.[10]

Much of the legislation over the years has focused on improving the transparency of the industry. In 2005, Congressman Strickland introduced the Private Prison Information Act. The legislation required that any nongovernmental entity contracting with the federal government to run a correctional facility must release information about its operations under the same requirements that government agencies abide by—the Freedom of Information Act (FOIA). The legislation has been introduced in every Congress since then but has never moved past a committee hearing. In 2007, Senators Clinton and Lieberman cosponsored the bill. CCA campaigned against the legislation, arguing that government oversight of private prison contracts is sufficient to ensure good performance. Facing opposition from the Reason Foundation and the Department of Justice, the bill died in subcommittee.

During a hearing for the legislation in the summer of 2008, Representative Bobby Scott, chair of the subcommittee on Crime, Terrorism, and Homeland Security, acknowledged that the subcommittee had held a hearing on the bill the previous fall in conjunction with a hearing on the Prison Litigation Reform Act. "Shortly after the hearing, the Corrections Corporation of America contacted the subcommittee staff to express its strong opposition to the legislation and question the necessity of the bill."[11] The advocacy group Private Corrections Institute and the ACLU supported the legislation, claiming it was difficult for them to obtain information from private prisons through the regular FOIA process of submitting the request to the federal Bureau of Prisons.

Although declining to testify at the hearing during the summer of 2008, CCA submitted written testimony that the Private Prison Information Act was "a solution in search of a problem" and would "impose upon the private sector an unprecedented requirement to respond to requests for information from the general public."[12] Their view was (and still is) that the federal agencies they contract with are the "gatekeepers" of sensitive materials and law enforcement, and that the federal monitors ensure compliance with contracts. Despite CCA's claim that enough transparency exists, neither CCA or GEO Group are subject to the open records laws with which the Freedom of Information Act requires state correctional agencies to comply.

Texas Democratic Representative Sheila Jackson Lee has emerged as the Private Prison Information Act's champion, introducing it year after year, most recently in 2015.[13] Since 2012, seven separate bills have been introduced on Capitol Hill seeking to improve the transparency and accountability of private prisons. Each bill has died in committee.

Frustrated at how little private prison corporations are accountable, Representative Lee, introduced the legislation in 2015 with a letter of support signed by thirty-four criminal justice, civil rights, and public interest organizations. The Southern Poverty Law Center, the ACLU, the Center for Constitutional Rights, and the Sentencing Project argued that private prisons should be subject to the same standards of transparency as government agencies. "This lack of public transparency is indefensible in light of the nearly $8 billion in federal contracts that Corrections Corporation of America (CCA) and the GEO Group (GEO)—the nation's two largest private prisons firms—have been awarded since 2007."[14]

In September 2015, Senator Sanders introduced a sixty-four-page bill, the Justice Is Not for Sale Act, which would ban all federal government contracts with private prison companies at the federal, state, and local level.[15] The bill would have (1) banned all state, local, and federal private prison contracts within two years, (2) eliminated private immigration detention centers within one year, (3) ended the current law that the federal government is required to maintain a certain number of beds for immigrant detainees, (4) increased the monitoring and oversight of immigrant detention facilities, and (5) reinstated federal parole.

Other policy makers have attempted to make the industry more accountable. In July 2016, Senate Finance Committee Ranking Member Ron Wyden (D–Ore.) introduced legislation aimed at making it tougher for private prison companies to benefit from Real Estate Investment Trusts (REITs), federal tax breaks for special real estate firms. Both GEO Group and CCA received this status in 2013 (see chapter 6). On January 2, 2013, GEO Group announced that it had "completed all the necessary restructuring steps" to convert to a REIT, and the company's CEO George Zoley said the "management team strongly believe that these important steps will maximize our company's ability to create shareholder value given the nature of our assets, help lower our cost of capital, draw a larger base of potential shareholders, provide greater flexibility to pursue growth opportunities, and create a more efficient operating structure."[16] That same day CCA announced that "it had completed an internal reorganization of its business operations so that it now has the ability to elect to qualify as a real estate investment trust ("REIT") for the taxable year commencing January 1, 2013."[17]

REITs were created during the Eisenhower administration to assist companies that focus their business on real estate holdings by reducing—and in some cases eliminating—corporate taxes. Common REITs include shopping centers, hospitals, malls, and office buildings, which reap enormous tax advantages through the status. According to the Securities and Exchange Commission (SEC), a REIT is "a company that owns—and typically operates—income-producing real estate or real estate-related assets." To qualify as a REIT, a company must have the majority of its assets and income connected to real estate investment and is required to distribute at least 90 percent of its taxable income as dividends.

As REITs, private prison companies must separate the operational side of running prisons from the real estate portion of their businesses. REITs are structured as passive owners of real estate, but the IRS permits corporations to restructure or break themselves up to benefit from the low corporate tax rate the status provides. Both CCA and GEO Group hold and operate certain assets through taxable REIT subsidiaries that are subject to corporate income taxes. For example, CCA holds TransCor (its inmate transportation business) as a subsidiary to the REIT. In 1997, CCA tried for the first time to restructure as a REIT. The company created separate operating structures, boards of directors, and management teams for the arm of the company that managed its operations and for the arm that oversaw its real estate holdings. This 1997 conversion to a REIT produced unsuccessful results. The REIT, named Prison Realty Trust, eventually defaulted on its debt, and the company's stock dropped to under $1.00 a share, "putting it at risk of being delisted from the New York Stock Exchange." CCA eventually reversed its REIT conversion.[18]

As the IRS has expanded its favorable treatment of this tax status, prison corporations have taken advantage of REIT status by claiming that the money they receive from governments for housing prisoners is the same as collecting rent. After Senator Wyden introduced the Ending Tax Breaks for Private Prisons Act of 2016, he wrote:

> I am very concerned that the US prison system has become a way for private enterprises to turn an unfair profit. Our broken down tax code has made this possible by allowing the private prison industry to take advantage of tax rules aimed at REITs. As part of rethinking our criminal justice system, particularly as it results in the mass incarceration of low-income and minority individuals, the tax rules for

REITs must be changed so that we are not encouraging companies to unjustly profit from prison detention services.[19]

CCA issued a statement in response, claiming that "the rationale for this bill is deeply misguided. . . . The fact is, we provide problem-solving alternatives that help our government partners address some of their biggest corrections challenges, such as dangerous overcrowding and skyrocketing costs."[20]

The United States taxes the profits of resident corporations at graduated rates ranging from 15 to 35 percent; however, most corporate income is taxed at the maximum rate.[21] Before converting to a REIT, CCA was subject to the maximum tax rate, but the REIT tax advantages dropped that to a 3 percent rate in the first quarter of 2015.[22] Even if Senator Wyden successfully pushes through his legislation, the private prison REITs could replicate almost the same structure by morphing into a private real estate limited partnership. They just wouldn't have access to the same public capital. Changing the tax code to eliminate the tax benefits of private prison corporations is not a likely scenario.

These initiatives represent extraordinary efforts on the federal level to improve the transparency and accountability of private prisons. States have also waged their own battles to improve transparency in their relationships with private prison corporations. In 2012, seventeen religious and nonprofit organizations created a group that stopped a proposal to privatize twenty-seven facilities in Florida.[23] In Vermont in 2016, Representative Barbara Rachelson introduced a state House bill to prohibit the state from contracting with a "for-profit contractor or private vendor for the provision of services relating to the operation of a correctional facility."[24] Representatives in Vermont have tried and failed to pass similar bills over the years. Because of overcrowded facilities in the state, Vermont inmates have been shipped to private prisons in Kentucky and Michigan. Former Representative Suzi Wizowaty sponsored a bill proposing that all Vermont inmates should be incarcerated in correctional facilities that are owned and operated by the federal, state, or local government.[25] That bill also died in committee.[26]

In California, Democratic State Senator Ricardo Lara introduced the Dignity Not Detention Act, which would prohibit counties or cities from entering into or renewing contracts on behalf of the Department of Homeland Security (DHS) with a private corporation to house immigrant detainees.[27] The California State Assembly passed the legislation in 2016, and it bans California cities and counties from contracting out the management of immigration detention centers to private companies. The bill went even further and required localities holding undocumented immigrants on behalf of DHS to adhere to Immigration and Customs Enforcement (ICE) best practice standards. In California, 85 percent of the state's immigrant detainees (3,700 people) are held in one of four privately operated detention facilities.[28]

A month later, California Governor Jerry Brown vetoed the bill. If the governor had signed the legislation, California would have been the first state to outlaw local government contracting with private companies to operate immigration detention centers.[29] In vetoing the bill, Brown wrote, "I have been troubled by reports detailing unsatisfactory conditions and limited access to counsel in private immigration detention facilities. The Department of Homeland Security, however, is now considering whether private contracting should continue for immigrant detention, and if so under what conditions. Their recommendations are expected in November. These actions indicate that a more permanent solution to this issue may be at hand. I urge the federal authorities to act swiftly."[30] Under President Obama, the Department of Justice and DHS attempted to roll back its reliance on private prisons; with Trump in office, Governor Brown's willingness to wait for the federal government to curb its dependence on private corporations to house immigrant detainees is likely to prove futile.

The intense scrutiny of private prisons on the campaign trail and in state legislatures has not gone unnoticed by the for-profit prison industry. CCA's 2015 annual report details the political opposition their industry continues to face. Under the heading, "Risk Factors," the SEC filing states:

The operation of correctional and detention facilities by private entities has not achieved complete acceptance by either governments or the public. The movement toward privatization of correctional and detention facilities has also encountered resistance from certain groups, such as labor unions and others that believe that correctional and detention facilities should only be operated by governmental agencies. In the past, legislation has been proposed in the United States Congress to prohibit the federal government from entering into contracts with private prison operators, and to eliminate state and local contracts for privately run prisons. Such legislation runs contrary to our primary business purpose and, if passed, would have a material adverse impact on our business. Moreover, the belief or market perception that such legislation could be passed could have a negative impact on our stock price.[31]

Conversely, corporate offices do not seem rattled by the heightened attention paid to private prisons. Speaking at a REIT week investor forum in 2016, CCA's CEO Damon Hininger appeared nonplussed: "I would say that being around thirty years and being in operation in many, many states, and also doing work with the federal government going back to the 1980s, where you had [a] Clinton White House, you had a Bush White House, you had [an] Obama White House, we've done very, very well."[32] Similarly, in a GEO Group investor conference call, CEO George Zoley answered a question about how sentencing reform in the states may impact his company. He acknowledged the wave of criminal justice reforms taking place in the states: "So these reforms are going on, but they are fairly modest, and they don't seem to have impacted us in any meaningful way."[33]

Can the President Ban Private Prisons?

The executive branch is limited in its power to "end private prisons and private detention centers," as Secretary Clinton vowed to do. Federal policy makers are hamstrung partly because the private prison industry has diversified from merely owning and operating state prisons to capitalizing on the growing need to find prison beds for immigration detainees.

How entrenched are these companies in federal and state bureaucracies? Federal private prison facilities can be a bit of a black hole: different agencies contract with the corporations to house different populations. For example, the Bureau of Prisons (BOP) contracts with private corporations to house inmates, the majority of whom are sentenced criminal aliens who may be deported upon completion of their sentence. Their crimes are usually immigration violations rather than drug trafficking offenses. The U.S. Marshals Service (USMS) detains those awaiting trial for federal crimes, and ICE detains those charged with violating immigration laws, entering the country illegally, or awaiting deportation. If that's not complicated enough, the USMS has authority over some of its inmates who are housed in beds at BOP facilities, for which USMS does not pay, and houses some of its inmates in different state prisons, some of which are privately owned or operated.

Breaking it down even further, the two companies with the lion's share of private prison beds in America—GEO Group and CCA—own and operate prisons that contract with individual state governments and three different federal agencies. GEO Group has contracts with eleven states: Alaska, Arizona, California, Florida, Georgia, Indiana, Louisiana, Oklahoma, New Mexico, Texas, and Virginia. Contracts with Florida alone accounted for a little more than 5.2 percent of its revenue. GEO Group also contracts with the three federal government agencies with correction and detention responsibilities (BOP, ICE, and USMS), which accounted for a little more than 47.2 percent of the company's 2016 revenue.[34]

CCA's 2016 Annual Report acknowledges that the BOP, ICE, and USMS accounted for 52 percent of its total revenues ($953.9 million). Approximately 9 percent of total revenue was generated from BOP contracts, and 8 percent of total revenue was generated from ICE contracts. Business from state contracts constituted 38 percent of total revenue in 2016, worth $710.4 million.[35]

If some future president made headway on this issue and reduced the number of federal contracts with private prisons, would that chip away at mass incarceration? Would conditions of confinement improve?

A future administration or Congress could exert its influence to curb the states' reliance on private prisons; it could attach strings to the $4 billion in funding the federal government doles out to states each year for criminal justice. Congress could penalize states that contract with private prisons to house inmates. In reality, this tactic is unlikely to get past a Congress that has spent decades sending money to the states for almost any criminal justice purpose they deem appropriate. Such a proposal would not sit well with the nation's directors of corrections either, some of whom have no choice but to send their overflow inmates to private prisons.

President Trump's administration has a favorable stance toward private prison operators. Within months of taking office, Trump began to ramp up the private sector's role in building more immigrant detention centers to accommodate his immigrant enforcement policies. As the next chapter reveals, a vast infrastructure exists whose roots will not easily be torn out.

CHAPTER EIGHT

Shadow Prisons: Inside Private Immigrant Detention Centers

Moreover, we believe that the government will tighten its security regarding illegal residents. New initiatives in this area will require secure facilities for a group composed of several thousand illegal immigrants, thereby driving a need to outsource key detention operations to companies such as ours.

GEO GROUP, 2002 ANNUAL REPORT

SAN ANTONIO AND Laredo sit almost 200 miles apart in South Texas. The land is peppered with low green bushes, a handful of hundred-acre ranches, and an equal number of dilapidated one-story houses. The route between these towns runs along I-35 until it reaches mile marker one, where the United States ends and Nuevo Laredo, Mexico, begins. At the border, a Union Pacific cargo train scrawled with graffiti inches north, laden with goods picked up at the border. The frontage roads approaching the final thirty-mile stretch of I-35 are dotted with white and green U.S. border patrol trucks parked between mile markers. Camouflaged in the low-lying vegetation and dusty roads, border patrol agents watch for people crossing the border illegally, many of whom have walked across the Rio Grande, which in some stretches is only 100 feet wide.

This corridor between San Antonio and Laredo is marked by federal immigration detention centers warehousing men, women, and children detained because they entered the United States illegally. Immigration and Customs Enforcement (ICE), an agency under the umbrella of the Department of Homeland Security (DHS), has the authority to detain undocumented immigrants but has contracted out the supervision of more than 60 percent of these detainees to for-profit prison corporations. ICE facilities are "administrative detention facilities," not prisons. The distinction is slight: immigration is a civil issue, not a criminal one. In 2016, more than 408,000 people were apprehended by U.S. border patrol agents.[1] ICE placed 352,882 immigrants in civil detention facilities, and ICE and the border patrol together removed or deported 450,954 undocumented immigrants.[2]

Laredo is home to two immigration detention centers. The Laredo Processing Center is an all-female ICE facility owned and operated by Corrections Corporation of America (CCA). The Rio Grande Detention Center, on the banks of the Rio Grande, is owned and operated by GEO Group. This 1,900 bed facility has a contract with the U.S. Marshals Service to house pretrial detainees bound for federal court, and a contract with ICE to house immigrant detainees. In 2014, GEO Group won a contract to expand their capacity to 400 beds, which was expected to generate $38 million in annual revenues.[3] A third private detention facility in Laredo, the Webb County Detention Center, is owned and operated by CCA and is under contract with the U.S. Marshals Service to house 480 male and female pretrial detainees. This facility is not an immigrant detention center, but some of the pretrial detainees also may have ICE detainers.

The South Texas Residential Family Detention Center (STRFDC) is a mammoth facility with 50 acres of land in Dilley. An irrigation system marks the border between this detention center and a Texas state prison. Combined, the inmates in these two facilities make up more than half of the town's population. STRFDC is the largest immigrant detention center in the nation. A hundred miles north of the border, it is perched on flat green land previously used as a camp for oilfield workers. Opened in December 2014, it can hold 2,400 women and children, most of whom fled Central America. DHS signed a four-year, billion-dollar contract delegating authority to CCA to manage the detention center. STRFDC is one of three detention centers in the United States that house women and children. The second is the Karnes County Residential Center, south of San Antonio, which is owned and operated by the GEO Group, and can hold more than 500 people. The third is the Berks County Residential Center, northwest of Philadelphia, which ICE runs. It can house about one hundred men, women, and children.

Sixteen miles from Dilley is the sleepy town of Pearsall, population 9,000. Pearsall is home to the South Texas Detention Complex, owned and operated by the GEO Group. The facility houses about 1,900 immigrant detainees, including 1,450 males and 454 females. Pearsall has always been a prison town. The oldest building in Pearsall is the former Frio County Jail, built in 1884. Next to the jail's front door a plaque declares its status as a historic landmark:

> Oldest building in town. Built in 1884 for $11,000. Style typical of era. Used as jail and jailer's residence until 1967. Second story and part of the first housed jail. Two separate cells were added in 1885 for female or juvenile prisoners or for the insane. For years a well on the premises supplied water. During prohibition in early 20th century, confiscated bootleg liquor was stored by law officers in one of cells.

The South Texas corridor is a cash cow for the private prison industry. Since 2001, GEO Group and CCA have relied more and more on federal government contracts. Today 62 percent of all ICE immigration detention beds in the United States are operated by for-profit prison corporations, a huge jump from a decade ago, when just 25 percent of immigration detention beds were operated by for-profit prison corporations.[4] In fact, CCA has earned $689 million from ICE contracts since 2008 and GEO Group has earned $1.18 billion.[5]

As Bob Libal, executive director of Grassroots Leadership told me, "The corridor between Laredo and San Antonio is a corridor of criminal prosecution and migrants feeding the economic boom of for-profit prisons in South Texas."[6] The San Antonio–Laredo corridor is a microcosm of the network of immigrant detention facilities spread across the states. In total, there are more than 180 detention centers, housing more than 33,000 people each day.[7]

Life at Laredo

Private detention centers frequently receive complaints of substandard conditions: bad food, inadequate medical care, allegations of sexual abuse, too few lawyers, and no due process. The prisons are part of the federal infrastructure, but the companies that run them operate under a different—and less stringent—set of rules and can cut costs.

As a retired Bureau of Prisons (BOP) contracting official explained, "the more specificity you put in the contract, the more money the contractors are going to want for performing the service."[8]

In the summer of 2016, I toured two private DHS detention centers in South Texas. I met with an assistant field director at ICE who did his best to explain the complicated relationship between the border patrol's authority to detain undocumented individuals, ICE detention, U.S. Marshal detention, and federal BOP Criminal Alien Prisons.

Border patrol agents who apprehend illegal immigrants within fourteen days of their entry and within 100 miles of a U.S. land or coastal border are authorized to expedite the immigration process and deport the individuals to their home countries through "extra-Constitutional" authority. ICE provides administrative detention, overseeing the care and housing of undocumented immigrants awaiting deportation or a decision by a judge that they can stay. Once an immigration judge has authorized the deportation—ICE officials often use the term "removal"—ICE coordinates the immigrant's transportation and departure. When ICE deports to Mexico from Laredo, ICE officers walk immigrants across the bridge to Mexico with the proper documentation and ensure that they leave the country. In Texas, he explained, the private prison corporations contract directly with the counties who then sign intergovernmental service agreements with DHS. This complicated relationship allows DHS to delegate the management of this population to CCA and GEO Group. Every one of the private facilities is monitored by ICE, the official explained.

The U.S. Marshals Service has responsibility for federal defendants, almost half of whom are charged with immigration or drug offenses. Because the agency does not have its own detention facilities, it relies on public and private facilities with which it has agreements, housing about 18 percent to one third of its prisoner population in 40 private facilities.[9] The U.S. Marshals' use of private prisons has skyrocketed since the 1990s. Whereas in 1994 only 1 percent of its detainees were in private prisons, by 2000 that number had risen to 16 percent.[10]

The ICE official walked me outside the DHS building on a 91-degree day that felt like 102 degrees, and guided me across the dusty parking lot to the CCA detention center. Wedged next to an abandoned gas station and across the street from a car dealership, the brown walls of the detention facility blend into the cracked brown parking lot. The structure could be a warehouse or a shipping facility except for the barbed-wire perimeter and the dueling American, Texas, and dark red CCA flags flapping above the building. A horizontal white sign announces that the property exists under the auspices of U.S. Immigration and Customs Enforcement. Another sign reads Laredo Processing Center.

The small lobby had two benches of connected red plastic chairs and a soft drink machine. A mustached CCA officer in a khaki uniform greeted me behind a glass window. Above him on the wall hung portraits of executives smiling down onto the dingy waiting area. They were CCA CEO Damon Hininger; Executive Vice President and Chief Corrections Officer Harley Lappin; Vice President, Facility Operations, Steven Conry; and Operations Managing Director Jason Ellis.

I was ushered into the warden's office and greeted by the Laredo Processing Center's Chief of Security, Julio Chapa. I asked Chapa how the facility was monitored by ICE. He explained that an ICE monitor, called a detention service manager, is assigned to the facility eight hours a day, forty hours a week. The facility is also inspected annually by the Office of Detention Oversight division of DHS. Specifically, ICE's Office of Professional Responsibilities audits the private detention centers. According to the 2015 Compliance Inspection, the facility was found to be compliant with thirteen of the fifteen DHS new detention standards. The two areas they failed were detainee grievance procedures and staff–detainee communication.[11]

Chapa walked me around the facility, explaining the detainee classification system, which is color coded according to security risk. Women wearing blue jumpsuits are low risk and were mostly cases of illegal entry or reentry. Women wearing orange jumpsuits were considered medium risk and were mostly criminal aliens. Women in red jumpsuits were considered high risk and presented a serious risk to the safety, security, and operation of the facility. Some of the women in red jumpsuits also suffered from mental illness. Although immigration detention facilities provide administrative civil detention, the distinction between a minimum security prison and the immigrant detention center was difficult to discern.

We passed a small room used as a medical office where a doctor sees detainees about once a week and a nurse sees detainees about twice a week. Near the medical office, a detainee in a blue jumpsuit worked as a hair stylist cutting other detainees' hair. I peered into the housing units and saw women sitting or lying down on bunk beds and in chairs watching TV. Because these facilities are designed for short stays, there is almost no programming. Similar to a jail (also designed for short-term stays), men and women at immigration detention facilities don't have many ways to occupy their time.

We passed Ana, a woman wearing a blue jumpsuit, busily mopping the hall. She smiled at me when we passed, and I asked Chapa if I could speak to her. She spoke perfect English and explained that she was brought into the country illegally when she was one month old. She was twenty-six now. Five days ago, for a payment of $2,000, she tried to drive two Mexican citizens, an eighteen-year-old and a child, across the border. Ana had planned to start South Texas College in the fall. Detained in Laredo, CCA paid her $1.00 a day to mop floors while her case wove its way through the complicated immigration criminal justice system.

Most of the 382 women detained at Laredo spoke Spanish. Eighteen women under capacity, the facility was nearing full occupancy. Even though the detention center was only a few miles from Mexico, the majority of the women in the facility came from El Salvador. In recent years, the Congressional Research Service has reported a large increase in "credible fear" claims of persecution by undocumented immigrants: 36,000 in 2013 compared to just 5,000 in 2009,[12] and the increase is primarily from El Salvador, Guatemala, Honduras, and Mexico—countries embroiled in gang and drug violence.[13] A group of eight women wearing blue jumpsuits who fled from El Salvador and Honduras stood in an office with CCA officials, calling their friends and family. They explained that they had been at the facility about a week and had entered the United States from Mexico.

Chapa walked me by the laundry facility where two detainees stood folding laundry along with a CCA female guard. Margaret, wearing an orange jumpsuit, was one of the detainees folding sheets in the laundry room for $1.00 a day. An African American woman with her hair in two buns on the top of her head, she came from Sierra Leone in West Africa. She had been in the Laredo Processing Center since December. Eight months later, she felt she didn't have the energy to appeal a judge's denial of her asylum in the United States. Her eleven-year-old daughter lived with family friends. She has served six months for a criminal charge, but the asylum process appeared to have taken its toll. "I'm tired," she said. She felt she had no choice but to accept deportation and return to Sierra Leone with her daughter.

Because many undocumented individuals claim they fled their home country because of domestic violence or fear of political violence, ICE facilitates asylum interviews. For those lucky enough to be granted asylum in the United States, ICE officials work with nonprofits and community and faith-based organizations to find home placements. In 2014, the average stay for undocumented individuals in ICE custody was one month—29.6 days to be precise. At eight months, Margaret was an extreme outlier.

Criminalization of Immigration

The story of immigrant detention is inextricable from the story of for-profit prisons. In the early 1980s, the U.S. government passed a series of laws that increased the punishments around illegal immigration. Human rights and political crises in Central America brought more and more immigrants across the border outside the usual channels. In the late 1990s and early 2000s, private prisons were receiving lots of bad press, and state budgets were shrinking. Desperate to stay afloat, the private prison industry saw a new market ripe for privatization—immigrant detention. Immigrant detention centers are not required to offer rehabilitative programming or other services prisons need to provide, so the Bureau of Prisons thought it was a good fit. Today the for-profit industry only manages about 8 percent of prison beds across the nation, but they manage a whopping 62 percent of immigration detention beds. Of the ten largest immigration detention facilities in the United States, private prison corporations manage nine of them. Cost-cutting meant skeleton crew services for immigrant detainees, and allegations of abuse and neglect in private detention facilities now threaten contracts for the whole industry.

Immigration law is complex. In fact, some argue it is the most complicated part of the U.S. legal system, more bewildering even than tax law in its statutory complexity. As Michael Wishnie of Yale Law School explains, "The entangling of immigration and criminal law is as old as the nation itself, although since the terrorist attacks of September 11, 2001, immigration enforcement has become more entangled with routine police enforcement."[14] This knot has widened the intersection between traditional law enforcement and immigration officers, including the often strange scenarios in which multiple agencies hand off undocumented citizens to each other, trying to navigate the gray zone between criminal and immigration law.

The criminalization of immigration has created a new body of law—"crimmigration." Legal scholar Juliet Stumpf traced the history of this trend:

> The "crimmigration" merger has taken place on three fronts: (1) the substance of immigration law and criminal law increasingly overlaps, (2) immigration enforcement has come to resemble criminal law enforcement, and (3) the procedural aspects of prosecuting immigration violations have taken on many of the earmarks of criminal procedure.[15]

In the late 1970s, the Immigration and Naturalization Service (INS) started to contract with private corporations to build and operate holding facilities for undocumented individuals awaiting hearings or deportation.[16] By 1986, 25 percent of the INS detention facilities were in private hands.[17]

Crimmigration began in the 1980s, when Congress passed laws creating harsher punishments around illegal entry and reentry. The Anti-Drug Abuse Act of 1988 was the nation's first mandatory immigration detention law. It required the detention of noncitizens who had committed aggravated felonies, requiring federal immigration officials to detain those individuals on bond pending their removal proceedings instead of releasing them.[18]

President Clinton's signature 1994 crime bill not only funded more police on the streets and more prison beds in states nationwide, it also allocated new federal money to pay for the deportation of "criminal aliens." The added enforcement authority and funding mobilized the U.S. Marshals' and ICE's immigration enforcement practices. Today federal spending on immigration detention and deportation has reached $2.8 billion a year, more than doubling since 2006.

The law also toughened the penalties for immigration-related violations. The crime bill raised the maximum penalty for the crime of illegal reentry after deportation following a felony conviction to ten years and raised the maximum for previously deported aggravated felons to twenty years. The law also required "deportation of an alien provided lawful permanent resident status who is convicted of a crime involving moral turpitude committed within ten years after the date of entry."[19]

In addition, the definition of what constitutes an "aggravated felony" has expanded to include a slew of nonviolent and minor felonies along with some misdemeanors.[20]

Gloom and Doom for Private Prisons

When the 1994 crime bill started leveraging funding and enforcement power against undocumented immigrants, the private prison corporations were focused on state prison populations. But in the late 1990s, despite a decade of tremendous growth, CCA and GEO Group's stock prices dipped—and began a steady decline that would bring CCA to the brink of bankruptcy in the early 2000s. After an overbuilding spree in the 1990s, CCA and GEO Group were sitting on thousands of empty prison beds. Spec prisons across the country stood empty as states faced budget cuts and were reluctant to sign new contracts with these companies.

Bad press around high-profile escapes and riots at private prisons from Arizona to Texas reduced the industry's credibility as well. In August 1996, two incarcerated sex offenders from Oregon housed at a CCA-run prison in Texas escaped. They were caught eleven days later near Dallas, having fled nearly 200 miles from the prison. "Jail officials did not notify Houston police for at least two hours after the escape."[21] In fact, until the escape, local and state officials had no idea that the facility, which was designed to house immigrant detainees, housed more than 200 sex offenders. After the incident, Oregon transferred all their inmates from the CCA-run facility back home.[22] CCA released a statement after the incident: "The company is not obligated to notify local authorities or state corrections officials of out-of-state inmates being housed there. . . . However, considering the interest by those officials, the company believes that notification in the future is appropriate."[23]

In the summer of 1997, a videotape surfaced of jail guards kicking inmates in a Texas jail run by a private corporation. The video appeared to show the guards "zapping them with stun guns and forcing them to crawl around on their stomachs. In at least one instance, a guard dog was seen biting an inmate's leg as the man writhed in pain."[24] The private firm, Capital Correctional Resources Inc. (CCRI), contracted with Missouri to house the inmates in a Texas jail because of overcrowding in Missouri prisons. Once the video was made public, the Missouri Department of Corrections canceled its contract with CCRI.[25] Missouri Attorney General Jay Nixon filed a lawsuit charging officials in Brazoria County, Texas, with a cover-up, and the FBI investigated the allegations for possible abuse and civil rights violations.[26] The FBI announced indictments; a jury in federal court acquitted one deputy, failed to reach a verdict against another guard, and returned a misdemeanor conviction against a third civilian jailer.[27] Despite the acquittals, the private prison industry's brand suffered and bad press continued.

In August 1997, prisoners from the Northeast Ohio Correctional Center, a CCA-owned medium security facility in Youngstown, Ohio, filed a lawsuit alleging that they were abused and denied adequate medical care. A federal judge approved a $1.6 million settlement in March 1999.[28] In 1998, six maximum security prisoners—including four convicted of murder—cut through a gate and escaped the Youngstown facility.[29] The episode came under scrutiny because the Youngstown prison was only set up to house medium security inmates. Compounding the negative press, Youngstown Mayor George McKelvey admitted that the "prison guards didn't even notice the escape until an inmate disclosed it."[30]After the incident, approximately eighty of the maximum security prisoners at Youngstown were transferred to the Torrance County Detention Facility in New Mexico, which was also run by CCA.

In August 1998, a group of the transferred inmates attacked and injured five guards at a CCA facility in New Mexico,[31] and in January the Wackenhut-owned and -operated Lea County Prison in Hobbs, New Mexico, reported its eighth stabbing, and the second stabbing death, in the six months since it opened.[32] Violence at private and public prisons in New Mexico was so high in the late 1990s that the Department of Corrections convened a task force to investigate the increase in violence in public and privately run prisons in the state.

In June 1999, two Montana inmates escaped from the CCA-owned and -operated West Tennessee Detention Facility, kicking off a seven-day search by the highway patrol and the Shelby and Tipton County sheriffs' departments.[33] In August, several Wisconsin inmates at a CCA prison in Whiteville, Tennessee, filed lawsuits alleging "they were repeatedly beaten, choked, sprayed with pepper spray and shocked with electrical devices following an assault on a guard the year earlier."[34] The lawsuits alleged that CCA had cut costs and increased profits by "inadequately staffing its prisons with poorly trained guards and resorting to unlawful, physical force when trouble occurs."[35] In December 2000, a federal jury in South Carolina awarded $3.1 million to a teenage inmate who was "hogtied and thrown against a wall by CCA corrections officers."[36] Beyond these high-profile incidents, the states were not certain that these contracts even saved them money.

California canceled an agreement in 1999 with private corporations to run four 500-bed prisons, and Georgia canceled a contract to use a 1,500-bed facility CCA had built on speculation in rural south Georgia.[37] In 2000, Louisiana's Department of Corrections took control of the Jena Juvenile Justice Center, a Wackenhut corrections facility, following reports of widespread brutality. Also in 2000, North Carolina canceled contracts at two CCA facilities due to staffing shortages and other administrative problems.[38]

CCA's stock peaked in 1998 at $40 a share, only to lose 93 percent of its value by 2000. GEO Group's shares nosedived too, losing more than two-thirds of their value (figure 8.1). In the fall of 2000, *Business Week* wrote that "today, the industry is in a rut, and its prospects have been severely trimmed. Overbuilding and ill-fated financial schemes have hammered stock prices. States, once eager to outsource their inmates,

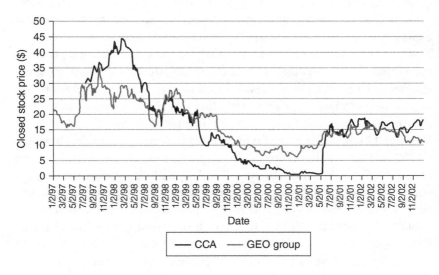

Figure 8.1 CCA and GEO Group Stock Prices, 1997–2002

are backing out of private prison contracts. News of escapes and violence at private prisons adds to a climate of distrust."[39] Although the article suggested that this downward trend might be permanent, it noted that CCA was targeting federal contracts and that Wackenhut's prisons overseas in South Africa and Australia were profitable.[40]

The gloom and doom for the private prison industry was short-lived. The industry began to look to the federal government, and a new market emerged—privatization of federal prisons. In the wake of the Oklahoma City bombing, in 1996 President Clinton signed the Antiterrorism and Effective Death Penalty Act. The legislation expanded the grounds for detaining and deporting immigrants, including long-term legal residents of the United States. Timothy McVeigh, convicted of the 1995 bombing, was a U.S. citizen, but the act aimed to calm fears about undocumented criminals. That fall, President Clinton took a further step and signed the 1996 Illegal Immigration Reform and Immigrant Responsibility Act, which expanded the list of crimes designated as "aggravated felonies" for which a noncitizen would be deported after serving his or her sentence. Those subject to deportation even under the pre-1996 legal code now had no line of defense, no relief—in many cases, deportation was automatic. Any conviction carrying a sentence of one year or longer, whether suspended or served, required deportation.[41] This included minor drug offenses, some cases of drunk driving, and even shoplifting. Within a few years these immigration laws were fully implemented, and the federal government experienced a surge in demand for immigration detention facilities.

The federal Bureau of Prisons (BOP) issued a request for a proposal for companies to manage low security private prison beds to meet the needs of its "criminal alien requirements" (CAR).[42] CAR prisons are "low-custody institutions with lesser security requirements than the medium and maximum-security institutions run directly by the BOP."[43] This was the first of what would become a profitable business model in the years to come. BOP awarded two contracts to CCA to manage 7,500 CAR beds. In 2000, CCA signed two additional massive contracts with the federal government: one for an immigration detention center in San Diego, and one to house noncitizen convicts at a 2,300-bed speculative prison that had long stood empty in California City.[44] Both CCA and GEO Group snapped up these contracts, which essentially bailed out the two largest private prison corporations from their financial woes.

GEO Group's stock prices steadily rose from about $7.00 in May 2000 to over $14.00 just one year later. CCA's growth was even more dramatic. Nearing bankruptcy in December 2000, in a desperate attempt to raise stock prices enough to retain its listing on the exchange, shareholders approved a reverse stock split at their annual meeting. Shares in CCA leapt from about 75 cents to over $14.00 in just two weeks.[45]

At the same time, the nonimmigrant BOP population was also growing. Between 1980 and 2012, the federal prison population ballooned by almost 800 percent,[46] increasing, on average, by nearly 6,000 inmates annually.[47] With this massive increase and a budget so bloated that BOP now accounted for 25 percent of Justice Department spending, the department turned to private prison companies to operate facilities for noncitizen inmates convicted of federal crimes. The logic was simple: BOP would run prisons with citizens convicted of federal crimes and provide required reentry programming and other services. Facilities to house the vast majority of noncitizens convicted of federal crimes, however, were contracted out because noncitizens didn't need—or at least were not required to receive—services such as educational programming and mental health care. A private corporation was best suited to operate these facilities in which the majority of inmates would eventually face deportation.

The Bush Years and the Creation of Homeland Security

September 11, 2001, reinvigorated the private prison industry. In an almost immediate response to the attacks, President George W. Bush created the Office of Homeland Security. When Congress passed the Homeland Security Act in November 2002, the Department of Homeland Security (DHS) was born, consolidating twenty-two federal departments and agencies into one cabinet-level agency. Steve Logan, CEO of Cornell Companies (a for-profit prison corporation acquired by GEO Group in 2010), spoke on an investor conference call about the terrorist attacks:

> It's clear that since September 11 there's a heightened focus on detention, both on the borders and in the U.S. What we are seeing is an increased scrutiny of . . . tightening up the borders. . . . So I would say the events of 9/11 . . . um . . . let me back up. The federal business is

the best business for us. It's the most consistent business for us—and the events of September 11 is [*sic*] increasing that level of business.[48]

When immigration enforcement was transferred to DHS in 2003, annual immigrant detentions skyrocketed.[49] This federal crackdown on immigration violations was key to the revival of the private prison industry. Finally, President Bush signed the Intelligence Reform and Terrorism Prevention Act in December 2004, ostensibly aimed at preventing future terrorist attacks on U.S. soil. This immense piece of legislation authorized DHS to hire more border patrol agents and add 40,000 detention beds over five years. CCA's 2004 Annual Report applauded passage of the bill:

> The Intelligence Reform Bill authorizes the Department of Homeland Security to, subject to appropriations, hire a total of 2,000 new border patrol agents over each of the next five years and increase the total available detention beds by 40,000 over the next five years. We believe these initiatives could lead to meaningful growth to the private corrections industry in general, and to our company in particular.[50]

In 2005, the federal government increased its prosecutions of immigrants through a joint initiative of DHS and the Justice Department, called Operation Streamline. Under the initiative, border patrol refers undocumented immigrants to the Justice Department for criminal prosecution. Operation Streamline began in the West Texas town of Del Rio near the Mexican border in late 2005, and immigrants who had illegally crossed the border were rounded up and subject to criminal prosecution. This was a reversal from the previous policy of "expedited removal," sometimes referred to as "catch and release," that allowed an undocumented person to be deported without a formal hearing. The former approach used civil law provisions for removal from the United States and avoided the criminal justice process entirely.

Since the program's inception, Customs and Border Protection has partnered with federal prosecutors to prosecute undocumented immigrants for misdemeanor illegal entry and felony illegal reentry. The decade-old program has drawn significant criticism for its fast-tracked mass prosecutions, in which dozens of undocumented individuals receive a group hearing in court.

Private Prisons Step In

In 2006, President George W. Bush told the nation he was ending the "catch and release" policy whereby undocumented citizens from Mexico were driven back across the border. Additional immigration detention space was needed, and federal officials opened the T. Don Hutto Family Detention Center near Austin, Texas. The 512-bed center, operated by CCA under a $2.8 million-per-month federal contract, represented the Bush administration's tough approach to immigration enforcement. But the Hutto center quickly drew scathing criticism for its treatment of women and children. Within a year, the Bush administration faced a lawsuit over the detention center's conditions. Court papers describe children "forced to wear prison jumpsuits, to live in dormitory housing, to use toilets exposed to public view and to sleep with the lights on, even while being denied access to appropriate schooling."[51] In 2009, the Obama administration closed Hutto, leaving only a single, small family detention center in Berks County, Pennsylvania, to house refugee families in exceptional circumstances.

Also in 2006, county commissioners in Willacy County, Texas, signed a contract with ICE to develop a $50 million detention center in Raymondville, Texas. The workers were under strict orders from ICE to finish the project quickly. The facility would house 500 illegal immigrants within thirty days, and up to 2,000 within ninety days. Ten Kevlar-covered pods were put up that could house 200 prisoners each. "It looks like a tent—it's not a brick-and-mortar type building," Raymondville City Manager Eleazar Garcia said. "They pour a slab, then put up an (aluminum) beam support system and then blow this structure up like a tent."[52] The facility earned the nickname "Tent City" and housed 120 detainees in each air-conditioned tent. At Willacy, most "dormitories" were Kevlar tents that housed about 200 men in bunk beds spaced only a few feet apart.[53]

Management and Training Corporation (MTC) won the contract to operate the facility. The *Texas Observer* called the town "prisonville," noting that within its boundaries it contained "a privately run, 1,000-bed state prison; a county-run, 96-bed jail with space for federal inmates; a private, 500-bed federal jail; and a recently opened private, 2,000-bed detention center for undocumented immigrants that is a crown jewel in the Bush administration's border-enforcement policy."[54] In 2007, an American Bar Association delegation flagged detainee complaints, including "lack of access to lawyers and medical care, rodents, flooding toilets and water seeping underneath the tents during rainfall."[55] In 2010, the Inter-American Commission on Human Rights and Texas Appleseed documented complaints by immigrant detainees at the prison for a lack of medical care, and in 2011, the PBS series *Frontline* cited sexual abuse by guards and other physical and racial abuse in Willacy.[56]

The facility was taken over by the BOP after complaints of abuse in 2011 and was expanded to 3,000 beds and transformed into a CAR prison—one of thirteen around the country—to house undocumented immigrants serving sentences for low-level offenses, including crimes related to crossing the border.[57] These low security facilities in the federal system detained noncitizens serving the final stretch of their criminal sentences before being transferred to immigration authorities and deported. The contract to operate Willacy guaranteed a minimum payment based on a 90 percent capacity rate ($48 million in 2015)—even if the prison sat empty. For inmates beyond that 90 percent threshold, the federal government would pay MTC a per diem. The guaranteed payments meant BOP had an incentive to fill the prison, even beyond its capacity.

In 2014, the ACLU released a report on for-profit detention centers, condemning Willacy for its poor conditions—specifically, overcrowding. Despite a capacity of 2,000 the facility was detaining 2,834 immigrants by early 2015.[58] In February 2015, detainees seized control of the facility during a riot that lasted for two days. Using pipes as weapons, inmates set fires and damaged property. Correctional officers responded with tear gas.[59] The facility was destroyed, and detainees were transferred to other federal facilities. BOP ended its contract with MTC, and nearly 400 employees were laid off.[60] At least 150 of the facility's 400 employees lived in the county of 22,000. According to the U.S. Census Bureau, the county suffers a 35 percent poverty rate.[61]

In late March, Standard and Poor downgraded the prison bonds to "junk" status.[62] The town was devastated. The economy had depended on the prison industry, floating millions of dollars in bonds through a "Public Facilities Corp." to build the correctional center.[63] But the election of Donald Trump proved a blessing for the Texas town. In March 2017, Willacy County commissioners approved the sale of the facility for $68 million (the amount owed on its bonds) to MTC, who will also pay Willacy County $3 daily for each inmate held there.[64] MTC also announced it would create about 275 jobs. When the county selected MTC over the GEO Group, Willacy County agreed to drop a multi-million-dollar lawsuit alleging that MTC's failure to address problems at the prison led to the February 2015 riot.[65] At the time of the agreement, MTC didn't have a contract with any state or federal agency to hold inmates, but ICE had expressed interest in the facility. In April, MTC and Raymondville officials inspected Willacy, which had been closed for about two years after the last inmate uprising. After the inspection, it was announced that Willacy's infamous tents would be torn down and the facility redeveloped.[66]

The Bed Mandate

Senator Robert Byrd (D–W.V.), chair of the Senate Appropriations Committee, introduced the bed mandate into the DHS Appropriations Act of 2010.[67] Congress then allocated funding for ICE to "maintain a level of not less than 33,400 detention beds through September 30, 2010."[68] This marked the first time Congress had designated a specific number of total detention beds for ICE to maintain.

Despite its obscurity, the results of this quota are staggering. From 2001 to 2011, the total number of immigrants who passed through ICE detention per year more than doubled, from 204,459 to a record-breaking 429,247.[69] In 2015 alone, almost half a million people were held in immigrant detention facilities, and the average number of daily detention beds nearly doubled, from 18,000 in 2004 to 34,000 in 2014 (figure 8.2). Noncitizens held in civil detention can be found in an extensive system of more than 200 facilities, mostly in private detention, county jails, and federal facilities. The federal government now spends $2.8 billion on immigration detention and deportation every year.[70]

The legislation states "not less than," and DHS and Congress have debated whether the agency is merely required to maintain capacity for 34,000 detainees or to actually detain and house 34,000 people each day. At the House Judiciary DHS Oversight Hearing in May 2014, DHS Secretary Jeh Johnson clarified that he did not interpret the bed quota to mean that 34,000 beds must be filled but rather maintained.[71] The bed mandate has produced enormous revenue for private prisons,

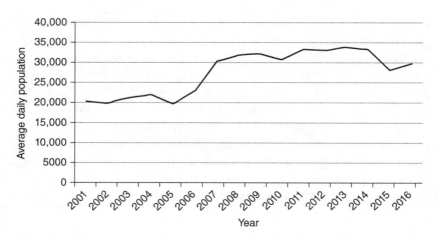

Figure 8.2 ICE Average Daily Population, 2001–2016 *Source*: "ICE ERO Facts and Statistics," ICE ERO Report, U.S. Department of Justice Report and Recommendations, and National Immigrant Justice Center, various years.

which have increased their portion of immigrant detention beds by 13 percent. In fact, nine of the largest ICE detention centers are privately operated. With a near-monopoly on immigrant detention, CCA and the GEO Group operate a combined 72 percent of the privately contracted ICE immigration detention beds.[72]

Central American Crises Surges Immigration

Since 2008, violence in Central America has brought a surge of migrants fleeing Honduras, El Salvador, and Guatemala that far eclipses the immigrants crossing the border from Mexico. In 2011, San Pedro Sula, Honduras, overtook Ciudad Juárez, Mexico, as the most violent city in the hemisphere, with 159 homicides per 100,000 residents.[73] In response to this latest influx of refugees, DHS significantly expanded its detention of mothers and children by more than 4,000 percent, from approximately 85 detention beds to nearly 3,800 beds in 2015.[74] Parents and children who are detained are kept together—a major policy shift from congressional action in 2005.[75]

By early 2014, a broader humanitarian crisis was apparent. Between October 2013 and June 2014, 39,000 adults with children were detained at the border.[76] The Obama administration sent Vice President Joe Biden to Guatemala to meet with the leaders of El Salvador, Guatemala, and Honduras—the three countries responsible for the majority of the incoming migrants—to ask for their help conveying the message that there were no new legal recourses for these populations to enter the United States.[77] That summer, the situation at the border had become a crisis. The Obama administration built more family detention centers in South Texas and issued a $3.7 billion emergency request to address the influx of Central American migrant families. The budget allocations included $879 million for more than 6,000 new family detention beds. Rushing to stem the influx of undocumented immigrant families through the South Texas border, the administration opened a makeshift family detention center in Artesia, New Mexico, to hold 700 immigrants—a stopgap measure until bigger detention facilities were built.

DHS wanted a facility built quickly, and they turned to CCA. In an odd contractual arrangement the most knowledgeable contract attorney would be hard pressed to explain, the federal government did not engage in a public bidding process but amended an Intergovernmental Service Agreement between the City of Eloy, Arizona, and ICE to house up to 2,400 detainees at the South Texas Family Detention Facility.[78] NPR reported: "Watchdogs who monitor for-profit immigrant jails say they've never seen anything quite like it."[79] CCA is now the biggest employer in Eloy, Arizona, a small town of 17,000 people nearly 1,000 miles away from Dilley: it operates three prisons and the Eloy Detention Center, which is an ICE jail for immigrants. CCA pays Eloy $438,000 annually just for amending its contract. CCA's payments make up 5 percent of the revenue for Eloy's general fund.[80]

The deal is structured with two separate agreements: one between ICE and the town of Eloy, and the other between Eloy and CCA. Pursuant to the contract and Intergovernmental Service Agreement, ICE sends the city of Eloy $290 million a year in agency pass-through funds, including $37 million to operate the Eloy Detention Center and $253 million to run the South Texas Detention Center in Dilley.[81] DHS pays CCA for 100 percent capacity, even if the facility is not full. The contract states that "CCA is assured of a predictable payment, collecting a fixed amount of around $20 million per month—even when the facility's population drops."[82] CCA spokesperson Jonathan Burns justified the contract because it requires CCA to provide full staffing and other services no matter how many detainees are housed in the facility at any given time.[83]

Dilley City Administrator Noel Perez stated that the city took on $5 million in debt in 2014 to upgrade water and sewage in the town to accommodate the detention center.[84] The family detention center boasts bunk beds and cribs that can sleep up to eight, and flat-screen TVs and kitchens in the cottages, although cooking is prohibited to avoid fires.[85] The vast detention complex contains makeshift classrooms in trailers and basketball courts and playgrounds for its nearly 1,000 children. It employs a staff of 700, including teachers, pediatricians, and psychiatrists.[86] At full capacity, the detention center can hold 3,000 immigrants.[87] When DHS Secretary Johnson stood outside STRFDC in 2014 to announce its opening, he delivered a stern message to undocumented immigrants: "It will now be more likely that you will be detained and sent back."[88]

CCA received $36 million in revenue from the Dilley facility during the first quarter of 2015.[89] In May, CCA announced that its "revenue for the first quarter of 2015 was $426 million compared to $404.2 million in the first quarter of 2014. The increase in revenue was primarily attributable to the operational ramp of our South Texas Family Residential Center."[90] A year later, the Dilley facility brought in more than $70 million during the first quarter, almost double its revenue during the previous year's first quarter. CCA's CEO Damon Hininger explained: "Our financial performance was driven primarily by stronger than anticipated demand from our federal partners, most notably Immigration and Customs Enforcement."[91]

GEO Group, which owns and operates Karnes, the 500-bed capacity family detention center plagued by complaints since it opened in 2014, announced in an earnings call that "revenues for the first quarter 2016 increased to approximately $510 million from $427 million a year ago."[92]

Family Detention

The practice of keeping so many undocumented families and their children in immigrant detention centers has immigrant advocates up in arms. In 2015, U.S. District Court Judge Dolly Gee found ICE in breach of the 1997 class action *Flores v. Meese* settlement, which, among other things, proscribed holding immigrant children "for prolonged periods in secure, unlicensed facilities."[93] The court ordered the agency to comply with the agreement by October 2015.[94] But in September, the Texas Health and Human Services Commission found a backdoor. They adopted an emergency rule aimed at *Flores* compliance[95] that relaxed living standard requirements for facilities seeking child care licenses. Specifically, the rule exempts facilities that (1) house over four occupants to a room, (2) allow children to share a room with unrelated adults, or (3) allow children of opposite genders to share a room from identical limitations that would bar them from obtaining a child care license.[96]

Both Karnes and STRFC applied for child care licenses.[97] The state of Texas issued Karnes a license "despite allegations of child sexual abuse at the facility and inspections that turned up safety deficiencies."[98] Before STRFC could obtain its license, mothers detained in Karnes and Dilley in conjunction with the nonprofit organization Grassroots Leadership filed suit against the Texas Department of Family and Protective Services (DFPS), arguing that the agency had no authority to issue child care licenses under the emergency rule.[99] In June 2016, Travis County Judge Karin Crump issued an injunction against DFPS, enjoining Dilley's license.[100] Karnes kept its license. A final judgment, which prevented DFPS from licensing Karnes and STRFC, was issued in December 2016.[101]

Since the Obama administration announced its detention reform initiative in 2009, the number of noncitizens DHS detained yearly has increased by nearly 25 percent.[102] In 2012, DHS detained a record 477,523 adult noncitizens.[103] Prosecutions for illegal entry and reentry neared 100,000 in 2013, accounting for more than half of all federal criminal prosecutions, and they remained near those levels for the rest of Obama's time in office.[104] Cases against immigrants for illegal entry into the country accounted for half of all criminal cases in the nation's federal court system in 2015.[105] As a result, spending on immigration detention facilities climbed sharply, from $700 million in 2005 to more than $2 billion today.

Lobbying and Demand

Government policy created the immigration detention boom, but can we believe the narrative of for-profit prison corporations that they simply provide a service and sit on the sidelines? CCA says that it does not lobby for legislation that would increase incarceration:

> CCA's political and government relations activities are designed to educate federal, state and local officials on the benefits of partnership corrections, CCA's ability to assist them in meeting their corrections needs and our track record of success. Our company does not, under longstanding policy, lobby for or against policies or legislation that would determine the basis for or duration of an individual's incarceration or detention.[106]

For-profit prison corporations have not been shy about donating campaign funds to key legislators and meeting with federal agencies in Washington. Working hard for those contracts, the industry increased its lobbying to DHS and BOP. CCA, for example, increased its federal lobbying expenditures from $410,000 to $3 million between 2000 and 2004.[107] Legislators on the Appropriations Committee received campaign funds from GEO Group and CCA.[108]

In 2010, NPR investigated just how much influence private prison firms have on policy makers. A group of legislators and corporations met in December 2009 in Washington, D.C. at an American Legislative Exchange Counsel (ALEC) meeting to discuss a model immigration bill. ALEC describes itself as "America's largest nonpartisan, voluntary membership organization of state legislators dedicated to the principles of limited government, free markets, and federalism."[109] ALEC is a conservative organization known for writing model legislation with corporate partners and then encouraging their introduction through legislative members. NPR reported that the group voted to create a model bill on immigration and discussed and debated proposed language. "The 50 or so people in the room included officials of the Corrections Corporation of America, according to two sources who were there."[110]

Four months after the meeting, Arizona passed a bill based on that model legislation. In fact, Arizona's newest immigration law, "Support Our Law Enforcement and Safe Neighborhoods Act," was taken almost word for word from the ALEC model bill. SB 1070 made it a state misdemeanor crime for an undocumented citizen to be in Arizona and required local law enforcement officers to try to determine an individual's immigration status during a "lawful stop, detention or arrest" when there is reasonable suspicion that the individual is an undocumented immigrant. The U.S. Supreme Court later struck down most of its provisions. The bill was introduced by Arizona state Senator Russell Pearce (R) who had attended the ALEC meeting. In a further indication of the tangle of interests that private prisons create, NPR reported that thirty of SB 1070's thirty-six cosponsors received campaign contributions from lobbyists of the three major private prison companies: CCA, GEO Group, and MTC.[111]

In the 2011–2012 legislative session, twenty-three states introduced ALEC's model legislation on immigration, the "No Sanctuary Cities for Illegal Immigrants Act," which requires local law enforcement officials to uphold federal immigration law.[112] Again, it appears that the lobbying paid off.

In January 2015, GEO Group bought LCS Corrections, which owns a handful of immigration detention facilities in Texas and Louisiana. In announcing the $312 million industry deal, GEO Group's CEO George Zoley stated:

This important transaction represents a compelling strategic fit for our company. The recently announced reactivation of a significant portion of our beds in inventory is indicative of the growing need for beds around the country, and this important strategic transaction will further position GEO to meet the demand for correctional and detention bed space in the United States.[113]

In the fall GEO Group renewed a ten-year contract with ICE to continue to operate a 1,575-bed detention center in Tacoma, Washington. The deal was expected to generate approximately $57 million in annualized revenues at full occupancy.[114] The Northwest Detention Center made headlines in 2014 when more than 700 detainees conducted a hunger strike to protest low wages and high commissary prices.[115] The facility made national news again in 2017 when hundreds of detainees refused meals in a hunger strike to protest conditions at the facility in addition to protesting delayed immigration hearings.

In June 2016, ICE announced that it hoped to add 1,000 additional family detention beds in Texas and more than 3,000 beds at Karnes and the family detention center in Dilley. Responding to ICE's announcement, Texas officials submitted a proposal to ICE to build a new family detention center in a former nursing home in San Diego, Texas. Worried about the almost $1 million in revenue the town will lose because of a drop in oil prices, the detention center could bring much-needed jobs and economic opportunity to South Texas. UK-based Serco, which operates private prisons and immigration detention centers around the world hoped to win the contract and promised 200 local jobs if the center is opened.[116]

For private industry, the business model makes sense. Immigrant detainees have limited legal rights and are not guaranteed—in fact, are rarely provided—many programmatic services such as education, mental health or drug abuse counseling, or job training. They are also less likely to complain about the conditions of their confinement. Language barriers get in the way, and they're often without the money to hire attorneys to fight for their release. In terms of profit, immigrant detainees are low-hanging fruit.

Things Fall Apart

Three months before the 2016 presidential election, the private prison industry had its worst month since the late 1990s, when they were on the verge of bankruptcy. The Justice Department quietly declined to renew a contract with CCA for a facility in Cibola, New Mexico, that the company had operated since 1998. At the time, the Cibola County Correctional Facility employed a staff of 300 and housed 1,200 minimum security male inmates; most were Mexican immigrants and all were undocumented and convicted of federal crimes.[117] The Justice Department almost immediately began to transfer the inmates to other prisons and planned to do so until their contract ended in October, four years before it was set to expire in 2020. The department's decision not to renew the Cibola contract was a marked outlier; only three other private prison contracts had been terminated before they were set to expire. One of those was the Willacy County Correctional Center contract with MTC.

A mere eleven days later, the Justice Department's inspector general—the department's internal watchdog—called on BOP to more rigorously oversee its contracts with private prison companies. The inspector general found that privately run federal prisons are more dangerous than those managed by BOP and need more oversight, suggesting that BOP "needs to improve how it monitors contract prisons in several areas."[118] The report found that contract prisons consistently fail to measure up to federal standards in preventing dangerous conditions, intercepting contraband, and ensuring internal accountability for staff misconduct.[119] It also accused BOP of inadequate communication in monitoring the private prison: after one inmate died due to "delayed or incomplete treatment" at the contract facility, the monitors took no steps to "require corrective action . . . and corrective actions were delayed."[120] Although most of the report criticized BOP for failing to properly monitor and improve conditions in these private facilities, the investigation did find that the private prisons had fewer incidents of positive drug tests and sexual misconduct than BOP facilities.[121]

In 2013, the federal prison population was at its peak at 220,000 inmates, and BOP was housing approximately 15 percent of its population—nearly 30,000 inmates—in privately operated prisons. By 2016, contract prisons held more than 22,000 inmates, about 12 percent of the total federal prison population, and were run by three for-profit prison companies: CCA, GEO Group, and MTC.[122] The majority of these inmates are non-citizens subject to deportation.[123] A BOP spokesperson recently stated that 96 percent of inmates in their private prisons are non-citizens.[124] According to the BOP, they rely on private facilities to house many "criminal aliens in low security privately contracted correctional institutions." These inmates are "generally healthy, adult male criminal aliens with ordinarily 90 months or less remaining to serve on their sentences." An email a reporter forwarded to me from the public affairs division of the BOP provides more details:

> BOP private facilities do not provide for the same level of programming as BOP facilities, nor do they house inmates needing higher levels of medical care. While most low security criminal aliens (75% nationwide) are able to be housed in private facilities, approximately 25% require greater levels of medical or mental health care, or have security reasons requiring them to be housed in BOP facilities. Privately contracted facilities provide the BOP with an effective means of managing low security, specialized populations such as criminal aliens and other offenders; they provide the BOP with flexibility to ramp up or down our capacity and costs relatively quickly based on population and needs and funding.[125]

When all was said and done, the report recommended that the Department of Justice improve oversight and monitoring of the private prisons with whom it contracts.

Justice Department officials read the report and decided to do more than improve their monitoring of these facilities. A week after the inspector general issued its bombshell report, the Department of Justice made an announcement that shocked private prison industry analysts, private prison abolitionists, and the private prison corporations themselves. The Justice Department said it would gradually phase out the use of private prisons to house federal inmates at its thirteen privately run federal "contract" prisons, which primarily house noncitizens convicted of crimes.

Deputy Attorney General Sally Yates sent a memo to BOP directing it to decline to renew contracts with private prison corporations as they came up for contract renewal.[126] Although two of these facilities (prisons in Moshannon Valley, Pennsylvania, and Great Plains, Oklahoma) were contracted with private providers until 2024, most BOP contracts were set to expire earlier. Yates acknowledged that for the first time in decades the federal prison population had started to decline. Acknowledging that private prisons relieved overcrowding during the height of federal incarceration rates, Yates stated that they "simply do not provide the same level of correctional services, programs, and resources; they do not save substantially on costs; and as noted in a recent report by the Department's Office of Inspector General, they do not maintain the same level of safety and security."[127]

Because of the inmate population drop, BOP could begin transferring prisoners from the thirteen privately run prisons to its own facilities. Advocacy organizations were ecstatic, but still voiced concern that DHS held as many as 34,000 immigrants awaiting deportation. The majority of them were held in immigrant detention centers owned and operated by for-profit prison companies. The *New York Times* editorial board stated that private prisons are "notoriously violent and dysfunctional," called them "a national shame," and urged DHS to eliminate its contracts as well.[128] The *Boston Globe* followed suit a few days later, urging the Obama administration to eliminate private prison contracts with DHS.[129]

Soon after the announcement, Senator Bernie Sanders (D–VT.) issued a joint letter with Representative Raul M. Grijalva (D–AZ.), asking Secretary Johnson to phase out its reliance on contracts with for-profit prison corporations. Other advocates and journalists pointed out that the overwhelming majority of private prison inmates are held in state prisons. California journalists were quick to point out that their state had the lion's share of contracts with private prison industries, the majority with CCA. At the time of the announcement, nearly 6,000 inmates were held in private prisons within the state, 4,800 were held out of the state in private prisons in Arizona and Mississippi, and 3,700 immigrants were detained by the federal government in private prisons in four California cities.[130]

Shares of the private prison giants tanked. CCA and GEO Group stock lost nearly half their value ($13.22 and $13.80 per share, respectively), an indication that the nation's largest for-profit prison corporations profitability might be on the wane. CCA responded to the news immediately in an emailed statement to investors and the press:

> We value our partners, and we will continue to work with them, both through the types of management solutions we've provided for more than three decades, as well as new, innovative opportunities we've been exploring in recent years in a proactive effort to meet their evolving needs. It's important to note that today's announcement relates only to BOP correctional facilities, which make up 7 percent of our business.[131]

The day after the announcement, GEO Group CEO George Zoley said in a conference call: "There's been an overreaction to the news about the [Bureau of Prisons] contracts. We think, in time, this will correct itself."[132]

Despite the corporations' significant value losses, the Obama administration only targeted a few BOP contracts. At the end of the day, it affected only 15,000 prison beds operated by GEO Group, representing about 14 percent of the company's annual operating revenues, and 6,000 prison beds for CCA, about 7 percent of its revenue. The stocks quickly regained some of their initial losses in after-hours trading, and five days later both companies' stocks had rebounded. GEO Group saw a soaring 26.2 percent increase in its value, and CCA saw a 10.2 percent increase.

Then the other shoe dropped. Secretary Johnson succumbed to outside pressure from activists and editorial boards and inside pressure from the Obama administration and announced the formation of a DHS Advisory Council "to evaluate whether the immigration detention operations conducted by Immigration and Customs Enforcement should move in the same direction."[133] Johnson directed the advisory council to create a subcommittee to review DHS policy and practices concerning the use of private immigration detention and evaluate whether the practice should be eliminated. The report was due November 30, 2016. The day of Johnson's announcement, CCA relied on DHS contracts for 51 percent of its revenue, more than seven times the revenue it received from BOP contracts. GEO Group's numbers were about 34 percent, a little more than double its BOP contracts. The flailing stocks dropped again.

A week after the DHS announcement, A DHS attorney I spoke with told me there was little or no advance warning that this announcement was coming. As of August 8, ICE reported that "there were 33,676 immigrants in detention, with 24,657 of them in private facilities."[134] On September 5, the *New York Times* again urged the federal government to sever ties with private prisons. They knew Secretary Johnson would review the advisory council's report before making any decision and suggested that "to save time, Mr. Johnson could do the wise thing and end the contracts now."[135]

The private prison corporations were not alone in voicing concerns over the federal government's sudden scrutiny of their contracts. In mid-September, Rep. Randy Neugebauer (R–TX.) and five representatives from Texas, Georgia, and California sent a letter to Deputy Attorney General Sally Yates explaining their anxieties over the announcement to phase out privately operated prison contracts. Specifically, they noted their concern "with the impact this directive will have on the local communities we represent. In many of these areas, the contract prison is one of the largest employers, and citizens have few other job opportunities."[136]

DHS officials began speaking anonymously to the press, stating that "ending private detention for migrants would require Congress to spend millions more dollars because government-run operations are more costly."[137] An ICE official who spoke anonymously stated that transferring control of immigration detention centers to ICE "would require an 800 percent expansion of ICE capacity" to replace the privately run facilities. It would also, he claimed, cost billions of dollars.[138] Three weeks after Johnson asked the independent advisory council to review his agency's use of for-profit immigration detention centers, ICE Director Sarah Saldaña testified in front of the House Judiciary Committee that ending these contracts "would pretty much turn our system upside down," requiring ICE "to build detention centers" and "hire staff."[139]

In a draft report issued on December 1, a subcommittee of the advisory council recommended that ICE continue to rely on private prison firms to detain undocumented immigrants.[140] Unexpectedly, seventeen council members endorsed a split position—voting to approve sections recommending greater oversight and detention center monitoring but agreeing with the dissent expressed by Marshall Fitz (formerly of the Center for American Progress) criticizing "the conclusion that reliance on private prisons should, or inevitably must, continue."[141] Only five members voted to approve the report in its entirety.

A majority of council members agreed with the report's recommendations that ICE expand measures to provide more robust oversight of private facilities. Some of these recommendations include that "all inspections should make greater use of qualitative review of outcomes, rather than simply using a quantitative checklist," and "annual inspections done by ICE's Enforcement and Removal Operations (ERO) should move toward greater direct involvement by ICE officers and subject matter experts and not be left to implementation by the personnel of an inspection contractor."[142] The report and the council's vote are nonbinding.

South Texas Detention Center

I visited the South Texas Detention Center (STDC) in Pearsall, Texas, in 2016, a 1,900-capacity immigrant detention center owned and run by the GEO Group. The facility is co-ed and has fifteen male and six female dormitories. The visiting area had a portrait of President Barack Obama alongside one of GEO Group CEO George Zoley. Given the proximity of the portraits, one unfamiliar with U.S. politics could easily mistake the millionaire private prison entrepreneur for the nation's vice president. Dueling television sets in the waiting area showed *Live with Kelly* on one screen and the GEO Group logo on the other. The day I visited, STDC held 1,850 detainees, a mere fifty people short of capacity.

The ICE administration office is physically connected to the center, and a woman wearing a blue jacket with POLICE-ICE written in block letters crossed the threshold into the waiting room to greet me. She ushered me into a large conference room in the ICE part of the building. I was told that detainees stay an average of sixty days, and despite its proximity to the Mexico border most of the detainees hail from El Salvador and Honduras. I asked about the relationship with the GEO Group, and she said that DHS is not about to get in the business of owning prisons.

Far larger than the Laredo Processing Center, the facility at Pearsall felt almost like a small city. The four courtrooms looked identical to courtrooms anywhere in United States: rows of benches for families and attorneys, a judge's chair, a station for the judge's clerk with a computer, a desk for an interpreter, and podiums for ICE enforcement officers on one side of the room and defendants and their attorneys across the aisle. A Department of Justice plaque hangs from the wall behind the judge's seat alongside an American flag. During the hearings, records of proceedings are created, evidence is presented and marked, and decisions such as whether detainees are eligible for release on bond are conducted. The scene is replicated in courtrooms across the country, but this one takes place inside a secure detention facility, and a GEO Group officer stands between the respondent and the judge. The private prison guard delivers paperwork from the court clerk to the detainee, a representation of the sometimes strange melding of the justice system with private prison corporations.

There are fifty-eight immigration courts across the country, and nineteen are located in ICE prisons and detention centers.[143] Four immigration judges work here, and they determine whether an undocumented immigrant has committed an offense that is considered deportable and whether that person poses a flight risk or is a danger to society. About 86 percent of detained immigrants do not have lawyers representing them. Given how complex immigration detention policies are in the United States, winning a case without an attorney is unlikely.

Nine of those nineteen immigration courtrooms in prisons are inside detention centers run by GEO Group and CCA. Pearsall Immigration Court processes the most cases among immigration prison courts: more than 10,000 of the 87,000 cases handled in immigration courts in prisons.[144] In August 2016, U.S. Immigration Courts faced a backlog of

512,190 cases,[145] and the Justice Department ramped up hiring and employed an all-time high of 277 immigration judges.[146]

I sat through a bond hearing where the detainee, Mr. Gonzalez, requested bond to remain in the community while his immigration case weaved its way through the system. Gonzalez was arrested for a third DUI charge; he blacked out and woke up in county jail. The judge denied bond, determining that Gonzalez was a danger to the community. After consultation with his attorney, Gonzalez stated that he was not opposed to voluntary departure, a move that would avoid a formal order of removal, which could prove problematic if Gonzalez ever applied to legally enter the United States.

Alternatives to detention, particularly community-based support programs, provide better access to legal and social services at a fraction of the cost and have proven to ensure appearance for court dates in more than 90 percent of cases.[147] But what is life like for those who are detained? Detainees can take advantage of four to five hours of recreation time a day, with attached recreation areas right outside their housing pods. They can work to keep themselves busy, cleaning the common areas or working in the kitchen for $3.00 a day. According to the DHS officials who walked me through the facility, full-time doctors (who are also ICE employees) work at the facility, and ICE pays for outside treatment for detainees who need to leave the facility for medical help.

Pursuant to the agreement with DHS, GEO Group is not required to provide education or job programming. Because of the transient nature of the detained population, immigrant detention facilities housing adults do not focus on reentry and life skills. They are a hybrid form of detention, somewhere between county jail and federal prison. One of the DHS enforcement officers who guided me through the facility noted that STDC is not a prison, it's a processing center. "And don't forget, these people broke the law," she said, referring to how most of these detainees entered the country. It is a point that frustrates immigration advocates who don't think undocumented immigrants should be locked up while they await a decision on their deportation status, and a point that vexes ICE officials who are merely enforcing laws they did not create. "This is not a punishment facility, this is a detention facility," the ICE enforcement attorney said.

One of those undocumented immigrants at STDC was Cecilia, who was picked up six weeks earlier by U.S. border patrol officials. Wearing a blue sweatshirt with her hair in a bun, Cecilia explained that she was waiting for political asylum and hoped to stay in the country with her husband, who is a U.S. citizen. Cecilia, a citizen of Peru who had only a temporary Social Security card, flew back to her home country to visit her daughter and was picked up by the border patrol near the Mexican border in Piedras Negras, Texas.

Twenty-five-year-old Javier Fuentes fled Mexico in June by walking across the border and surrendering to U.S. border patrol agents. He had witnessed a murder in Mexico that involved Mexican police officers and fled to the United States hoping for asylum. When I spoke to Fuentes, he had been detained for sixty days, waiting patiently for an asylum interview. I asked him what he would do if he was deported to Mexico. "I would go to Canada, or another country," Fuentes said. "I can't go back there. It's not safe."

Inside one of the all-male dormitory pods with bunk beds for one hundred men, a Spanish soap opera played on the television as some detainees slept and others sat together on plastic chairs speaking Spanish. A silver video visitation phone operated by Telmate hung on a white brick wall near the booth where ICE officials guard the dormitory twenty-four hours a day. A sign hung nearby the phone: "All sessions are subject to recording and monitoring."

Driving north toward San Antonio, I tuned the radio to the news and a debate about whether Donald Trump was serious about his campaign promise to deport every single one of the estimated 11 million undocumented immigrants living in the United States. In September 2015, Trump spoke on *60 Minutes* about his deportation plan: "We're rounding 'em up in a very humane way, in a very nice way," Trump said, and continued, "and, by the way, I know it doesn't sound nice. But not everything is nice."[148]

CHAPTER NINE

Public Prisons Versus Private Prisons

*There is a mixed bag of research out there. It's not as black
and white and cut and dried as we would like.*

STEVE OWEN, SPOKESMAN FOR CORECIVIC[1]

RESEARCHERS AND POLICY MAKERS have attempted to compare private and public prisons for decades. So far, the studies do not provide compelling evidence that private prisons provide the promised cost savings and benefits the industry marketed to government at its inception. Vermont Department of Corrections inmate Colin was convicted of possessing child pornography and spent thirteen months at the Lee Adjustment Center, a CCA prison in Beattyville, Kentucky. Vermont attempted to resolve its overcrowding problems and saved money by shipping its inmates 900 miles away to a private prison in a two-square-mile town best known for its annual Woolly Worm Festival. In 2014, when Colin was housed at Lee, Vermont paid $65.47 per day for his stay, less than it cost to house inmates in its own public facilities.[2]

In Vermont, the correction officers wielded power through disciplinary reports (DRs), which were written up for the slightest infringements of facility rules. If staff wanted promotions or raises, prison correction officers had to prove they were in control. When Colin arrived in Kentucky, he didn't know what to expect, and to his surprise

Lee felt different. The guards worked for CCA, not the Vermont Department of Corrections, and had a different philosophy than their government counterparts in Vermont. "We have to be here for eight hours. We want to go home to our families at the end of the shift, intact," Colin told me on the phone, imitating them. "Whatever we can do to make your lives more pleasant, less awful, we will do if we can do it within the confines of what is safe."[3]

The idea at Lee was that happy inmates don't fight or steal. With fewer staff than the Vermont prisons and private guards who earned significantly less than state correction officers, guards didn't want inmates causing trouble.[4] In Vermont, one officer was assigned for every unit; in Kentucky, each correction officer oversaw three units. At Lee, Colin and a fellow inmate pooled their money to buy a gaming computer from another prisoner. According to Colin, the guards didn't mind as long as no one had been taken advantage of and it wasn't stolen. Colin went to the gym almost daily, played pool, foosball, ping-pong, and even used the weights from time to time. As an inmate in Vermont, he wasn't allowed to take a computer class because his crime involved computers. CCA didn't care. He earned 75 cents a day for attending computer class and $50.00 for getting his GED.

"They are kind of an easy target, right?" said Colin. "I mean, who doesn't hate a multi-million-dollar company? We all do. We are conditioned not to trust them, to hate them. 'They must be treating these guys like cattle, probably horrible conditions, how could we possibly do this to our men and women?' But I think if you interviewed a hundred guys who each spent two years in Vermont and two years in Kentucky, they would say, 'Give me Kentucky all day long.' "[5]

Despite these perks, Colin's mother couldn't afford to put money in his commissary account *and* visit him in Kentucky. She opted to fund his commissary account. With high blood pressure and the prospect of so many high-sodium, bland meals at the prison, Colin used the money to buy healthier foods from the commissary: tuna fish, canned chicken, vegetables, and pasta that he could keep in a cooler in his pod. Colin called home, and his fifteen minute phone call cost $2.70—pretty expensive, Colin pointed out, for someone earning 50 cents a day. Even so, Colin doesn't believe private prisons should exist. "I would like to see the privatization of our penal system go away. But I only say that because we no longer need these massive warehouse facilities for the hundreds and thousands of men and women that we incarcerate, so the states can maintain their own facilities, with their own inmates."[6]

Another Vermont inmate, Larry, received a twenty-five-years-to-life sentence for murder, spent fifteen years incarcerated, and was at Lee a decade earlier than Colin. He participated in horticulture classes, worked in a dog-training program for almost eight years, played video games, and listened to music on MP3 players. Not all of Larry's time at the private prison was marked with tranquility. Seven months after arriving at the prison, Larry had a bird's eye view of a riot that started when five Kentucky and four Vermont prisoners attacked a guard tower in the recreation yard. According to Larry, it was like watching a mob form. "It started with a small group in the middle, and everyone else wrapped against the fences, trying to initially stay as far away from it as they could . . . it led to the dorms being ripped apart and the main building being lit on fire and burned."[7] Despite the fire that toppled the guard tower, no inmates escaped; the riot ended within a few hours and without serious injury.[8]

Larry admits he preferred his time in the private prison. "I had more toys, an Xbox, more fun." Nevertheless, like Colin, Larry expressed revulsion that private corporations own and manage prisons. "There is a direct correlation between private prisons and the concept of incarceration. When you have a private corporation that has a vested interest in people going to prison, then how do you think they're going to spend some of their money? It's as much as saying Phillip Morris running a day care will push legislation that it's OK for kids to smoke."[9]

Comparing Public and Private Prisons

Studies comparing the cost savings and quality of public versus private prisons are plagued by uncertainty. In 1996, the General Accounting Office (GAO), an independent agency that reports to Congress and often is referred to as the "congressional watchdog," released a report noting that the few studies comparing operational costs or quality of service between private and public prisons "provide little information that is widely applicable to various correctional settings" and "do not permit drawing generalizable conclusions about the comparative operational costs and/or quality of service of private and public prisons."

Many of the studies suffer from flawed measures and designs, biases, and cannot be generalized to all prisons.[10] Because private corporations are not subject to the same disclosure laws as government agencies, researchers must evaluate public versus private prisons without equivalent datasets: escapes, staff ratios, and use of solitary confinement. Despite three decades of research studies, the differences between the facilities are still largely a black box, leaving policy makers unsure of private industry's value in corrections.

Costs

One common pro-privatization argument is that private prisons improve efficiency and cost fewer tax dollars. But the way costs are calculated on a public budgeting document and for a private company vary widely and are not easily comparable. CCA, for example, claims that contracting with them can save states money: "CCA provides federal, state and county corrections agencies comparable or improved services at a lower rate. CCA's operating cost per inmate per day averages from 5 to more than 20 percent lower than the average per diem of most states in which CCA operates."[11]

When conducting these comparisons, evaluations must account for staff costs: correctional staff salaries and benefits such as health care, pensions, and staff training. These inmate and facility costs must also be included: inmate health care, food services, educational and rehabilitative programming, and facility operations and maintenance such as repairs or renovations. How can we compare these costs across prisons when each facility contains a unique inmate population? For example, inmates with higher security classifications cost more to house behind bars than those with lesser security classifications because of the staff-to-inmate ratio and higher security measures. Similarly, elderly and sick inmates require more health care, additional staff, and often more services. The cost of incarcerating someone over fifty years old is two to five times the cost of incarcerating someone younger than forty-nine.[12] Private prisons frequently negotiate restrictions on the type of inmates they will house, for example, limiting the admission of inmates with medical conditions. These differences eliminate the possibility of finding a control group for comparison.

According to Emory Law School Professor Sasha Volokh, "sometimes no comparable facilities exist. Even where there are two prisons in the jurisdiction housing inmates of the same sex and security classification, they generally differ in size, age, level of crowding, inmate age mix, inmate health mix, and facility design. In particular, adjusting facilities to take into account different numbers of inmates is problematic, since facilities with more inmates, other things equal, benefit from economies of scale."[13]

The Reason Foundation found that public sector costs are spread out across multiple agencies:

> Public correctional agency budgets typically cover major operating costs (e.g., staffing, supplies, programming, etc.) but do not reflect the full range of costs paid by the government. Some costs—including risk management, pensions and other post-employment benefits, information technology, payroll, accounting and human resources—may be paid for out of other agency budgets. . . . By contrast, when the private sector contractors bid for prison contracts they include all the relevant costs up front in their bids.[14]

CCA suggests that the sheer size of their organization lets them take advantage of economies of scale.

> When a small state prison system negotiates with a medical provider for inmates' prescription drugs, they are only negotiating for a small number of inmates. But with CCA, we are negotiating for more than 70,000 inmates. Because of that, we're able to get a better rate—time and time again. And that's one reason our cost to house, clothe, feed, educate and provide medical care to each inmate each day is typically lower than the average government prison cost.[15]

Rick Seiter worked in corrections for most of his career, serving as assistant director at the Bureau of Prisons, director of the Ohio Department of Rehabilitation and Correction, and executive vice president and chief corrections officer of CCA. For Seiter, procurement is one huge value that the private sector brings to corrections: "In the private sector, we could combine purchasing of all kinds of things," he told me. "Where, mostly, so many times in the government, you'd do it almost prison by prison, or you do it state by state, or county by county, and we could save lots of money."[16]

Contract monitoring, an important expense borne by private corporations, often is omitted in studies of their revenue. Most private prison contracts require frequent monitoring of the facilities, from health care and quality of food to maintaining a proper staff ratio and ensuring that staff vacancies are quickly filled. The expense of this monitoring means more costs for private firms, who may need to add specialized staff or even pay states for its monitors to visit or join their permanent staff. Another cost almost never included in comparisons is prison litigation and its resultant settlement fees—or even jury-awarded damages—to plaintiffs who sue the for-profit corporations.

The GAO has concluded many times that there is insufficient data to determine whether public or private prisons are more cost effective. In 1996, they reviewed five studies that compared private and public costs and quality of service in correctional facilities in California, New Mexico, Tennessee, Texas, and Washington.[17] Four of the five studies analyzed operational costs, and only one concluded that the operational costs of private prisons were substantially lower (14 to 15 percent) than publicly run facilities.[18] The GAO found that the Texas study lacked the same diligence as the studies in California, Tennessee, and Washington, all of which indicated "little or some" difference in operational costs. It found the Tennessee study most reliable because it controlled for the most variables—all three facilities were in Tennessee and had comparable inmate populations by numbers and demographics (except race).[19] The GAO stated: "Regarding operational costs, because the studies reported little difference and/or mixed results in comparing private and public facilities, [we] could not conclude whether privatization saved money."[20] In 2007, the GAO determined that the Bureau of Prisons did not collect enough detailed information to determine whether private prison firms provided long-term cost efficiencies or comparable quality to the cost of government-operated facilities.[21]

In 1999, two University of Cincinnati doctoral candidates conducted a similar meta-analysis of thirty-three cost-effectiveness evaluations of private and public prisons from twenty-four independent studies.[22] They included all research studies assessing public versus private adult prison cost-effectiveness published in academic journals as well as federal, state, and local agency reports. The researchers concluded "that private prisons were no more cost-effective than public prisons."[23]

In a 2001 study on private prisons examining issues from cost savings to legal implications, the Justice Department concluded: "There is no consensus among academics and professionals in the field concerning the potential cost savings that privately managed operators can provide."[24] In fact, the study determined that cost savings were not significant in private prisons and that private prisons have lower staff-to-inmate ratios, less sophisticated information management systems, and a higher reported rate of serious incidents such as assaults.[25] Serious incidents typically include significant security threats such as inmate escapes, homicides, stabbings, operating on lockdown, and discovery of homemade weapons.

I asked criminologist James Austin, who authored the 2001 Justice Department study, whether he sticks by the Department of Justice's conclusion more than fifteen years later, and he said:

> Their share in the "marketplace" of prisons remains small and is unlikely to expand except in the boutique business of illegal immigrant detention. This is largely because private prisons operate the same way as public prisons except that they pay their staff somewhat lower wages and benefits. But this produces a less productive staff which limits their ability to manage medium and maximum custody inmates. There is no clear evidence that they are cheaper to operate than public prisons.[26]

All of these studies found that comparing private and public prison costs is complicated: "comparable public facilities may not exist in the same jurisdiction. Private facilities may differ substantially from other government facilities in their functions . . . or they may differ in their age, design or the security needs of inmates housed, all of which affect the cost of staffing them."[27]

This pattern of apples-to-oranges comparisons is evident in two attempts to evaluate GEO Group's facility in Taft, California, against state counterparts.[28] The first study, prepared for BOP, compared Taft with three federal public facilities—Elkton, Forrest City, and Yazoo City—from 1999 to 2002.[29] The second study, prepared for the Justice Department, compared Taft's contracting costs with what the government would have spent if BOP had operated the facility from 1998 to 2002.[30] The first study found that the cost difference was minimal—costs at Taft ranged from $33.21 to $38.62 per inmate each day, whereas the public facilities ranged from $34.84 to $40.71.[31] The second study found significantly higher cost savings for the privately run facility, with Taft's costs ranging from $33.25 to $38.37 and public costs ranging from $39.46 to $46.38.[32]

A 2007 Vanderbilt University study (partly funded by CCA and the Association for Private Correctional and Treatment Organizations) examined the role of privatization on the cost of government-provided services.[33] Surveying the cost of housing public and private prisoners from all fifty states between 1996 and 2004, they found that the existence of private prisons in a state reduces the growth in per-prisoner expenditures of public prisons by a statistically significant amount. Introducing private prisons into a state correctional system appears to slow the growth in public prison per capita expenditures by about 3 percent annually. The researchers found that states could save up to $15 million yearly for the management of public prisons if they used privately managed prisons.[34]

Erwin A. Blackstone and Simon Hakim, professors of economics at Temple University, analyzed government data from nine states that generally had higher numbers of privately held prisoners (Arizona, California, Florida, Kentucky, Mississippi, Ohio, Oklahoma, Tennessee, and Texas), alongside Maine, which does not contract out its corrections services. They calculated both short- and long-term savings per state and found that contracted prisons generate significant savings without sacrificing quality.[35] However, just like the Vanderbilt study, this research was funded by private prison firms. CCA acknowledges that the study received funding from members of the private corrections industry, but it nevertheless maintains that these "findings reveal that long-term partnerships with companies like CCA can cut costs by government from 12 to 58 percent."[36]

In 2009, MTC published a report examining the expansion of the private prison industry. For jurisdictions that contract with private correctional firms, the report stated that the savings accrued through lower daily inmate costs save millions of dollars in budget reductions for the public correctional systems.[37] However, in 2011 Arizona found that their minimum security public and private prisons cost approximately the same amount per prisoner after adjusting for medical costs incurred by public prisons whose inmates were in poorer health.[38] The results are inconclusive. At best, private and public prisons perform roughly the same.[39] Most of the studies finding that private prisons produce significant cost savings were funded by the private prison industry. In addition, the data are so haphazard that it is impossible to prove one sector is definitively better or cheaper. Prison researcher Gerald Gaes concludes: "The current weight of the evidence on prison privatization in the United States is so light that it defies interpretation."[40]

The Problem with America's Prisons and Jails

There are abuses in both public and private correctional facilities, and there is not enough data to say one is better (or worse) than the other. Many government-operated prisons have struggled with abusive guards and rampant sexual assault perpetrated by correctional employees on inmates as well as correctional staff not doing enough to prevent sexual assaults between inmates. Almost 10 percent of former state prisoners reported one or more incidents of sexual victimization during their incarceration.[41] A national inmate survey given to state and federal inmates between 2011 and 2012 found that the rate of sexual assault by correctional staff and by other inmates was pretty much evenly split.[42] And nearly one out of three deaths in jail is attributed to suicide.[43]

Consider Maricopa County's (Phoenix) notorious Tent City Jail, and its eccentric creator, Sheriff Joe Arpaio. Shortly after he was elected in 1993, Arpaio set up a series of outdoor tents to hold as many as 2,000 inmates. There was no heating or air conditioning. In 2003, when temperatures inside the tents hit 138 degrees and the inmates complained, Arpaio responded, "It's 120 degrees in Iraq and the soldiers are living in tents and they didn't commit any crimes, so shut your mouths."[44] Arpaio's treatment of inmates spawned a decades-long court battle with the ACLU over prison conditions. In 2008, a federal court assumed oversight of the county's jails, finding numerous violations of inmates' constitutional rights, including health care. One small portion of the decision by U.S. District Judge Neil Wake provides a vivid illustration of the conditions in Arpaio's jails. Wake noted that fruit "often is overripe or bruised and frequently inedible," and that bread "frequently is moldy and entirely or in part inedible."[45] The voters finally tired of Arapio's antics in November 2016, and he was replaced by Democrat Paul Penzone who has vowed to reverse several of Arpaio's most controversial policies.

New York City's Rikers Island Jail Complex, wedged between the Bronx and Queens next to LaGuardia Airport, is notorious for its abuse and neglect. Conditions at the jail are so unsafe that Rikers Island is considered one of the most dangerous correctional facilities for inmates. Five former correction officers at the facility were sentenced to prison in 2016 for beating an inmate. In 2014, U.S. Attorney Preet Bharara wrote that a "deep-seated culture of violence" was embedded in the very fabric of Rikers.[46] A wider campaign to shut down Rikers emerged after Kalief Browder, sixteen years old when arrested and later charged with second-degree robbery for allegedly stealing a backpack, spent nearly two of his three years at Rikers Island in solitary confinement, alone in a cell for twenty-three hours a day. Browder committed suicide at his parents' home in the Bronx in the summer of 2015. Although New York City Mayor Bill de Blasio has vowed to close Rikers, no one really knows how the process would work and even de Blasio concedes it would take at least a decade.[47]

In February 2016, the FBI arrested forty-six current and former correction officers across the state of Georgia for smuggling liquor, tobacco, and cell phones into inmates' cells in exchange for money. Officers and staff also were charged with facilitating drug deals in Georgia prisons, some of which involved kilos of cocaine and meth.[48] In October 2016, federal prosecutors filed charges against multiple correction officers at the Louisiana State Penitentiary at Angola. Prison guards allegedly stood by in January 2014 while other guards severely beat a handcuffed-and-shackled Angola inmate being held in solitary confinement.[49] These are just a few examples of how poorly some public correctional facilities are managed.

Such abuses are hardly the sole province of government-run prisons, of course. Private prisons also have their share of overly violent, corrupt, and negligent employees. Within months of opening a prison in Youngstown, Ohio, in 1997, CCA faced a class-action suit that alleged "high levels of violence and dangerous conditions" and resulted in a settlement of $1.6 million. In the late 1990s, GEO Group (called Wackenhut at the time) faced lawsuits over sexual abuse at juvenile facilities in Texas and Louisiana.[50] In a 2000 interview about violence in these facilities, George Zoley said that a "correctional organization is subject to numerous allegations of that nature. . . . That's part of the business; it's a tough business. The people in prison are not Sunday school children."[51] Zoley's comments appeared tone deaf as advocates and policy makers have clamored for years to increase transparency and accountability in private prisons, partly because of a worry about undertrained and unaccountable prison guards.

In July 2010, three inmates from Kingman Arizona State Prison, operated by MTC, cut the chain-link fence surrounding the facility and escaped into the Arizona desert. Within two weeks, two of the escapees had carjacked a couple vacationing in New Mexico, murdered the couple, and drove them in their truck to a rural farm where they left the trailer and truck on fire with the murder victims' remains inside. After the escape, an Arizona Department of Corrections investigation found that a "culture of complacency" existed at the prison that made the escape easier, in part due to the frequency of false alarms at the facility.[52] The investigation also found that MTC staff believed that they could not chase an escapee.[53]

One of the more notorious incidents at a private prison occurred in Idaho in 2010. A video revealed that prison guards at Idaho's largest prison, the CCA-operated Idaho State Correctional Institution, failed to halt an attack on a prisoner whose head was stomped several times, leaving him permanently disabled. The prison is so violent that inmates called the facility "Gladiator School." A study conducted by the Idaho Department of Corrections in 2008 found that there were four times as many prisoner-on-prisoner assaults at the private prison than at Idaho's other seven prisons combined.[54] In 2010, the ACLU filed a federal class-action lawsuit charging that officials at the prison promoted and facilitated "a culture of rampant violence that . . . led to carnage and suffering among prisoners at the state-owned facility operated by the for-profit company Corrections Corporation of America (CCA)."[55] In 2013, CCA officials acknowledged that the corporation had violated the state contract by understaffing the Idaho Correctional Center and having employees falsify documents to cover up the vacancies. And in 2012, a Mississippi federal judge called the GEO Group's Walnut Grove Correctional Facility "a cesspool of unconstitutional and inhuman acts and conditions."[56]

A Pennsylvania incident cuts to the heart of why so many advocates call for an outright elimination of private prisons. Between 2003 and 2008, two Pennsylvania judges accepted more than $2.5 million in payments from a for-profit juvenile detention facility owned by Mid-Atlantic Youth Services Corporation for sentencing juvenile offenders to the private facility—it became known as the "Kids-for-Cash" scandal. The detention center stood to profit from these placements, and the two judges involved pleaded guilty to tax evasion and wire fraud in the scheme. One victim of the scandal was fourteen-year-old Phillip Swartley, who was caught stealing change from unlocked vehicles one night to buy chips and soft drinks. One of the judges who was eventually found guilty sent the fourteen-year-old, who waived his right to an attorney, to a private juvenile detention center.[57]

Alex Friedman, the managing editor of *Prison Legal News* and an associate director of the Human Rights Defense Center, a group that advocates for prisoner rights, spoke to me many times as I wrote this book. He points to the "Kids-for-Cash" scandal as a textbook lesson in why private prisons should not exist. "That incentive doesn't exist in public prisons," Friedman stressed, and many others who believe the financial incentives tied up in the private prison industry make them morally reprehensible believe the industry is on par with slavery—a capitalist scheme that trades people for profits. Instead of the slave trading companies of the seventeenth and eighteenth centuries, corporations that manage prisons have emerged. Friedman sums up his argument this way:

> For all the faults of our public prisons, they are not financially incentivized to lock up as many people as they can and keep prisons full. Yes, they must operate within budgetary constraints, and there are certain financial incentives in all prisons—but public prisons do not exist to generate profit. Private prisons, like all private corporations, do exist to generate profit for their shareholders and executives.[58]

If one sets aside the moral argument, hard-headed practical questions still remain, said Eugene Volokh: "Somewhat surprisingly, for all the ink spilled on private prisons over the last thirty years, we have precious little good information on what are surely some of the most important questions: when it comes to cost or quality, are private prisons better or worse than public prisons?"[59]

There are a lot of unanswered questions about the effectiveness and value of private prisons. We don't know whether they save money. We don't know how or if they have innovated. We know next to nothing about the product other than how Wall Street values these companies. One of the reasons we know so little is because private prisons are far less transparent than their public counterparts. When things go wrong, private prisons have every incentive to cover it up.[60] A public prison—no matter how horrible the scandal—will never lose a contract; a private prison will. Worse, perhaps, private prisons are not covered by FOIA and open records laws (except in a few states) as are functions of government. Without the ability to file FOIA and open records requests, the public cannot learn the most basic information about what life is like inside these facilities.

CHAPTER TEN

Wrestling with the Concept of Private Prisons

The American Bar Association urges that jurisdictions that are considering the privatization of prisons and jails not proceed to so contract until the complex constitutional, statutory, and contractual issues are satisfactorily developed and resolved.

AMERICAN BAR ASSOCIATION RESOLUTION, ADOPTED FEBRUARY 1986

By the reckoning of the 17,000-member American Correctional Association, running a prison is just another traditional government service, like education or garbage collection, that can prosper in the hands of private management. Half the battle lies in convincing the public that private interests can handle felons as adeptly as they do college degrees and trash bags.

CHRISTOPHER ROSE, *NEW ORLEANS TIMES PICAYUNE*, JUNE 14, 1989[1]

IN 2010, LAYNE PAVEY, a twenty-six-year-old resident of Billings, Montana, was serving twenty months for conspiracy to possess with the intent to distribute cocaine. Pavey spent a month in a CCA-operated federal transfer center in Nevada, and she said that the facility seemed different than other prisons. Wearing "Corrections Corporation of America" badges, the guards looked like Verizon wireless representatives and were friendlier than government corrections officials. Pavey assumed this was because private prisons don't have enough staff to watch the bathrooms and walk around to check every cell. "They are cutting their costs to house you, so they try to keep the population peaceful."[2]

Pavey called her family and told them it was the nicest prison in which she had ever been held. But soon the more complicated reality of the situation hit her. "We realized that someone has found a way to make money off my mistakes, my pain, my misfortune. And that, right there, was the biggest blow to the head. It was, oh, my God, our country is so obsessed with incarcerating us and thinks we are such bad people that they are now making money off of us being bad. What sort of hope for us is there? What hope is there for the criminal justice system getting fixed if private companies are now making money off of our incarceration?"[3]

A thread emerged through all my conversations with former private prison inmates. Despite feeling a bit more at liberty in the private facilities with their MP3 players and video game consoles, everyone who spent time in private prisons believed the same thing: Private corporations that profit off of incarceration are morally wrong. As Pavey put it, "I'm shocked that prisons became private without really a large national debate. I feel like it happened under the nose of the public."[4] Given the immense responsibility corporations have for the safety, security, and well-being of prisoners, it is peculiar that the industry expanded with so little discussion.

Are Private Prisons Moral?

In 1985, Ira Robbins testified before Congress that government liability cannot be eliminated by delegating this function [incarceration] to a private entity.[5] A staunch critic of the practice, Robbins has argued that the "concept of privatization of corrections is bad policy, is based on a tenuous legal foundation, and has profound moral implications."[6]

The motivation for relying on private prisons in the first place was their promise to save governments money. But we must first ask a more fundamental question: What are the moral implications of for-profit firms overseeing hundreds of thousands of inmates? Political scientist Don DiIulio Jr. argues for a normative approach to thinking about the private management of prisons and jails. "Should the authority to administer criminal justice in prisons and jails, to deprive citizens of their liberty, and to coerce (even kill) them, be delegated to contractually deputized private individuals, or ought it remain in the hands of duly authorized public officials?"[7] DiIulio argues that the coercion of some citizens by others is exercised in the name of the "offended public," but that the agents of this punishment remain identified as state actors—just as a judge's robe and a police officer's badge identifies them as proxies of the state. These symbols, DiIulio argues, represent the public nature of crime and punishment. Robbins takes this line of inquiry a step further when he applies this paradigm to the case of private prisons. What happens "when an inmate looks at his keeper's uniform and, instead of encountering an emblem that reads 'Federal Bureau of Prisons' or 'State Department of Corrections,' he faces one that says 'Acme Corrections Company?'"[8]

University of Connecticut Professor Charles Logan, has written extensively on private prisons and defends the industry. He argues that "the state does not *own* the right to punish"—to the contrary, the state "merely administers it in trust, on behalf of the people and under the rule of law. Because the authority does not originate with the state, it does not attach inherently or uniquely to it, and can be passed along."[9]

Few courts have wrestled with the constitutionality of private prisons. In 2005 the Supreme Court of Israel heard a case brought by the Academic College of Law's Human Rights Department against the Israeli government and the private prison operator ALA Management. Israel had no experience with private prisons until 2004, when the Knesset (Israeli Parliament) adopted Amendment 28, which authorized the construction of a privately run prison.[10] Partly because of budget cuts and significant prison overcrowding, the Israeli government decided to contract with a private firm to alleviate costs and overcrowding. At the time, prisoners in Israel lived in an average of 3.4 square meters each, whereas the projected new private facility would provide 5.3 square meters per inmate.[11] By the spring of 2009, ALA had not only broken ground but had fully built the facility at Be'er Sheva when a High Court panel issued an order delaying the opening of Israel's first private prison, an 800-bed facility for low and medium security inmates.[12]

The lawsuit was brought by the Academic College of Law's Human Rights Department against Israel's Ministry of Finance and Ministry of Public Security, the Knesset, and private prison operator ALA Management. The petitioners alleged that transferring prison powers to a private company violated prisoners' fundamental human rights, and that private firms, focused on profits, might save costs by cutting corners on facilities and paying guards poorly and generally undermine those rights. ←

In 2009 the Israeli Supreme Court, in an 8 to 1 decision, found privately operated prisons per se unconstitutional.[13] The court held that a private, for-profit company executing the traditional state power to hold prisoners violated those prisoners' constitutional rights to liberty and human dignity, concluding that these powers restrict a person's liberty "on a daily basis" regardless of who is operating the prison—a private entity or the state. Imprisoning a person, in itself, the Court explained, violates an inmate's right to liberty.[14] However, the Court also found that when this power is executed and enforced by a private corporation that is motivated "first and foremost" by profit maximization, the legitimacy of the sanction of imprisonment is undermined.[15] In the words of the Court, this practice makes inmates "subservient to a private enterprise that is motivated by economic considerations" and "is an independent violation [of the right to personal liberty] that is additional to the violation caused by the actual imprisonment under lock and key."[16]

In June 2015, lawyers, academics, and community organizers in the United States founded an Arizona-based nonprofit called Abolish Private Prisons. They focus on challenging the constitutionality of private prisons, using a legal argument that is largely built on the *nondelegation doctrine*. Abolish Private Prisons claims that incarceration is a quintessential government function, and the delegation of this role is a violation of due process. Injecting financial bias into the carceral system turns prisoners into property, violating the Thirteenth Amendment's abolition of slavery and the Eighth Amendment's prohibition of cruel and unusual punishment.[17]

For many opponents of the private prison industry, these normative arguments make it difficult to defend private prisons just because they save money or are a quick way to build necessary capacity. Richard Harding, criminology professor and former director of the Crime Research Centre at the University of Western Australia, wrote that "it sometimes seems as if all the data in the world—even if they showed that private prisons were cheaper, prisoner health was better, recidivism rates were lower, and so on—would not convince some opponents."[18] These arguments aside, the fact remains that private prisons are a fixture of today's criminal justice system. The following pages examine the alleged benefits and the real and potential troubles of private prisons through the eyes of their stakeholders.

Perverse Incentives

The central premise for states to contract with private prison corporations is that they will save taxpayers money. To save money and turn a profit, these companies cut costs and find efficiencies that government officials—hamstrung by stringent procurement laws and union contracts—cannot.

For-profit prison company contracts have created perverse incentives. A *perverse incentive* produces unintended consequences at odds with the interests of the policy makers who created the incentives. For example, nineteenth-century paleontologists traveling to China paid locals for every fossil fragment that they brought to them. Because paleontologists paid per fragment, when locals found intact fossils, they smashed them. This increased their payments but decimated the scientific value of the fossils.[19] In the case of prisons, government officials outsourced the management of prisons to private firms to save as much money as possible while ensuring that these companies could take overflow inmates when their own state prison capacity was capped. They did not intend to create an unlimited market of inmates for the private sector, but private prison corporations have created a web of perverse incentives around a common financial interest—the steady growth of mass incarceration. Policy makers and departments of correction have done little to check the influence of private prison corporations.

Contracts and Guaranteed Occupancy

The incentive structure in many private prison contracts encourages states to keep the private prisons full, or very close to it. A number of private prison contracts include occupancy requirements mandating that governments keep the prisons between 80 and 100 percent full. If the state fails to supply enough prisoners, it must pay for each prison bed regardless of whether it holds an actual inmate. By contractually requiring states to guarantee payment, the prison companies are successfully insured against ebbs and flows in the prison population and are protected from ordinary business risks.

Consider this 2015 contract between CCA and the Arizona Department of Corrections.[20] Arizona agreed to pay CCA at a guaranteed 90 percent occupancy rate for a 1,000-bed medium security prison in Eloy. Even if the state of Arizona runs out of inmates, CCA is guaranteed revenue. In fact, three privately run prisons in Arizona are governed by contracts that contain inmate quotas of 100 percent, and the state is contractually obligated to pay for every bed, whether it's occupied or not.[21]

In 2013, In the Public Interest reviewed sixty-two state and local private prison contracts. Of these, forty-one contained clauses requiring the prisons to remain occupied between 80 and 100 percent. Oklahoma had three contracts containing a 98 percent occupancy guarantee provision, some of Louisiana's contracts contained occupancy requirements of 96 percent, and Virginia had a contract with a 95 percent occupancy guarantee.[22] These clauses force corrections departments to pay thousands, sometimes millions, for unused beds. In the Public Interest has labeled them a "low-crime tax" that penalizes taxpayers when incarcerations are reduced.

Lobbying

Enter the "bed brokers." In the 1990s, these brokers called around to different prison wardens and sheriffs (who run county jails) to find inmates to fill empty cells. Meanwhile, the private prison industry was expanding and quickly growing more sophisticated. The firms hired lobbyists and consultants (usually former corrections directors) who could gauge state leadership and correctional trends. For example, if impending criminal justice reform might cut the demand for prison beds or facilitate inmates' early release, these lobbyists would know. Private prison firms also hired government relations staff, which allowed them the flexibility to avoid registering as lobbyists.

A former director of corrections, who spoke on background, recounted to me how he received phone calls from former corrections officials asking about inmate population projections. Just after his retirement, he had dinner with a colleague who had made some of these calls, and the director asked who he had worked for at the time. The consultant explained that he was paid $30,000 a year simply to keep his ear to the ground: "It was my job just to check on you and make sure you were happy and to see if you had any complaints and to see if you had any insight on future beds". The former corrections director told me, "It wasn't surprising to me, but it was a lot of a retainer to make a phone call once in a while."[23]

Although for-profit prison corporations publicly claim that they don't lobby for changes in criminal justice policy, they spend large amounts of money every year on lobbying firms that advocate for their financial interests in Congress and in state legislatures. CCA spent more than $17 million in lobbying expenditures from 2002 through 2012; GEO Group spent $2.5 million from 2004 to 2012.[24] Since 1989, GEO Group, CCA, and their associates have spent almost $25 million on lobbying efforts and more than $10 million on campaign donations.[25]

Statewide lobbying disclosure laws vary, so it's difficult to determine how much these corporations spend on lobbying in individual states. However, between 2003 and 2010, CCA spent $1.5 million on state election campaigns, most of which focused on California, Florida, and Georgia. GEO Group spent $2.4 million on state election campaigns, primarily in California, Florida, and New Mexico.[26]

CCA and its hired lobbying firms have spent a little over $21 million lobbying Congress and federal agencies from 1998 to 2014 on bills relating to immigration, detention, and private prisons. In 2015, CCA lobbied Congress over legislation unfavorable to their industry, specifically the Justice Is Not for Sale Act, the Private Prison Information Act, and several appropriations acts that would affect their business.[27] In 2015 alone, the GEO Group lobbied Congress about the Recidivism Risk Reduction Act and the Corrections Act (criminal justice reform bills), and the Refund Act.[28] The previous year, GEO Group lobbied regarding the Border Security, Economic Opportunity, and Immigration Modernization Act and the Consolidated Appropriations Act.[29]

CCA issued a report about political activity and lobbying, the first page of which states:

> Transparency is a critical part of the relationships we have with our government partners and the taxpayers we ultimately serve, as well as our shareholders, and we are committed to transparency regarding our government relations and political efforts. In addition to complying with applicable disclosure laws, CCA is going a step further to produce this annual report, which we believe will bring further clarity to our activities. We believe it is the right thing to do for our business, our partners and our shareholders.[30]

CCA indicated that it spent $1.1 million on lobbying activities (both state and federal) in 2014. In addition to CCA employees registered as lobbyists, the corporation retained consultant lobbyists in the federal government and in twenty-two states.[31] "CCA works with a number of consultant lobbyists to ensure that public officials are made aware of the issues impacting our industry."[32]

In 2015, GEO Group and the firms it hired to lobby spent $560,000 on lobbying the federal government, employing eight lobbyists, six of whom have "revolving door" connections.[33] The Center for Responsive Politics explains this term "as a revolving door that shuffles former federal employees into jobs as lobbyists, consultants and strategists just as the door pulls former hired guns into government careers."[34] During the 2016 election year, GEO Group spent a million dollars on lobbying expenditures for the federal government alone, employing twelve lobbyists, ten of whom have "revolving door" connections.[35]

Former Oklahoma state Senator Cal Hobson called private prison lobbying "rotunda dynamics."[36] He saw how lobbyists from four private prison firms were regularly at the statehouse, walking the halls of the capitol building on Lincoln Boulevard in Oklahoma City, meeting with legislators. Between 1995 and 2000, the state increased its investment in the private prison industry by more than $95 million.[37]

The Revolving Door

From their inception, for-profit prisons knew the value of recruiting correction officials from the federal government and from well-regarded state departments of corrections. This government-to-industry revolving door provides income for retired government correction officials and ensures that the industry remains connected to the government. CCA cofounder Tom Beasley was a former chairman of the Tennessee Republican Party; he also served on a committee that selected the head of Tennessee's prison system. Beasley joined forces with Don Hutto, former director of corrections in Arkansas and Virginia and former president of the American Correctional Association, and the two founded CCA with businessman Robert Crants (see chapter 3). In 2001, Harley G. Lappin retired as director of the Bureau of Prisons (BOP) and joined CCA for a reported salary of $1.5 million. Another former BOP director, J. Michael Quinlan, joined CCA in 1993, a year after his retirement from BOP.

Of course, these transitions through the revolving door aren't always smooth. Conflicts of interest have existed since the industry's first days. Oklahoma's Department of Corrections was placed under a federal court order in 1974 after a U.S. district judge ruled that Oklahoma's prison conditions were unconstitutional. The order specifically prevented double-bunking of inmates. In 1985, in response to prison overcrowding, the Oklahoma state legislature passed the Oklahoma Prison Overcrowding Emergency Powers Act.[38] The legislation authorized the early release of lower-security inmates convicted of lesser crimes to free up prison space, specifically when the prison system had sustained 97.5 percent of capacity for at least ten days. Inmates with a violent conviction and repeat offenders were not eligible for early release under this law.

In 1996, Lamonte Fields was serving a fifteen-year sentence for distribution of cocaine. He was among fifty-seven inmates the department released that August to curb prison crowding.[39] As a teen, Fields had been convicted and sentenced to a juvenile facility for shooting a classmate. He was back in prison on a drug charge as an adult. Five days after he left prison, Fields shot and killed his eighteen-year-old girlfriend, her mother, and her stepfather before the police killed him. The incident received widespread press coverage and prompted Governor Frank Keating to call for Corrections Director Larry Fields's resignation. Keating called for repeal of the law: "I'm certainly not going to let anybody else out"; inmates released early "had murder in their eyes."[40] Horrified that the Department of Corrections knew about Fields's violent juvenile record but released him anyway, Keating said he had "no faith" in the management of state prisons.[41]

What happened after the retirement of Director Fields surprised everyone. Governor Keating called on his friend J. Michael Quinlan— CCA's director of strategic planning and former director of BOP—to examine the Oklahoma prison system and recommend improvements. According to Keating, Quinlan offered to study the state system at no cost, whereas another expert bid $400 per day. The governor asked Quinlan to examine everything from inmate placement to inmate classification methods.[42] In a letter to corrections board members, Senator Hobson balked at the deal. In particular, he pointed to Quinlan's clear conflict of interest: "Asking a top official of CCA to make recommendations on the future of Oklahoma's prison system is somewhat like asking the president of General Motors to recommend whether the state should purchase more Ford or GM vehicles for its motor pool."[43]

Two months later, Quinlan issued a report detailing his recommendations to improve the safety and security of Oklahoma's prisons. Quinlan projected that the prison system would need about 1,300 more medium and maximum security beds in 1997 and a little more than 4,000 more by 2001. He suggested that the Department of Corrections reduce the space given to each inmate in state prisons to add additional prison beds to accommodate more prisoners.[44] The report found that Oklahoma's prison population was projected to rise for at least ten years, but Quinlan was careful not to make any recommendation about the state's use of private prisons. He did recommend implementing a more stringent classification system, however, which would require more space.[45]

Nevertheless, Keating said that the use of private prisons "is certainly a solution I would like to see discussed and debated" because private prisons give states "the best bang for their buck" and would keep the state from building a surplus of prison space should crime and incarceration rates ever drop.[46] Tara Herivel and Paul Wright note that "By 1998 CCA had constructed two more prisons in Oklahoma and Wackenhut had built one." By the end of the following year, Oklahoma had signed contracts to place one-quarter of its prison population in private prisons.[47]

Government and private prison companies enjoy an almost symbiotic relationship; boards of directors at private prison firms often include former state and federal corrections administrators. CCA's board of directors includes Thurgood Marshall Jr., former cabinet secretary to President Clinton and son of Supreme Court Justice Thurgood Marshall; Chief Corrections Officer Harley Lappin, former director of the federal Bureau of Prisons; and Chief Development Officer Tony Grande, former Tennessee commissioner of economic and community development. Two former BOP directors, Harley Lappin and J. Michael Quinlan, serve as CCA executives: CEO and senior VP, respectively.

Similarly, GEO Group's board of directors includes former Democratic Mayor of South Beach, Florida, and Executive Director of the League of Cities Clarence Anthony; Republican and Chairman and CEO of ElectedFace Inc. Richard Glanton; and former Under Secretary of the United States Air Force Anne Newman Foreman. Recently retired from GEO Group's board but acting as director emeritus and still consulting for the company is Norman Carlson, who served for seventeen years as the director of BOP.

Former director of the U.S. Marshals Service, Stacia Hylton, also served as federal detention trustee. During her tenure the Office of the Federal Detention Trustee awarded a number of contracts to GEO Group, the nation's second-largest private prison firm. Between her role at the Office of the Federal Detention Trustee and the U.S. Marshals, Hylton went to work for GEO Group as a consultant and was reportedly paid at least $112,500. GEO also hired Daniel Ragsale, who left his post as Deputy Director of ICE in 2017, where he joined David Venturella, another ICE official who serves on GEO's management team. The private prison industry exerts enormous influence, often in subtle ways. A former director of corrections who spoke on the condition of anonymity told me how the governor of his state asked that officials from a private prison corporation meet the potential candidates who might succeed him.[48]

Given the close connections between government officials and the leadership of for-profit prison corporations, it is not surprising that private prison companies have fared so well. These relationships sustain the industry. In 2014, Florida Governor Rick Scott headlined a $10,000 per person fund-raiser at the home of George Zoley, CEO of the Boca Raton–based GEO Group. Governor Scott has supported prison privatization and a plan to expand the GEO Group's role in the state. The dinner attracted protestors who were angry at the reports of abuse, sexual assault, and neglect at GEO Group facilities. The protestors demonstrated outside Zoley's home in Boca's Royal Yacht & Country Club community.

Not all policy makers support these tight-knit relationships. Texas state Senator John Whitmire spoke out about it: "It poses a conflict of interest if they don't have an arm's-length relationship when they're doing their official duties. . . . You certainly wouldn't want people lining up their next job doing favors for the people they want to go work for."[49]

The American Correctional Association (ACA) is a trade association for corrections, but it also serves as the accreditor and regulatory organization governing the standards for prisons across the country.

The standards ACA auditors address include programs and operations, staff training and development, physical plant inspections, safety and emergency procedures, sanitation, food service, and rules and discipline. The ACA itself has a close relationship with for-profit prison companies such as CCA and GEO Group (see chapter 4). These companies sponsor the ACA's biannual conferences, advertise in ACA's magazine *Corrections Today*, and mingle with correction officials at conferences and cocktail parties.

The ACA publishes twenty-two different manuals of standards, guidelines ranging from adult to juvenile to community corrections. Private correctional companies highlight their ability to gain ACA accreditation for their facilities. In fact, almost every private prison contract now requires ACA accreditation, although the process is criticized by the ACLU for its "paper audit" feel. Auditors make appointments to show up weeks if not months ahead of time to inspect facilities. A prison may receive accreditation for checking simple boxes: food served at a regulated temperature and adequate recreation time for inmates, even while issues such as sexual assault are rampant. The ACA depends on these accreditation fees for its income.

Mother Jones journalist Shane Bauer spent four months undercover as a correction officer in a CCA-run prison in Louisiana. ACA auditors visited his prison during one of his shifts, and Bauer described the inspection:

> The only questions they ask Bacle and me are what our names are and how we're doing. They do not examine our logbook, nor do they check our entries against the camera footage. If they did, they would find that some of the cameras don't work. They do not check the doors. If they did, they would see they need to be yanked open by hand because most of the switches don't work. They don't check the fire alarm, which automatically closes smoke doors over the tiers, some of which must be jimmied back open by two guards. They do not ask to go on a tier. They do not interview any inmates. They do a single loop and they leave.[50]

Richard Gagnon, a former manager at a food co-op in Vermont, spoke to me from a Vermont prison about his two years at a CCA-owned and -operated prison in Kentucky. According to Gagnon, when inspectors from the Vermont Department of Corrections made the trip to Beattyville, Kentucky, to inspect the Lee Adjustment Center housing about 400 Vermont prisoners, it wasn't "like they were trying really hard to find anything or fix anything." Gagnon imagines the inspectors walking through the prison and observing, "Yep, looks fine to me. No one is hanging from the rafters. We'll go back to Vermont and give you a clean bill of health." Frustrated about the inspections, Gagnon pointed out that despite the clean bill of health, a toilet in their bathroom overflowed at least once a month with "a small pond of feces . . . erupting onto the floor." Gagnon added that "mostly, everyone just pretended like everything was fine, because repercussions would be immediate. You would be sent to the Hole, to solitary, and you wouldn't know how long you would be there."[51]

A former corrections director told me that the public relations departments at private prisons are very careful, very calculating:

> They are like any other major oil company. They want to minimize the effect of the oil spill. They don't market themselves as cheaper anymore because they are not. They will say they think they are one of the better options. . . . You may want to ask how many homicides have you had? They will say that they are fully ACA accredited and still have the highest suicide rate and homicide rate in the world because the standards don't say you can't have highest suicide rate in the world. That is one of the issues with ACA, you can't have food at a certain temperature, but twenty-five murders, that will not make you fail ACA accreditation.[52]

Reggie Wilkinson is known for his groundbreaking work implementing state of the art treatment for prisoners diagnosed with a mental illness in Ohio. He sits on the board of MTC, the nation's third largest prison firm, which is privately owned rather than publicly traded. Wilkinson points out that the close relationship between the private sector and the public sector can have benefits. "Once upon a time, many of them were heads of agencies in state and corrections. I can tell you that they don't go to a private company and instantly change their view on corrections because they are now working for a private prison. They don't compromise their integrity about what's good for inmates just because they work for a private company."[53]

In 2015, MTC hired Bernie Warner as their senior vice president of corrections, luring him away from his role as secretary of the

Department of Corrections in Washington, D.C. Wilkinson argues that recruiting government correctional staff like Bernie Warner should be encouraged. Warner was well known for transforming his state's use of solitary confinement. Through programs that trained guards how to manage gang members and reduce violence, and by developing specialized housing for prisoners suffering mental illness, the number of inmates held in the most restricted isolation units was cut by more than 50 percent, from 612 in 2011, when the program for violent inmates began, to just 286 by 2015.[54]

I met with Warner not long after he joined the ranks at MTC, and he told me that he was drawn to the innovation, freedom, and flexibility of working in an environment unconstrained by government. He joined the private prison sector to bring the passion and energy that had served him well in state corrections, but he worried about the stigma he felt the private prison industry suffered. "State directors of corrections struggle with the same issues the private industry faces," he told me. "How to motivate, engage, and retain staff in creative ways." We discussed the differences between state and private corrections, and he said to me, "I'm the same person I was in government. We need to get past people's ideology."[55]

Rick Seiter, who has worked for both government and private corrections (specifically for CCA), shares this belief about the positive side of comingling private and public sector staff. As Seiter put it, "So, it's the same people in leadership, quite frankly you see both mixing out. It's not like there's a public sector group and a private sector group; it's a group of correctional professionals that know the best way to do things, that are experienced and talented, that do it for whoever they're working for."[56]

The American Legislative Exchange Council

For-profit prison companies have been so successful in part because of how well they exert local power through their partnership with the American Legislative Exchange Council (ALEC) to design bills that increase incarceration. ALEC is a conservative organization known for writing model bills, often with the assistance of corporate partners. Legislative members associated with ALEC introduce hundreds of these model bills annually in state capitols across the nation. Nearly one-quarter of the country's state legislators, mostly conservative law-makers who believe in privatizing government services, are members of ALEC. Both CCA and GEO Group have paid for many years of membership, but GEO Group currently claims they have not been a member for more than a decade, and CCA cut ties with the organization in 2010.

In its 1995 Model Legislation Scorecard, ALEC noted that its busiest task force was working on criminal justice and introduced 199 bills. ALEC boasted that twenty-five states enacted "truth-in-sentencing" laws based on its model legislation, which requires prisoners to serve 85 percent of their sentences in prison, and eleven states enacted habitual-offender or "three-strikes" laws, which require a life sentence for a third felony.[57] Until 2000, the task force was cochaired by CCA Vice President John Rees. Brad Wiggins, CCA director of business development, and Brian Nairin, of the National Association of Bail Insurance Companies, became cochairs in 2000.

Beyond supporting legislation to increase the size of the national prison population, ALEC encourages policy positions that earmark correctional funding for private corporations. For example, the Private Correctional Facilities Act authorized contracts between state and local governments and private prison companies: "This Act would allow any unit of government to contract with the private sector to perform services currently performed by a corrections agency."[58]

During the long partnership between for-profit prison corporations and ALEC, especially during the tough-on-crime era of the 1990s and early 2000s, the industry actively worked to increase the incarcerated population in the United States. In particular, private prison companies drafted model legislation to detain rising numbers of undocumented immigrants. In 2005, UCLA Professor Sharon Dolovich wrote about the intimacy of this former relationship with ALEC and other legislative agendas: "It is clear, however, that each company pays thousands of dollars in annual membership dues for a seat at the drafting table with influential legislators. They do so, furthermore, under the auspices of an organization committed to policies certain to increase prison populations nationwide in a way that is consistent with the contractors' own financial interests."[59] Nevertheless, CCA states that it "does not actively participate in the public debate over sentencing and many other criminal justice issues."[60]

Lack of Transparency

Oversight of prisons, both public and private, is complicated. Inmate privacy, security, and even whether prisons can comply with the public's need for information make it difficult for the press and the public to find out what happens behind prison walls. Questions typically asked of prisons are about staffing levels, escape statistics, health care, programming, and solitary confinement. Government prisons are required to comply with the public's requests for information under public records laws, but private prisons usually are not required to comply. Few state courts have grappled with whether private prisons should be considered the functional equivalents of government entities.[61]

Private facilities do not have to report how many inmates they hold in isolation or release the policies dictating who is placed in isolation.[62] At federal criminal alien requirement (CAR) facilities, prisoners reported not only that they are punished with isolation for minor infractions but that the isolation unit (or segregation) is commonly used for overflow when the general population dorms are full.[63] According to ACLU staff attorney Carl Takei, "it required going in and interviewing scores of prisoners that were able to speak about their experiences. [The Bureau of Prisons] didn't produce any documents in response to our FOIA request."[64]

Some state courts have started to rule in favor of increased transparency, requiring private prisons that accept public money to comply with disclosure requests. In late 2014, a district court judge in Texas found that CCA prisons counted as a "government body" and therefore must comply with the Texas Public Information Act. Judges in Vermont, Tennessee, and Florida have issued similar decisions.[65]

Based on a lawsuit filed by Prison Legal News, Tennessee's Court of Appeals ruled in 2013 that CCA was required to produce records under the state's public records law because it was the functional equivalent of a government agency.[66] Lawsuits in Vermont and Texas resulted in similar court rulings requiring CCA to comply with public records laws.[67]

Private firms don't exist in a vacuum outside of any regulatory authority. Through government contracts, private prison corporations must comply with standards promulgated by the ACA and the

National Commission on Correctional Health Care (NCCHC). CCA spokesperson Steve Owen believes the Prison Information Act is unnecessary. "The Department of Justice, the Bureau of Prisons and the Department of Homeland Security already have in place explicit procedures for making applicable information available to the public," he wrote. "The result could be a breakdown in the now collaborative process between private sector contractors and the federal government to determine what information is appropriate for release."[68] Private prison corporations continue to spend money lobbying against laws that would increase transparency, which makes one wonder what these companies are hiding.

Getting Inside Private Prisons

How opaque are these companies? I reached out to the leadership of GEO Group and CCA for interviews. I tried to contact GEO Group CEO George Zoley and was told by his secretary to send her an email and she would make sure she printed it for Zoley. I sent her three emails requesting an interview with Zoley or someone on his staff.[69] I never received a response. I contacted another GEO Group official a colleague referred me to and was told he couldn't discuss the corporation with me without Zoley signing off on the conversation. I contacted the Florida Department of Corrections to see whether I could visit GEO facilities in Florida and was referred to the Florida Department of Management Services "as they oversee the operations of privately run prisons."[70] Many emails and phone calls later, I connected with the director of the Division of Specialized Services at the Florida Department of Management Services, an independent agency that monitors private prisons in the state of Florida. They sent me a PowerPoint presentation they created on private prison monitoring and answered a list of questions I had sent to them, but they denied my request to follow around a monitor at a GEO Group facility in Florida: "We would not allow someone to shadow an OCM at this time."[71]

So I tried a different tack. I purchased one share of GEO Group stock for $30.92 in January 2016. When the shareholders meeting was announced on March 18, 2016, my brokerage firm informed me that in order to produce an admittance ticket, I would need to vote my share.

I confirmed with GEO Group through their shareholder services a few days before the April shareholders meeting, and they informed me that they could not admit me because I had not sent my request to GEO Group five days before the meeting. Despite assurance from my broker that my ticket was sufficient and my own email to GEO Group five days before the meeting confirming I would attend, GEO Group claimed I had not complied with the proxy materials.[72] They would not allow me to attend the meeting.

CCA was more receptive but still largely a black box. I reached out to the warden of the Winn Correctional Facility in Louisiana in March 2015. Neither the warden nor his secretary returned my emails or calls. I also reached out to CCA, and Jonathan Burns, a representative from the Public Affairs Department, contacted me a few weeks later. I explained my purpose in visiting some prisons, and he offered to facilitate my visit. I toured CCA state facilities in Colorado and New Mexico through the departments of correction for those states. I also let myself into the vacant CCA prison in Appleton, Minnesota. Through the Department of Homeland Security, I toured a CCA detention center in Laredo, Texas, and a GEO Group detention center in Pearsall. I contacted Burns February 17, 2016, requesting interviews with their leadership. I reached out to one of their executives directly who informed me I would need to work through public affairs before he could speak to me on the record. On March 30, 2016, Burns responded:

> While we can't accommodate an interview with Mr. Lappin or other CCA executives, we will be happy to serve as your single point of contact at CCA going forward, and are happy to provide you with written responses to any questions you'd like CCA to address. Please send those questions to me and our Public Affairs office will work to get you responsive information on behalf of the company asap.[73]

On April 6, 2016, I sent a list of twelve questions to Burns: How had CCA innovated? What obstacles to innovation exist? Could they give me information about what they would consider model facilities and programming? Could they point me to studies that compare cost savings for private versus public adult correctional facilities? I didn't hear from CCA for months, prompting me to send a follow-up email on June 22 and another on July 7. Nothing. I sent a fourth request on August 8, and on September 12 Jonathan Burns replied: "I know we owe you information responsive to the questions you submitted a while back and we should have that information to you shortly." I sent a fifth email requesting the answers to my questions on February 14, 2017. I never heard back.

I also corresponded with two CCA board members who declined to speak to me about this project. One of the board members wrote to me, "I've copied Tony Grande on this e-mail who is Chief Development Officer and Executive Vice President of CCA. Please feel free to contact him on this matter." I sent an email to Grande, but he never responded.

I have cataloged my efforts here to illustrate just how challenging it is to peek inside the world of private prisons. Proving that an industry is or is not transparent is difficult, and many of these contracts contain provisions for monitoring, mandate stringent staffing requirements, and require certain health care for inmates. Getting answers to my research questions—many of which would have given the corporation a platform to advertise practices they believe are a credit to them and to the field—was impossible, and interviewing current officials and board members equally so. The wardens and correctional officials I met on my tours of these prisons were friendly and open to questions, but my access to these facilities was always through the state departments of corrections, not through the private prisons themselves.

What Are the Potential Benefits of Private Prisons?

Private prisons have existed in the United States for almost four decades, but evidence of their benefits remains sparse. Wilkinson, who formerly ran the Ohio Department of Rehabilitation and Correction and now sits on the board of MTC, explained: "Yes, any for-profit organization has a motive to not lose money, to make money. But that doesn't mean that they don't focus on all the things that are important—like training and education and rehabilitation and other things."[74] The benefits of privatized corrections include their ability to reduce overcrowding in state prisons and their ability to close quickly when the prison population wanes. There is very little evidence that the private prison industry promotes competition among companies that manage prisons, however, and there is no evidence that the private prison industry has innovated beyond what government prisons provide.

Reducing Overcrowding

Perhaps more than anything else, overcrowding motivates governments to contract with private prisons. Due to overcrowded prisons, California started shipping several hundred inmates to private out-of-state prisons in late 2006. By the end of 2010, the state had sent more than 10,000 inmates to private prisons.[75] In 2011, the U.S. Supreme Court found that the conditions in California's overcrowded prisons violated the Eighth Amendment's ban on cruel and unusual punishment.[76] Justice Kennedy's majority opinion included photographs of inmates crammed into large warehouse-style rooms he called "telephone-booth-sized cages without toilets."[77]

In 2016, more than 4,000 inmates were held in private prisons in California, and 2,000 were held in private prisons out of state, mostly in Eloy, Arizona, and Tutwiler, Mississippi.[78] In addition, about 3,700 undocumented immigrants were held in private detention centers throughout the state.[79] Continuing to move inmates to private prisons played a role in allowing Governor Jerry Brown's administration to reach court-ordered prison population levels in early 2015. But other reforms also reduced the size and scope of the state's prison population: Assembly Bill 109, signed by Brown in 2011 and commonly called "Realignment," dramatically shifted the state of California's responsibility for tens of thousands of convicted individuals by delegating responsibility to the counties, and a November 2015 ballot initiative, Proposition 47, downgraded many drug possession and theft crimes from felonies to misdemeanors, which kept certain people convicted of low-level drug and property crimes out of jail.

Critics of private prisons say the industry promotes incarceration because private companies can quickly build jails and prisons at their own expense. Another huge boon for government officials is that legislators can in effect go behind their constituents' backs, by-passing voter approval for bond issues to construct new facilities. As happened in Appleton and Hardin, impoverished rural areas fight for the opportunity to lure private prisons to their towns. For policy makers, private prisons all but assure their reelection.

The private prison industry is an escape valve that relieves the pressure on states with overcrowded facilities, but it defers the debate about unnecessary incarceration. Legislators, governors, and corrections leaders can send their overflow across town to a private prison or out of state to a private facility. As long as private prisons are an option, difficult choices about reforming criminal laws and practices—how to reduce revocations to prison for probation or parole violations, whether to roll back mandatory minimum sentencing laws or reduce some felonies to misdemeanors—don't have to be made.

Closing with Flexibility

When state and federal prisons go largely unoccupied, closing these institutions is politically difficult. Most governors and legislators face backlash from constituents who balk when prisons—usually situated in economically hard-pressed, rural areas—are closed. Losing jobs and tax revenue can devastate the local economy. Almost all correctional staff participate in a union, which protects their salaries and their jobs, and policy makers who want to shutter prisons may face months, if not years, of resistance from unions.

Private correctional staff, on the other hand, almost never receive union protection and have little recourse if the facility where they work closes. It is politically less risky to close a private prison than a government one—the government can simply terminate the private contract. The government did just that in the summer of 2016. With the number of federal inmates dropping, the Justice Department realized it no longer needed to pay so many private firms to house inmates they previously didn't have capacity to hold in their own facilities. With the simplicity of a memo and a press conference, Deputy Assistant Attorney General Sally Yates announced that the Justice Department would slowly work toward not renewing its contracts with private prison companies. This guidance was reversed in February 2017 when new Attorney General Jeff Sessions issued a memo to the Bureau of Prisons directing the agency to return to "its previous approach," noting that Yates's guidance "impaired the Bureau's ability to meet the future needs of the federal correctional system."[80]

Competition

Private prison advocates argue that by introducing competition to incarceration, private companies provide innovative solutions that lower costs and improve quality. A Brookings Institute report found, however, that this competition—which is supposedly the source of innovation—is "fairly minimal." The three largest private prison companies account for more than 96 percent of the total number of private prison beds.[81]

Hypothetically, a more diverse market for private prisons could spur competitive innovation. For example, if governments could choose from multiple private prison companies, they could compare recidivism rates, cost savings, and reputation. But the reality is that the three largest private prison companies have very little competition. Twelve for-profit prison companies ran adult correctional facilities in 1999, but eight of the companies were eventually bought by other companies, with GEO Group and CoreCivic (formerly CCA) leading the way in those acquisitions.[82] With fewer private firms managing prisons, and the ones that do growing more powerful, there is less incentive to prove significant cost savings or better outcomes.

Innovation

Private prison corporations claim to be innovating, but a 2004 Department of Justice report examining state and federal government practices of contracting with private firms to manage prison found that "the existing studies of comparative costs and of comparative recidivism rates to [sic] not support any strong inferences about the state's obtaining more innovative imprisonment from the private sector."[83]

GEO Group's mission "is to develop innovative public–private partnerships with government agencies around the globe that deliver high quality, cost-efficient correctional, detention, community reentry, and electronic monitoring services while providing industry leading rehabilitation and community reintegration programs to the men and women entrusted to our care."[84] Similarly, CCA claims that "our approach to public–private partnership in corrections combines the cost savings and innovation of the private sector with the strict guidelines and consistent oversight of the public sector."[85] MTC claims that it "advocates for innovation and continual improvement within correctional systems and supports broader reform efforts to responsibly reduce prison populations."[86] However, there is little evidence that this is actually the case, which is probably due to private prison contracts themselves.[87] Private prisons are highly constrained in how they operate. Professor Volokh notes that "private prison contracts essentially " 'governmentalize the private sector,' reproducing public prison regulations in the private contract. Privatization can come to resemble an exercise in who can better pretend to be a public prison."[88]

A 2011 performance audit of the Arizona Department of Corrections points out that the department requires private prisons to "mirror state-operated facilities," conducting extensive oversight to ensure compliance. The report found that "in order to maintain uniform standards for state and private prisons, the Department requires contractors to follow Department Orders, Director's Instructions, Technical Manuals, Institution Orders, and Post Orders. These requirements extend to specific details, such as following the same daily menus as state-operated facilities."[89]

A Brookings Institute report found that although those in favor of private prisons focus on operational innovation, in reality the primary way the industry sees cost savings is by paying lower salaries for correction officers, who are generally not members of a union.[90]

Accountability and Monitoring

The two largest private prison corporations, GEO Group and CoreCivic, are publicly traded, but smaller companies such as MTC and LaSalle Corrections are not accountable to shareholders. GEO Group and CoreCivic stocks rise and fall based on press reports and rumors, and this encourages them to maintain good public relations. Criminologist Richard Harding explained that "the knowledge that one can fail so completely as to go out of business altogether or to lose major profits imposes a discipline to which the public sector has never been subject."[91]

Beyond their accountability to shareholders, private prisons also must contend with monitoring by state corrections departments and the Bureau of Prisons. But how consistent is this monitoring? Florida, Colorado, Georgia, and Ohio require full-time monitors at private prisons. Colorado's Private Prison Monitoring Unit, in the state's Department of Corrections, assigns monitors to each private facility and requires them to spend a minimum of twenty hours per week in the facility.[92] Georgia has a full-time private prison monitor at each private prison, ensuring that contract conditions are met and "that the facility operates with a continuous focus on sanitation, safety, and security."[93]

Florida is the only state that requires an independent agency that sits entirely outside of its corrections department to monitor its seven private prisons. In fact, Florida ensures that a full-time contract monitor who works for the Department of Management Services (DMS), Bureau of Private Prison Monitoring, is on site at these private prisons.[94] DMS is an executive agency, and the head of DMS is appointed by the governor and confirmed by the state Senate.

The Bureau of Private Prison Monitoring is charged with entering contracts with private prisons in Florida and ensuring that these contracts improve the efficiency and effectiveness of those prisons. The bureau may only enter into such contracts if it determines that the facility will save the state at least 7 percent compared to a state prison. This cost savings has been criticized by the Florida Center for Fiscal and Economic Policy: "there is no compelling evidence that the privatization of prisons has actually resulted in savings. . . . It is very difficult to ensure that a private prison is in fact 7 percent less costly to operate than a comparable public prison."[95]

Florida onsite contract monitors are paid between $40,000 and $57,000 a year and work full-time at the prisons. In addition to their forty-hour work week, these monitors must perform unannounced visits during nonstandard business hours.[96] Despite onsite monitors, Florida's private prisons have come under significant scrutiny over the last few years. In 2017, Florida Democratic Representative David Richardson asked Governor Rick Scott to use his emergency powers to replace the leadership of the MTC-owned and -operated Gadsden Correctional Facility, which houses 1,500 male inmates. Richardson stopped by the prison twice in March (legislators in Florida are permitted to enter prisons at any time) and observed "55-degree temperatures in inmate cells; no hot water; care being withheld from ill inmates; a tooth extraction without sedation; an inmate who contracted pneumonia after being housed in a unit with no heat or hot water; and reports that guards who impregnated inmates were allowed to remain on the job."[97] The prison is one of seven privately operated prisons in Florida. Richardson, who some say is on a one-man crusade to expose the harms of private prisons in Florida, also exposed that CoreCivic's Lake City Correctional Institution had overcharged the state at least $16 million over the past seven years.[98]

Ohio also relies on an independent agency to monitor prisons. Although Ohio correctional employees are already tasked with monitoring prisons, the state legislature created the Correctional Institution Inspection Committee to oversee Ohio's prisons and youth services facilities. Established in 1977, it inspects and reports on adult and juvenile prisons and investigates a wide range of issues from staffing and medical care to prison violence and inmate gangs. Ohio's statute mandates that any contract with a private prison must include "a requirement that the public entity appoint and supervise a full-time contract monitor, that the contractor provide suitable office space for the contract monitor at the facility, and that the contractor allow the contract monitor unrestricted access to all parts of the facility and all records of the facility except the contractor's financial records."[99]

In 2011, the Kasich administration sold the state-owned and -operated Lake Erie Correctional Facility for $72.7 million to CCA, which was also hired to run the facility. Around the same time, Ohio contracted with MTC to run the North Central Correctional Complex in Marion. Similar to the legislation in Florida, the private prisons in Ohio are required to save at least 5 percent over what it would cost the state to run the two prisons.

Although flawed, Florida's and Ohio's models that strive for some independent monitoring are rare. A growing chorus of academics and organizations support an independent oversight body to monitor jails and prisons. In 2008, the American Bar Association passed a resolution calling on all levels of government to establish public entities to systematically monitor and report publicly on conditions of confinement in all places of detention.[100] In 2006 the Commission on Safety and Abuse in America's Prisons asserted that "the most important mechanism for overseeing corrections is independent inspection and monitoring. Every US prison and jail should be monitored by an independent government body, sufficiently empowered and funded to regularly inspect conditions of confinement and report findings to lawmakers and the public."[101] In fact, the commission recommended creation of a national nongovernmental organization that could inspect prisons and jails at the invitation of corrections administrators. The idea drew its inspiration from the International Committee of the Red Cross, which carries out inspections of detention centers around the globe. More than a decade later, the United States still lacks such an independent body, and very few states have an independent agency or committee to inspect jails and prisons.

The New Mexico Case

New Mexico offers an interesting case study on monitoring private prisons. In New Mexico, each private prison in the state is equipped with a full-time monitor who is a Department of Corrections employee. I visited CCA's New Mexico Correctional Center in Grants, New Mexico, in 2016. The city has a population of less than 10.000 and is about 80 miles west of Albuquerque. After the collapse of the mining industry threw the town into a depression, it turned to tourism for revenue. The area has incredible natural beauty, national parks, Native American pueblos, and Indian ruins. It is also home to a privately owned women's prison with roughly 600 inmates, and more than 500 of those women have at least one mental health diagnosis.

The contract between the state of New Mexico and CCA details how much the state will pay the private firm for each of its female inmates. If the facility holds 300 or more female prisoners, the state Department of Correction pays CCA $68.20 a day. However, if the state sends between 323 and 585 inmates to the prison, they pay only $59.27 a day. The highest incentive is for the state to send at least 586 inmates to the prison because that number triggers a payment of just $15.99 a day per inmate. However, the contract explicitly states that if "the average monthly population of the Facility falls below 580 inmates, the parties will renegotiate the per diem rates for the month during which such event occurs."[102]

New Mexico houses about 6,600 inmates in its state Department of Corrections, and the state sends 44 percent of its inmates to its five private prisons; three are operated by GEO Group, one by CCA, and one by MTC. I walked around the facility with the warden, assistant warden, and the full-time contract monitor, Jerry Smith, who previously served as the assistant warden of the facility for CCA. In a typical day, Smith ensures that the food is served at the right temperature and that the freezer is working, that the inmates get adequate recreation time, that temperatures in the housing units and showers are correct, that the segregated housing decisions are justified, that the eligible inmates are released on time each month, and that all the posts are filled. Walking around the women's facility with Smith, he greeted each inmate we passed in the hall by name.

New Mexico fines CCA if they have a staff vacancy of more than 10 percent. The assistant warden noted that they are held to different standards than their state counterparts. Staffing levels are a problem nationwide among government operated and privately operated facilities. Most prisons are in rural areas, often hundreds of miles from large cities. The long commute, low wages, and tough working conditions are a hard sell for correction officers, medical staff, and other critical corrections workers. With salaries as low as $13.65 an hour and little opportunity for raises, most New Mexico officers leave within three years.[103] Although New Mexico prisons are at approximately 98 percent of capacity, one in three officer jobs remains vacant. With little hope of filling these staffing positions, CCA will pay these fines. In the women's prison, the contract stipulates that CCA can be fined if more than 10 percent of its correction officer positions are vacant for more than thirty days.

I spoke to some women housed in the facility about the conditions of their confinement. One woman, originally from Carlsbad, New Mexico, was transferred from another prison and told me there were thieves at the other prison but not here. At the state prison they stole her snacks and radio. She said the warden at the CCA facility tries hard. Ana, who had been at the prison for five years, explained that she earns between 60 cents and $1.00 an hour for a Microsoft education class that is paid for by CCA. She told me, "They are fair and reasonable here." CCA also contracts with a workforce program that brings a reentry van to the prison where inmates can learn about jobs they could be eligible for upon release. According to the assistant warden, this feature is not a requirement of the state contracts.

David Shichor discusses the risk of revolving-door syndrome, in which private prison firms promise jobs to government correction officials, including monitors. This can occur in reverse, as in Smith's case, where a former private prison official takes a job working for the state at the same facility. According to Shichor, the danger is that "a degree of intimacy may develop between the regulators and the company's personnel they regulate."[104] This concept is also sometimes called "regulatory capture" or "co-opt," meaning that the monitor will become so close to the corporation that he overlooks contract failures. Smith believes he is in a great position to monitor the private facility because he knows how it operates and what to look for.

After touring the facility, I spoke to the New Mexico audit manager, Irwin Wolkomir, who oversees monitoring of prisons across the state. Since January 2012, the state has assessed financial penalties against all five private prisons in New Mexico for noncompliance with certain aspects of their contracts with the state. Wolkomir said that before Secretary Gregg Marcantel took the reins of the New Mexico State Department of Corrections, private firms didn't often face penalties for breaches in their contracts. When Marcantel took over, however, the secretary decided to enforce the contracts with private firms more stringently than did his predecessors.

Wolkomir sent me the state's contract with CCA for the women's prison so I could see just how much Smith had to monitor. The contract was vague in places, such as requiring that "outdoor recreation will be permitted on a daily basis, weather permitting," or in the stipulation that the contractor "will provide discharge ("gate") money, discharge clothing, and discharge transportation when inmates are released."[105]

"These contract monitors are our eyes and ears," Wolkomir told me. "They approve releases. They approve and recalculate good time earned." Despite the talk of enforcement, I wasn't quite sure what the state's real stance was toward the private firms. After all, with five private prisons scattered across the New Mexico landscape, it seemed that the state may have needed the private firms more than the industry needed the state contracts. Wolkomir and his team however seem to hold CCA accountable for strict compliance to the contract. A few days after I visited the women's prison, Marcantel sent the warden of the New Mexico Correctional Center a letter with an attached penalty worksheet, fining CCA $24,000 for extended vacancies of correction officers, security supervisors, noncustody staff, and mandatory posts— not to mention keeping several inmates beyond their release dates.[106]

Financial penalties are an important tool for governments to ensure better conditions at private prisons, and the largest private prison operators set aside funds to settle lawsuits and pay financial penalties. These fines are considered part of doing business. In some cases, it is cheaper to pay a financial penalty for noncompliance with a contract because of inadequate staffing than it is to pay the salaries for those correction officers.

Despite volumes of research studies, creative monitoring, fines for noncompliance, legislation mandating cost savings, and transparency requirements, it is difficult to pinpoint a state in which private prisons produce more humane and better outcomes than their public counterparts. Even in Florida, where private prisons are required to prove cost savings when compared to government prisons, the evidence that the private prisons are in fact saving taxpayer dollars is questionable. For all the money the private prison industry earns, shouldn't we demand more transparency, more accountability, and better outcomes?

CHAPTER ELEVEN

The Future of Private Prisons

The degree of civilization in a society can be judged
by entering its prisons.

FYODOR DOSTOYEVSKY

FORMER REALITY SHOW star and real estate mogul Donald
Trump was elected the forty-fifth president of the United States on
November 8, 2016. The next morning the *New York Times* reported
that the election represented "a decisive demonstration of power
by a largely overlooked coalition of mostly blue-collar white and
working-class voters who felt that the promise of the United States
had slipped their grasp amid decades of globalization and multicul-
turalism. In Mr. Trump, a thrice-married Manhattanite who lives in
a marble-wrapped three-story penthouse apartment on Fifth Avenue,
they found an improbable champion."[1] Private prison companies contract solely with governments, making them vulnerable to the political
winds of presidential and gubernatorial administrations. How will the
industry fare under President Trump? Also, what does the future of
the private prison industry look like beyond the inner workings of the
nation's capital?

On the campaign trail Trump vowed to "get rid of gang members
so fast your head will spin."[2] In his speech at the GOP Convention in
July, despite crime being at historic lows, he vowed to "liberate our

citizens from the crime and terrorism and lawlessness that threatens their communities."[3] He also promised to deport 3 million immigrants and pledged to push Congress to increase the mandatory minimum for illegal reentry into the country to five years.[4]

Banking on Trump making good on his rhetoric, and with for-profit prison firms in charge of the majority of ICE detention centers, CoreCivic and GEO Group's stocks soared after the election (figure 11.1). CNBC called Trump "nothing short of a game changer for the beleaguered private prison contractor industry."[5] On November 9, GEO Group's stock rose 9 percent and CoreCivic's (which has fewer international holdings) increased by almost 20 percent. This continued in the days to follow: by November 23, CoreCivic's stock had jumped 57 percent and GEO Group's by 35 percent since election day.

Beacon Policy Advisors announced a positive outlook for private prison operators after Trump nominated Alabama Senator Jeff Sessions to serve as his attorney general, noting that Sessions would likely "very early" reverse the Bureau of Prisons memo that gradually phased out private prison contracts with the Justice Department. With Sessions leading criminal justice policy, Beacon expected "an increase in the number of federal inmates if some laws were to be more vigorously enforced, including federal drug laws; [this] would be [a] "materially positive" catalyst for private prisons."[6]

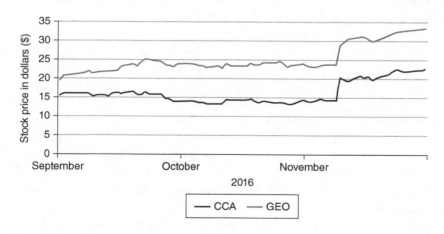

Figure 11.1 CCA and GEO Group Stock Prices, September 1, 2016–November 30, 2016 *Source*: NASDAQ.

In a prescient move, in October GEO Group hired two former Sessions' staffers to lobby on its behalf: David Stewart and Ryan Robichaux. These lobbyist connections to Sessions, whose role also encompasses overseeing the federal prison system, was important because Sessions had the power to reverse the Obama administration's phase-out of private prisons.[7] This gamble paid off when Sessions reversed this decision in February. Despite the inspector general's report, Sessions wrote that the Yates memo "changed long-standing policy and practice, and impaired the Bureau's ability to meet the future needs of the federal correctional system. Therefore, I direct the Bureau to return to its previous approach."[8]

A few weeks before the election, I spoke with an investment analyst who had covered the private prison industry for ten years. He asked that I not disclose his name. He believed Hillary Clinton would be elected, and even operating under that assumption he projected that private prisons would remain lucrative. The analyst pointed to rising anxiety about crime in rural America, a heroin crisis that may drive up prison populations, and polling data indicating that Americans feel unsafe. On the eve of President Trump's inauguration, financial analyst Michael Kodesch wrote to investors: "In our view, GEO and CXW [CoreCivic's stock ticker] are preparing to enter a sustained period of pro-private, tough-on-crime policies alongside comprehensive immigration reform. We believe the present shortage of [Immigration and Customs Enforcement] beds, in addition to pockets of capacity constraints and/or criminal justice reforms pushing for alternative corrections at the state level, create a material external growth opportunity not seen in years."[9]

Damon Hininger appeared on CNBC to discuss how his company may fare under Trump. "If there's need for more detention capacity on the border, we can provide that solution or if there's a unique population that we need to help serve with ICE," he said. When asked whether he thought the Trump administration would be friendlier to the idea of private sector involvement in prisons than the Obama administration had been, Hininger said, "I believe that is the case . . . especially if there is a real push to replace old, antiquated facilities, which has been a theme in this administration."[10] Hininger was onto something. Five days after Trump took office he signed two executive orders that signaled an expansion of the U.S. immigrant detention infrastructure. The Border Security and Immigration Enforcement

Improvements order outlines details "to immediately plan, design, and construct a physical wall along the southern border" and directs the secretary of Homeland Security to "immediately construct, operate, control, or establish contracts to construct, operate, or control facilities to detain aliens at or near the land border with Mexico."

During CoreCivic's fourth quarter 2016 earnings call, Hininger acknowledged the importance of these executive orders to the company's profits: "When coupled with the above-average rate [of] crossings along the Southwest border, these executive orders appear likely to significantly increase the need for safe, humane and appropriate detention bed capacity that we have available in our existing real-estate portfolio, as well as an increased demand for our detention facility design, development, and facility maintenance expertise."[11] Just as predicted, more immigrant detention cells are about to be built. GEO Group will build a new detention center in Conroe, Texas, as part of a ten-year renewable contract with ICE. GEO Group expects the new facility to generate $44 million in yearly revenue for the company.[12]

Rebranding the Private Prison Industry

Immigrant detention facilities are on the rise under a Trump administration, but the for-profit prison industry remains nimble because they believe their core business—state corrections—is in jeopardy. The industry must leverage its business plan to reflect the growing reality that more than half of the states have reduced their correctional populations in the last decade.[13]

In October 2016, CCA restructured, laying off fifty-five people and announced it had changed its name to CoreCivic.[14] This rebranding effort began in 2015, and just days before the Department of Justice's announcement phasing out their reliance on private prisons CCA's board of directors authorized changing the company's charter to reflect a move toward a wider set of government contracts. CoreCivic now consists of three distinct work streams: (1) CoreCivic Safety, continuing CCA's corrections works; (2) CoreCivic Properties, growing government real estate solutions; and (3) CoreCivic Community, developing residential reentry offerings.[15] These three divisions represent where the company believed it was headed in late 2016 and included an expansion of its reentry services. "Rebranding as CoreCivic is the culmination of a multi-year strategy to transform our business from largely corrections and detention services to a wider range of government solutions," said Hininger.[16] The new logo (an American flag stylized in the shape of a building) and brand identity attempts to remove the idea of incarceration from the company's identity.

Hillenby, the PR firm CoreCivic used for its rebranding, specializes in reputational management: "Our campaign-style approach is designed to aggressively defend your reputation, marginalize ill-intentioned interests, and promote a positive narrative that will move decision-maker sentiment in your favor."[17] CoreCivic's rebranding effort is more than just optics. It is core to a business strategy that its biggest competitor, GEO Group, has also internalized. It takes a diversified approach to delivering services for those who cycle in and out of the criminal justice system.

CoreCivic and GEO Group are diversifying largely as a result of a criminal justice reform wave that has taken over large swaths of the country. States, and federal government to some extent, have begun to examine how to safely reduce prison populations by investing in alternatives to prison, reduced revocations to prison for violating probation or parole, and reforming draconian sentencing laws. Because of this, these companies have focused on the profits to be made in overseas correctional markets and on providing services in the United States that go beyond incarceration.

Community Corrections and the Widening Net

In 2015, an estimated 6.7 million people were under the supervision of U.S. adult correctional systems, but almost 4.7 million of those were under parole or probation supervision in the community.[18] "We kind of read those tea leaves," said Tony Grande, CCA's chief development officer. As prison populations have shrunk, governments indicated a need for large private providers to offer less punitive, shorter-term facilities that are less like traditional prison and more like community-based operations that include rehabilitation.[19]

Community corrections describes correctional control outside of jails and prisons, and it refers to many institutions and services: halfway houses, where inmates may spend the last remaining days of their sentences before being released back home; drug or mental health treatment facilities, where inmates must engage in intensive programming; intermediate sanctions facilities that oversee the formerly incarcerated who violated the terms of their probation or parole but don't need to return prison; and more traditional probation and parole in which individuals are monitored by probation officers but remain at home in their communities. Fearing that bipartisan support for criminal justice reform may significantly reduce the national prison population, and as deferred sentences and alternatives to incarceration are on the rise, private corporations have started to invest in community corrections.

By moving away from traditional incarceration services and diversifying their efforts, for-profit prisons may survive reform. They are entering new markets, including drug and alcohol treatment, mental health treatment, day-reporting centers, job training, reentry services, electronic monitoring, and transportation of those involved in the criminal justice system. Carl Takei calls this trend of investing in reentry services "the Wal-Martification of reentry."[20] Other groups have coined the private industry's trend toward buying up treatment centers as the "treatment industrial complex." In fact, GEO Group boasts that it is the second largest provider of privatized correctional and detention facilities around the globe and the largest provider of community-based reentry services, youth services, and electronic monitoring services in the United States. Its 2016 annual report claims: "We believe these leading market positions and our diverse and complementary service offerings enable us to meet the growing demand from our clients for comprehensive services throughout the entire corrections lifecycle."[21]

Since 2009, GEO Group has significantly expanded its GEO Care division, which provides mental health services to those in the criminal justice system. In 2009, GEO's mental health subsidiary, GEO Care, acquired Just Care, Inc and that year's annual report noted that "through our GEO Care subsidiary, we have been able to grow this business to approximately 1,900 beds and $121.8 million in revenues from 325 beds and $31.7 million in revenues in 2004."[22]

GEO Care offers intensive residential treatment, youth services, electronic monitoring equipment and technical support, and community-based correctional services.[23] GEO Care's revenues accounted for 18 percent of the company's total in 2016.[24]

Continuing its flurry to diversify, GEO Group purchased Community Education Centers in 2017, which provides rehabilitative services through reentry and in-prison treatment programs to state and federal inmates. This $360 million deal added 12,000 additional beds to GEO Group's portfolio.[25] The company also branched out to provide surveillance services by purchasing Behavioral Interventions Inc. in 2010, which makes GPS ankle monitoring devices to monitor parolees, probationers, pretrial defendants, and undocumented immigrants.

CCA soon followed this trend and has worked to gain a foothold in community corrections in recent years. In 2013, they spent $36 million to acquire Correctional Alternatives Inc., a privately held community corrections company based in San Diego, California, that includes residential reentry programs and home confinement services. A year later Hininger said, "This is a watershed moment for our company and we hope it will be for our entire industry. We are determined to prove that we can play a leadership role in reducing recidivism and that we have every incentive to do so. The interests of government, taxpayers, shareholders, and communities are aligned. We all just need to recognize that and commit to that."[26] Today CCA owns twenty-five similar facilities with a total of 5,000 beds in six states. In 2015, CCA acquired Avalon Correctional Services, a privately held community corrections company that operates eleven community corrections facilities with approximately 3,000 beds in Oklahoma, Texas, and Wyoming. Community corrections has proved to be a lucrative business, and CCA's Avalon acquisition was expected to bring in $5 million per year.[27]

The private prison industry's segue into community corrections doesn't sit well with advocates and academics who study these companies. Critics caution that the bottom-line focus of publicly traded corporations will undercut decades of work by criminal justice reformers to shrink the size and scope of the U.S. correctional system. Takei believes that "relying on a private prison company to help end mass incarceration is like asking a drug dealer to help curb your addiction. This is vertical integration, not real reform."[28]

Market trends may indicate the profitability of providing services to the more than 4 million Americans caught in some sort of correctional supervision outside of prisons, but critics worry about private prison corporations expanding into the community corrections world. The danger they fear is that these services are merely "net-widening," an expansion of the community corrections system that catches more people for longer periods of time. These companies now have a financial incentive to trap as many people as they can for as long as they can, monitoring them through ever-more sophisticated surveillance.

CCA and GEO Group have diversified into inmate transportation services as well, operating the two largest transportation companies and transporting inmates between different institutions and to work-release programs. Founded in 1990, TransCor America, a wholly owned subsidiary of CCA, generated more than $4 million in revenue in 2015 alone.[29] GEO Group's in-house transportation division, GEO Transport, Inc., provides transportation to federal, state, and local government customers in the United States and internationally and operates a fleet of 320 transport vehicles, from vans to buses and even airplanes.

International Expansion

GEO Group and CCA are hedging their bets in the United States and diversifying internationally, building and operating prisons overseas, especially in the United Kingdom and Australia, countries that are increasing their use of private prisons. In 2016, the GEO Group earned $410 million from international markets, approximately 19 percent of their revenues. GEO Group's 2016 annual report states: "We believe we are well positioned to continue benefiting from foreign governments' initiatives to outsource correctional services."[30] GEO Group will soon complete its project in Australia, operating a new 1,300-bed prison in Ravenhall near Melbourne. The facility is expected to provide $75 million in annualized revenues for GEO Group under a twenty-five-year management contract.[31]

At least eleven countries across North America, South America, Europe, Africa, and Oceania participate in some level of prison privatization.[32] The UK, Australia, Scotland, and New Zealand all now have a higher proportion of prisoners housed in private prisons than does the United States, although the United States houses a higher absolute number of prisoners in private facilities.[33] England and Wales lead the pack with just over 18 percent of prisoners in for-profit prisons. Australia followed the United States and became the second nation to outsource its prisons to private firms. The United States turned to private firms due to overcrowding in the early 1980s, but privatization in Australia was driven by the need to replace deteriorating facilities, many more than a century old.[34]

The UK is home to fourteen private prisons.[35] The growth of private prisons in the UK has slowed, however, pushing some of the largest private prison firms to expand into Australia, where the government is increasing its outsourcing of prison management. The Australian immigrant detention system is entirely operated by for-profit firms. Australia boasts a higher proportion of inmates in privately operated prisons than any other country. Their first private prison became operational in January 1990.[36] Today, GEO Group, G4S, and Serco are responsible for more than 6,000 Australian prisoners. Nearly 40,000 people were incarcerated in Australia in January 2016, and the national imprisonment rate stood at 162 prisoners per 100,000 people.[37] Australia now imprisons more people than at any point in its history.[38]

Private prison contracts overseas provide some valuable insight into how to creatively contract with private prison companies in the United States to ensure better outcomes for the inmates housed in private prisons.

Reforming Private Prison Management Through Contracts

How can we make private prisons better? Is it fair to ask the private sector to succeed when public prisons have so clearly failed? One important answer can be found in measuring performance: how the contract between the government and the prison firm is structured. It's rare for these contracts to demand innovation, recidivism reduction, and outcomes that outperform the public sector. Most contracts require the private operator to replicate the government prison system's policies and procedures. But this is wrongheaded. A good first step would be to structure contracts around reorienting incentives, something that we might call *performance-based contracting*. States and the federal government should write contracts with economic incentives that focus on reducing recidivism and improving reentry outcomes.

Some have argued that private prisons should be held accountable for employing evidence-based practices proven to reduce recidivism.[39] This is perhaps a wonky policy suggestion, but such contracts could require evidence-based programming such as 24–7 Dads, a fatherhood program designed to help men improve their parenting skills, or cognitive behavioral therapy to treat depression. These programs aim to ease the reentry of the formerly incarcerated into the community and reduce their chance of returning to prison.

Kristofer "Bret" Bucklen, director of the Pennsylvania Department of Corrections, Bureau of Planning, Research & Statistics, has worked to change incentives in how his state's Department of Corrections contracts with private corporations to run halfway houses. Bucklen thinks it makes more sense to simply encourage the bottom-line, the outcome. In his view, incenting intermediate outputs such as practices or program has limitations. "Sometimes so-called evidence-based practices don't work," Bucklen told me. "They are not implemented correctly, they only work in certain limited environments, or they don't work when brought to scale. Thus it would be misleading to incentivize their use and just assume they'll reduce recidivism." Bucklen also pointed out that requiring "evidence-based" practices precludes innovation, meaning that corporations wouldn't have the freedom to try new programming that might not be on an approved list of "what works." "The use of evidence-based practices is limiting because it implicitly assumes we already know everything that works," Bucklen said. "By going straight to the end result and incentivizing recidivism reduction, this allows contractors to use a combination of already proven approaches and new innovations in order to have a better portfolio of approaches to reduce recidivism. In the end, the proof is in the pudding: recidivism reduction."[40]

[Although it would be ideal to hold the private sector accountable through statistics on recidivism rates of inmates, that is unrealistic.] Jails and prisons are transient places, and inmates can be transferred between facilities (both public and private) for any number of reasons: programming, medical care, security. If an inmate spent two years at a state prison, three years at a private prison, and six months back at a state prison receiving reentry programming before release, which prison is on the hook if that inmate lands behind bars again within three years?

Despite the challenge, some practitioners have started to think of creative solutions to the transient nature of inmate shuffling. In Pennsylvania, inmates typically move between two or three different prisons during their stay. Bucklen came up with an algorithm to calculate how much time inmates spend at each facility. Using this, his office can correlate recidivism rates with time spent in each prison. Bucklen explains it like this:

> Let's say we have two inmates. Inmate #1 spent two years at Prison A and one year at Prison B. Inmate #2 spent one year at Prison A and two years at Prison B. Let's say Inmate #1 recidivated and Inmate #2 did not, and let's say that they are both released from Prison B. Traditional recidivism measures would say that Prison A has a 0 percent recidivism rate (since nobody was released from Prison A) and Prison B had a 50 percent recidivism rate (since 1 out of the 2 inmates recidivated). Instead we could say that across the two inmates, three years were spent at Prison A and three years were spent at Prison B. Further, Inmate #1 recidivated and spent two years at Prison A and one year at Prison B. So under an adjusted recidivism rate (the model I developed), Prison A has a 66 percent recidivism rate (2 years/3 years) and Prison B has a 33 percent recidivism rate (1 year/3 years)."[41]

Pennsylvania does not have private prisons that hold state inmates, but if they did, this formula would prove useful to encourage the industry to reduce recidivism rates.

Leonard Gilroy at the Reason Foundation thinks private prisons should be held to a higher standard than their government counterparts. "This is what privatization is for," Gilroy told me. "Right now contracts are replicating the public sector. They are contracting a mini-me."[42]

The government is contracting everything down to the type of boots guards should wear, which impairs flexibility and innovation. Gilroy suggests that the true "innovation" private prisons afford is the opportunity to create performance-based contracts that incentivize operators to provide "job training, educational opportunities and rehabilitation programs, and better prepare inmates to reenter society."[43] If recidivism rates are more important than the temperature of food and the kind of boots guards wear, shouldn't contracts focus on those policy goals and perhaps even eliminate the compliance requirements that don't consider the big picture?

Recidivism is complicated, and even the best programming does not guarantee results. Too many prisoners are released into their communities with little education, few job skills, and oftentimes no social network. In addition, the many conditions of supervised release, such as drug testing, parole check-ins, and required classes, may interfere with steady work. The private sector has some advantages over the public sector in meeting these challenges, and they should be required to ramp up programming and treatments that have a track record of success. For example, contracts could include cash bonuses when private prisons do something right and financial penalties or even contract termination when they do something wrong.

Some promising models to build incentives into private correctional contracts are being introduced. In 2013, Pennsylvania Governor Tom Corbett's administration announced it would cancel all of the state's Department of Corrections contracts with private companies and rebid them on a performance basis. Providers were to be evaluated and paid according to their success in reducing the recidivism of those just released from prison. Facilities are now paid a 1 percent increase per client per day if their overall recidivism rate falls below a certain level. The state can cancel a contract if the recidivism rate increases over two consecutive years. Since these contracts were implemented, the recidivism rate for private facilities fell about 11 percent in the first year alone.

Bucklen, who spearheaded this incentive structure, told me that "it is not going to be the cure-all for any state looking at it; but we have finished three consecutive years with these contracts, and we have extended all the contracts as they have all reduced recidivism or maintained a baseline recidivism rate." I asked Bucklen how he made this happen. The results certainly seem like something other government agencies would want to replicate. But he said that he didn't quite know. "We are paying these contractors to be the professionals to figure that out," Bucklen said. "We have never simply asked them to figure it out. It should have been implicit all along, but it was never made explicit. These contracts state here is the end goal; you are the claimed experts at running halfway houses and reentry. We need you to figure this out with this goal."[44]

Recently, New York and Massachusetts explored performance-based contracts aimed at improving outcomes of those who cycle in and out of the criminal justice system. In August 2012, New York City announced the first U.S. social impact bond aimed at reducing recidivism among juvenile inmates released from Rikers Island Jail. *Social impact bonds* allow the private sector to partner with governments and philanthropies to fund social programs that help address public policy issues. In this public–private partnership, investors are repaid (and can make a profit) if the public policy outcome is achieved. Social impact bonds are in the spirit of privatization—leveraging private money for the public good.

A social impact bond funded the Adolescent Behavioral Learning Experience (ABLE) program, which serves sixteen- to eighteen-year-old juveniles detained in Rikers. Goldman Sachs funded the project's delivery and operations through a $9.6 million loan over four years to MDRC, a leading social policy organization. Bloomberg Philanthropies provided a $7.2 million grant to MDRC to guarantee a portion of the loan, reducing the lender's risk. The financial structure of these bonds is complex, but Goldman's incentives were clear: the lower the program's recidivism rate, the greater the interest paid. Goldman would earn up to $2.1 million in profit if the program cut participant recidivism by more than 10 percent.[45] Bloomberg Philanthropies and Goldman Sachs paid $7.2 million for the initiative, and if the program reduced recidivism by 10 percent or more, the city would save more than $20 million in the deferred cost of housing inmates, and Goldman would receive a $2 million windfall. Social impact bonds "bet on the success" of prisoners instead of betting on their failure, which tends to be the norm in private prison contracts. Social impact bonds are mainly used to address complex problems where "outcomes are simple to measure, such as homelessness, foster care, and prison recidivism."[46]

In 2015, the Vera Institute of Justice evaluated the program and determined that it "did not lead to reductions in recidivism and therefore did not meet the program's pre-defined threshold of success."[47] Despite the program's failure to reduce recidivism rates more than the control group, many deemed the experiment a success. The program cost taxpayers nothing because the intervention was funded by private dollars, and it permitted government to innovate, which will surely produce failures along the way to successes. The UK piloted similar recidivism-based contracts for prison operations, and the Peterborough prison reported a drop in reconvictions after experimenting with a social impact bond.

Gilroy thinks an ideal private prison contract would look at the current recidivism rate and raise the bar for a private prison contract, but he is not aware of any U.S. private prison contract with that structure.

He thinks it's imperative to push the envelope on these contracts: "Are we all cool with just doing nothing, or is someone going to step up and try to figure this out?"[48] To improve outcomes, private prisons need to evolve and experiment. Pushing the envelope will encourage more dynamism. Providing incentives to private firms to exceed baselines such as improved recidivism rates provides the right "carrot"; the "stick" of creating penalties for contract breaches such as failing to receive basic accreditation or meet minimum standards has failed to improve the system.

In Melaleuca, a new women's prison in West Australia run by French-based Sodexo, the company will earn a cash bonus of $15,000 (11,000 USD) for every inmate who doesn't return to prison within two years.[49] Currently a third of all Australian women prisoners return to prison following their release. Sodexo has held the contract to operate the 250-bed Melaleuca Remand & Reintegration Facility since June 2016. Western Australia's two other private prisons are run by UK-based Serco.

At Victoria's Ravenhall Prison, built under a public–private partnership and due to open in 2017, GEO Group, who will operate the prison, will be compensated on the basis of the rate of reoffending among its released prisoners.[50] The GEO Group has been promised a $2 million bonus payment per year if the rate of reoffending among inmates released from Ravenhall is 12 percent lower than at other prisons. In Australia, the recidivism rate has reached a ten-year high of 40 percent. The contract includes a target of a 14 percent reduction in recidivism among indigenous prisoners.[51] This medium security men's prison with a 1,000-bed initial capacity will expand to house 1,300 prisoners. GEO Group Australia will operate and maintain the prison for twenty-five years. "We welcome the Victorian government's unique scheme to encourage rehabilitation and reduce recidivism and look forward to partnering successfully with them," stated Managing Director Pieter Bezuidenhout.[52]

Wilkinson, a board member of MTC, agrees that performance-based contracts could work if they focus on achievable benchmarks. He suggested that the contracts incentivize private operators to meet certain benchmarks or even threshold levels of service, "for example, if a private operator achieves a certain number of successful GEDs or a certain number of inmates successfully complete alcohol or substance abuse abatement therapy, or how many contacts you have had with persons who have been diagnosed with mental illness," Wilkinson said. "I think you can quantify a lot of stuff in prisons if a contract is incentivized for that to happen." For Wilkinson, however, recidivism reduction is a tough goal for private prisons because private firms have no control over where these inmates go when they are transferred.[53]

Private prison operators point out that they don't control outcomes, especially when they house inmates for a year or two between state-operated facilities. Restructuring contracts around the nation's public policy goals would ensure that private operators provide more educational programming, job training classes, and work with inmates to ensure they are set up to succeed when released. When halfway house contracts in Pennsylvania were rebid, Bucklen said that "the contract providers screamed bloody murder." The companies argued that Pennsylvania couldn't hold them accountable for recidivism rates because there were too many people involved in reentry: parole supervisors, the police, and different service providers in the community. "That is a fair point," Bucklen told them, "but you have some role in reducing recidivism, otherwise we wouldn't work with you."[54]

Three years may be too long into a contract to wait for results if government wants to incentivize outcomes with private providers. Governments could build in shorter follow-up periods to assess recidivism in performance-based contracts, such as one year or six months. The first six months to a year after release presents the biggest risk for recidivism. The percentage of those rearrested after release drops considerably the longer individuals remain out of prison. In the first year after release from prison, the rate of arrest is about 43 percent compared to 20 percent in the third year of release.[55]

How can we measure recidivism when so many things can lead someone back to prison? The list is endless: trauma, peer pressure, poor or no programming, a strict parole or probation officer, poverty, family trouble, and so on. Private prisons have more than three decades of experience now. It is time for them to show that they can rehabilitate inmates, not merely warehouse them for the government.

Better Contracts

In 1987, the Supreme Court wrestled with two policies created by New Jersey prison officials that barred inmates from attending a Muslim service on Friday afternoons. The inmates argued that this violated their rights under the Free Exercise Clause of the First Amendment.

In *O'Lone v. Estate of Shabazz*, the Court came down on the side of the prison officials, holding that its policies were reasonably related to legitimate penological interests. Writing for the dissent, Justice William Brennan penned this:

> It is thus easy to think of prisoners as members of a separate neth-
> erworld, driven by its own demands, ordered by its own customs,
> ruled by those whose claim to power rests on raw necessity. Nothing
> can change the fact, however, that the society that these prisoners
> inhabit is our own. Prisons may exist on the margins of that society,
> but no act of will can sever them from the body politic.[56]

Justice Brennan's words are as important today as they were two decades ago. We can't simply cast aside the men and women who languish behind bars until they are released. We owe them a duty and a responsibility to constantly monitor their condition. Beyond that, we owe them the promise that we will push the envelope as far as we can to incentivize prison operators to provide better programming and outcomes. The primary focus of this book is on private prisons, but we need to do a much better job of improving conditions and providing better programming at both government run and privately run institutions.

Contracts are legal instruments, pieces of paper that can or cannot be complied with, but with strict monitoring contracts have the power to make wholesale changes in how we conduct the business of providing care and services to inmates in private prisons. Contract terms have to be tightly written and provide enforceable service agreements that protect essential life safety and security functions, including staffing, medical and mental health care, nutrition, sanitation, facility maintenance, and provision of counseling, education, and recreation. Penalties for violation of these agreements must be sufficient to make compliance more profitable than noncompliance. Private entities that perform public functions should be subject to the same transparency, accountability, and oversight as public entities.

Having explored the problems and some potential solutions for improving the lives of U.S. prisoners and immigrant detainees, the ten concrete requirements that end this chapter provide a starting point for more robust state and federal government contracts with private industry. The federal government would be wise to incorporate these recommendations in its contracts not just for privately operated BOP prisons but also for private prison companies that operate immigrant detention facilities. Even though immigrant detention centers house civil detainees, the people are not free to come and go. They are trapped behind bars every bit as much as those convicted of crimes.

1. *Contract Monitors*

The most important assurance of accountability at private prisons and detention centers is the contract monitor. It is imperative that government agencies provide multiple monitors (not just one on site) and ensure their independent judgment. Contracts should require monitors to pop-in unannounced at private prisons so facilities are not preparing for the visits in a way that obfuscates the true conditions of confinement. Some states, such as New Mexico, require a full-time contract monitor who works for the New Mexico Corrections Department. Other states, such as Louisiana, employ contract monitors who visit private prisons periodically. Although rare, some states, such as Florida, rely on an independent agency to monitor prisons. No model is perfect. A full-time staff monitor may become friendly with private prison staff and be reluctant to recommend fines; an independent agency may not have the authority to make changes because the contract is between the Department of Corrections and the private prison. At the very least, an objective monitor should spend significant time at the prison and be empowered to judge inadequate conditions of confinement and noncompliance with the contract. In addition, the monitor's reports should be made public and provided to the state's auditing entity and to the legislature.

2. *Termination of Rights*

Every private prison contract must have an escape clause. This ensures that the state can terminate the contract for a justified cause, such as poor performance on the private prison operator's part or a reduction in inmates that empties out the private prison.

3. *No Guaranteed Bed Payments*

States should negotiate contracts that pay a fixed rate per inmate but do not compensate firms for empty prison beds. These guaranteed payments waste taxpayer dollars and fly in the face of the claim that private prisons save taxpayer money. This should be combined with an incentive to reduce recidivism. Otherwise the pressure will be to fill beds either by inadvertently encouraging recidivism or by lobbying for longer sentences.

4. Maximum Capacity Levels

Agreeing on a maximum capacity at the private prison protects the firm from overcrowding and the government from liability. The primary reason to rely on a private prison is to reduce overcrowding; therefore, it's imperative that private prisons do not house more people than they have the capacity to handle.

5. Lengthening of Sentences

Staff at private prisons should not be authorized to take actions that increase time inmates serve in prison. For example, if a correction officer at a private prison gives an inmate a disciplinary sanction, officials at the private prison should not be able to extend that person's sentence for behavioral infractions. These decisions belong to the government correctional authority. If private prison operators have this authority, they are incentivized to dole out disciplinary sanctions that may result in inmates spending more time at their facilities. One way to implement this recommendation would be to require that hearing officers from an independent agency, such as the state or municipality's counsel's office, adjudicate disciplinary hearings.

6. Notice of Inadequate Performance

Government must create a means to provide notice of inadequate performance and devise a plan to remedy it.

7. Fines

Government must clearly define situations in which a private firm will be fined, how much the fine will be, and—most important—enforce these fines. Government should use this lever as a way to ensure humane and adequate conditions of confinement at private prisons.

Fines should be large enough that corporations find it less costly to comply with the contract than to pay fines for noncompliance.

8. Access and Transparency

Most prisons do not accommodate the press, and often press must contact the state public information office or the public relations office of the private firm. To ensure accountability, government contracts should require that private prisons allow the press to speak to inmates and tour the facilities. Outside stakeholders should be given access even with short notice, and no part of the prison should be off limits. Government contracts should require that private prisons comply with the same Freedom of Information Act and open records requests as state prisons.

9. Process Measures

Government should require private firms to provide vocational and educational classes. An ideal contract would distribute bonuses to private firms that provide more programming than their public counterparts.

10. Outcome Measures

Perhaps the boldest change government could make to private prison contracts is to pay bonuses to prisons that improve outcomes for the individuals leaving their prisons. A performance-based contract would reward private firms that reduce recidivism and sexual and physical assaults and that can prove their former inmates landed employment after release.

These recommendations will not solve every problem of contracting with private prisons, but they are a step toward opening the doors on what happens inside the nation's for-profit prisons. Once these recommendations are adopted in contracts, contract monitors are essential to ensure compliance and to confirm that conditions of confinement are humane.

Conclusion

WHEN I BEGAN this project in 2015, criminal justice reform was a hot issue. President Obama wanted his legacy to include a less punitive society. By the next summer, his administration had taken on the private prison industry. Deputy Attorney General Sally Yates sent a memo to the federal Bureau of Prisons (BOP) in August to curb its reliance on private prisons: "This is the first step in the process of reducing—and ultimately ending—our use of privately operated prisons."[1] A *New York Times* editorial argued that this was "a watershed step that should be the beginning of the end of an industry that has had an insidious effect on the American justice system."[2]

Six months later, President Trump's newly confirmed Attorney General Jeff Sessions sent a one-paragraph memo to BOP reversing the Obama Justice Department's guidance. The next day, CNN reported that the value of the stocks of the two biggest private prison corporations, CoreCivic and GEO Group, had doubled since Election Day.[3] By the summer of 2017, the BOP actively sought opportunities to contract with private corporations to house more inmates. The BOP posted a request for proposals for contract facilities to house more than 9,000 prisoners, most of whom are non-citizens with criminal convictions.[4] In April, GEO Group announced that ICE had awarded them a contract to build and run a $110 million, 1,000-bed immigration detention facility in Conroe, Texas, a town 40 miles north of Houston.[5] And in a further sign that the private prison industry would benefit from the Trump administration's policies, its 2018 proposed budget asked for $1.2 billion to expand immigrant detention capacity, which would greatly benefit GEO Group, CoreCivic, and MTC Corp.[6] Privatization was back in vogue. Just as in the Reagan era push for privatization, President Trump made no secret of his love for increasing the private sector's role in historically government-run activities. Rumors flew that he would advocate for the privatization of the Corporation for Public Broadcasting.[7] Within months of taking office, Trump tasked his son-in-law, Jared Kushner, to oversee a new White House Office of American Innovation, designed in part to figure out how to privatize certain functions of the federal government. Administrations come and go, and for three decades the private prison industry has ridden the rollercoaster of media and political scrutiny, increasing their advantage when administrations favored more rather than less privatization. There is no reason to think the private prison industry will go away anytime soon.

◦ Our overreliance on jails and prisons as a tool to combat crime created space for private prisons to emerge, and ultimately to thrive. Private corporations are in charge of inmates from the food they eat to the programming they are offered. The country is of two minds about it: small towns across America succumb to the promise of hundreds of jobs in their communities and lobby to attract private prisons at the same time that students from the Pacific Northwest to the eastern seaboard are leading divestment campaigns aimed to break all ties between their institutions of higher learning and companies that profit from people behind bars. Front and center on the presidential campaign trail, the politics swirling around the private prison industry made it tricky for private firms to project certain profits, and the industry's incentives remain at odds with significantly reducing America's prison population.

Private prison corporations encouraged policymaking that helped fuel their bottom line and the immense rise in incarceration rates. By lobbying policy makers and participating in ALEC, the industry has grown more profitable. A CCA official cochaired the criminal justice task force committee that drafted model state laws encouraging a more draconian stance on sentencing and legislation friendly to the private prison industry. This opened the door to the industry and played an important role in ensuring a long-term need for their facilities. When private prison stock flagged in the late nineties as state correctional budgets shrank, the companies moved into the burgeoning immigration detention business. With the industry faltering, the untapped promise of immigrant detention saved these corporations. By building detention centers on former cornfields and prairies, the industry created a market for the thousands of undocumented citizens who are forced to live behind bars while their paperwork and cases are examined.

Despite their success at gobbling up more and more of the immigrant detainee population, private prison corporations are taking significant steps to diversify and expand into services that do not require keeping people behind bars. GEO Group and CoreCivic have acquired residential reentry centers, drug treatment centers, and electronic monitoring services, and this diversification intended to protect their profits when the political winds shift and states and the federal government focus on criminal justice reform. At the margins, when one peels back the layers, the industry is responsible for more and more people. The private prison industry did not create mass incarceration, but it has not sat idly by.

In this book I have asked, "What does it mean for a for-profit company to manage jails and prisons?" Arguments on both sides of this issue have been examined: the anxiety about delegating core government duties, the economics, the politics, the morals, and the future of the industry.

What does it look like for incarcerated individuals, their families, policy makers, corrections officers, towns, and industry officials themselves? Eric Daley, an inmate who told me his story, subsequently wrote to me and ended his letter with this: "I just hope and pray you take the correct approach and condemn the privatization of prisons in America, because there is no place for them in the land of the free."[8] Many of my conversations with inmates and former inmates echoed this sentiment. Even with better contract incentives and more stringent monitoring, they wanted to know what private prisons say about our society.

The tough-on-crime philosophy that pervaded U.S. politics for decades pushed policy makers to legislate tougher sentences but at the same time found them unwilling to fund the construction of new prisons. If the United States didn't have forty years of policy promoting mass incarceration, it couldn't have sustained a business model allowing for extensive profits on the backs of inmates. With the majority of states facing court orders to reduce overcrowding in prisons in the mid-1980s, the private sector played a pivotal role in building prisons quickly and taking in overflow inmates.

In 1985, Ted Nissen, a former San Quentin guard and owner of Behavioral Systems Southwest, declared: "We have built a prison industry based on concrete walls, guard towers and the overclassification of inmates, and the prisons, instead of being run so that people are in better shape to live in society when they get out, are run so that we have a 50 percent failure (recidivism) rate within five years."[9] Thirty years later, recidivism rates have not changed, and the private sector has not lived up to its promise to improve upon government's failure.

The distinction between private and public prisons is not as important as the distinction between warehousing individuals and rehabilitating them. For the three decades that private prisons have existed, we have asked little of the industry—only that they prevent escapes, provide some programming, and save us money. This partnership between government and private prison operators to safely warehouse prisoners has not worked. It is time to drastically change that partnership and to encourage private prisons to perform a new state goal: reducing recidivism and preparing inmates for life in the community. The irony is that by meeting these public policy objectives private prison companies may put themselves out of business. That doesn't have to be the case, however, as improving contract terms can incentivize changes that greatly enhance the futures of those who spend time in their prisons.

In November 1984, Morley Safer aired a *60 Minutes* story on the emerging private prison industry. He started the segment saying, "'The business of America is business,' said Calvin Coolidge, and this story more than confirms that wisdom. 'Crime Pays' is not how to get away with it; it's how to cash in on it. The care and feeding of criminals in this country costs about $10-billion a year. A number of bright entrepreneurs decided, with that kind of cash available and the heat the government's taking about overcrowding and rehabilitation, that maybe they could do a better job of running corrections than the government."[10]

Safer interviewed CCA President Tom Beasley on the question of incentives. "You—you get recompensed for every prisoner you take care of, look after. Surely, it's in your interest to keep the prison population high?" Beasley, who cofounded CCA the year before and previously served as chairman of the Tennessee Republican Party, replied, "You know, that's a question that people frequently put to us. There's no incentive at all for us to worry about that, because every prison is overcrowded."[11]

By the end of 1984, the entire prison systems of seven states and Washington, D.C. were under court orders to relieve crowded facilities.[12] In twenty-five other states, at least one major prison was overcrowded and ordered to reduce its inmate population.[13] "We want to stay in business for a long time," Beasley told Safer on *60 Minutes*. "The great incentive for us, and we believe the long-term great incentive for the private sector, will be that you will be judged on performance. Yet the—the effect of your rehabilitative efforts, your recidivism rate . . . we intend to be in this business from now on so we don't want to be guilty. We want the contract renewed next year and the year after."[14]

Notes

Introduction

1. Justice Anthony Kennedy, speaking at the annual meeting of the American Bar Association, August 9, 2003, https://archive.org/stream/325931-dcom5/325931-dcom5_djvu.txt.

2. Michael Muskal, "Colorado Bans Solitary Confinement for Seriously Mentally Ill," *Los Angeles Times*, June 6, 2014.

3. Rick Raemisch, "My Night in Solitary," *New York Times*, February 20, 2014.

4. Dominion Farms Limited, "Principals," http://www.dominion-farms.com/principals.html.

5. Marianne Goodland, "Buying and Drying: Water Lessons from Crowley County," *Colorado Independent*, July 9, 2015.

6. Ann Marie Awad, "When Looking at the Arguments Around Raising Colorado's Minimum Wage, Context Is Key," KUNC.com, July 19, 2016, http://www.kunc.org/post/when-looking-arguments-around-raising-colorados-minimum-wage-context-key#stream/0. Compare Crowley's unemployment rate of 16 percent to Colorado's (as of June 2016) rate of 3.7 percent. "Mountain-Plains Information Office: Colorado," Bureau of Labor Statistics, last visited August 18, 2016, http://www.bls.gov/regions/mountain-plains/colorado.htm#eag_co.f.P.

7. As part of the deal, CCA acquired the real estate for six of their seven facilities. Boulder County property records show the Longmont facility sold for roughly $2 million; the Boulder facility is owned by the county. Joshua Lindenstein, "Boulder-based Correctional Management Inc. Acquired for $35M," *Bizwest*, April 11, 2016, http://bizwest.com/boulder-based-correctional-management-inc-acquired-35m/.

8. In late 2016, only twelve states were in full compliance. Thirty-six other states said they are working to comply. Juan A. Lozano, "Jails, Prisons Still Trying to Meet Federal Anti-Rape Rules," Associated Press, September 11, 2016, https://apnews.com/284878b0b20945a8a1acac2310ad54b7/jails-prisons-still -trying-meet-federal-anti-rape-rules. Hawaii's 168 female inmates at a privately run Kentucky prison were reported to be removed because of charges of sexual abuse by guards. Ian Urbina, "Hawaii to Remove Inmates over Abuse Charges," *New York Times*, August 25, 2009.

9. E. Ann Carson and Elizabeth Anderson, "Prisoners in 2015," Bureau of Justice Statistics Bulletin NCJ 250229, December 2016, https://www.bjs .gov/content/pub/pdf/p15.pdf.

10. Marie Gottschalk, *Caught: The Prison State and the Lockdown of American Politics* (Princeton, N.J.: Princeton University Press, 2015), 14.

11. Carson and Anderson, "Prisoners in 2015," 16.

12. Ibid., 28. In 2015, private prisons held 91,338 state inmates and 34,934 federal inmates.

13. Ibid., 7, 16, table 4, 27, appendix table 1. The six states that house at least 20 percent of their inmate population in private prisons are Hawaii, Mississippi, Montana, New Mexico, North Dakota, and Oklahoma.

1. The Prison Buildup and the Birth of Private Prisons

1. Justin Jones, "How to Starve the For-Profit Prison Beast," *Speak Freely* (ACLU blog), April 24, 2014, https://www.aclu.org/blog/how-starve-profit -prison-beast.

2. Dana Liebelson, "Gary Johnson Has Been a Champion of Private Prisons Throughout His Career," *Huffington Post*, October 12, 2016, http:// www.huffingtonpost.com/.

3. Adam Gopnik, "The Caging of America: Why Do We Lock Up So Many People," *New Yorker*, January 30, 2012, http://www.newyorker.com /magazine/2012/01/30/the-caging-of-america.

4. Stephanie Mencimer, "There Are 10 Times More Mentally Ill People Behind Bars Than in State Hospitals, *Mother Jones*, April 8, 2014, http://www.mother jones.com/mojo/2014/04/record-numbers-mentally-ill-prisons-and-jails.

5. For recidivism rates for those who are returned to prison with or without a new prison sentence, see Matthew R. Durose et al., "Recidivism of Prisoners Released in 30 States in 2005: Patterns from 2005 to 2010," Bureau of Justice Statistics, 2014, http://www.bjs.gov/content/pub/pdf/rprts05p0510.pdf.

6. Marc Mauer, *Race to Incarcerate*, rev. ed. (New York: The New Press, 2006), 2.

7. LeRoy B. DePuy, "The Walnut Street Prison: Pennsylvania's First Penitentiary," *Pennsylvania History: A Journal of Mid-Atlantic Studies* 8, 2 (April 1951): 131.

8. Chai Woodham, "Eastern State Penitentiary: A Prison With a Past," *Smithsonian Magazine*, September 30, 2008, http://www.smithsonianmag.com /history/eastern-state-penitentiary-a-prison-with-a-past-14274660/. See also, Norman B. Johnston, "Pioneers in Criminology V—John Haviland (1792– 1852)," *Journal of Criminal Law and Criminology* 45, 5 (1955): 514.

9. Woodham, "Eastern State Penitentiary."

10. Herman Mannheim, ed. *Pioneers in Criminology*, 2nd ed. (Montclair, NJ: Patterson Smith, 1972), 111.

11. This idea is attributed to Dr. Benjamin Rush. Eastern State Penitentiary.org, https://www.easternstate.org/learn/research-library/history. Jimmy Stamp attributed this quote to the Philadelphia Society for Alleviating the Miseries of Public Prisons, which counted Benjamin Franklin as a member. Jimmy Stamp, "The Daring Escape From the Eastern State Penitentiary," *Smithsonian Magazine*, November 13, 2013, http://www.smithsonianmag.com/arts-culture/the-daring -escape-from-the-eastern-state-penitentiary-180947688/.

12. Eastern State Penitentiary.org. "History," https://www.easternstate.org /learn/research-library/history.

13. Charles Dickens, *American Notes for General Circulation: Vol. 1* (London: Chapman and Hall, 1842), chap. 7.

14. Ibid., 239.

15. David J. Rothman, "Perfecting the Prison," in *The Oxford History of the Prison: The Practice of Punishment in Western Society*, ed. Norval Morris and David J. Rothman (Oxford: Oxford University Press, 1995), 100.

16. Frederick G. Pettigrove, "State Prisons of the United States Under Separate and Congregate Systems," in *Penal and Reformatory Institutions*, Vol. 2, ed. Charles Richmond Henderson (Philadelphia: Press of William F. Fell, 1910), 34.

17. Gustave de Beaumont and Alexis de Tocqueville, *On the Penitentiary System in the United States and Its Application in France* (Carbondale: Southern Illinois University Press, 1979) First published in 1833.

18. Edgardo Rotman, "The Failure of Reform," in *The Oxford History of the Prison: The Practice of Punishment in Western Society*, ed. Norval Morris and David J. Rothman (Oxford: Oxford University Press, 1995), 166.

19. Ibid.

20. Todd Clear, George Cole, and Michael Reisig, *American Corrections*, 9th ed. (Belmont, Calif.: Wadsworth, Cengage Learning, 2011), 60.

21. Martinson attempted to qualify this statement in subsequent works, but his original thesis "stuck" and had the greatest impact on crime theory. See Cyndi Banks, *Criminal Justice Ethics: Theory and Practice* (Thousand Oaks, Calif.: Sage, 2004), 107, 116–17. See also Mauer, *Race to Incarcerate*, 48.

22. Robert Martinson, "Can Corrections Correct?," *New Republic* 166 (1972): 14–15.

23. Michael Tonry, ed., *Retributivism Has a Past: Has It a Future?* (Oxford: Oxford University Press, 2001), vii.

24. Miller, "The Debate on Rehabilitating Criminals."

25. Donna Selman and Paul Leighton, *Punishment for Sale: Private Prisons, Big Business, and the Incarceration Binge* (Lanham, Md.: Rowman & Littlefield, 2010), 34.

26. Lyndon B. Johnson, "Statement by the President on Establishing the President's Commission on Law Enforcement and Administration of Justice," July 26, 1965, http://www.presidency.ucsb.edu/ws/?pid=27110.

27. Heather Ann Thompson, "Why Mass Incarceration Matters: Rethinking Crisis, Decline, and Transformation in Postwar American History," *Journal of American History* 97, no. 3: 729–30.

28. Ibid., 731.

29. Elizabeth Hinton, *From the War on Poverty to the War on Crime: The Making of Mass Incarceration in America* (Cambridge, Mass.: Harvard University Press, 2016).

30. Naomi Murakawa, *The First Civil Right: How Liberals Built Prison America* (Oxford: Oxford University Press, 2014).

31. U.S. Census Bureau, "Quick Facts, United States," https://www.census.gov/quickfacts/table/ PST045215/00; E. Ann Carson, "Prisoners in 2014," Bureau of Justice Statistics, September 2015, 15, http://www.bjs.gov/content/pub/pdf/p14.pdf.

32. Marc Mauer, interview by Lauren-Brooke Eisen, February 21, 2017.

33. John Pfaff, *Locked In: The True Causes of Mass Incarceration—and How to Achieve Real Reform* (New York: Basic Books, 2017), 27.

34. Charles Blow, "Drug Bust," *New York Times*, June 10, 2011, http://www.nytimes.com/2011/06/11/opinion/11blow.html.

35. Message to the Congress Transmitting Reorganization Plan 2 of 1973 Establishing the Drug Enforcement Administration, March 28, 1973, http://www.presidency.ucsb.edu/ws/index.php?pid=4159#axzz1PCJydjl5.

36. "DEA History," https://www.dea.gov/about/history.shtml.

37. Full Text of Nancy Reagan Speech, September 14, 1986, http://www.pbs.org/wgbh/americanexperience/features/primary-resources/reagan-drug-campaign/.

38. Marie Gottschalk, *Caught: The Prison State and the Lockdown of American Politics* (Princeton, N.J.: Princeton University Press, 2015).

39. Michelle Alexander, *The New Jim Crow: Mass Incarceration in an Age of Colorblindness* (New York: The New Press, 2010), 52.

40. Ibid., 49.

41. David Dinkins campaigned for more police and more social programs, whereas Mayor Edward I. Koch campaigned solely on more police protection without social programs to combat drugs and crime. David Dinkins won the New York City mayoral election and was sworn in January 2, 1990. Celestine Bohlen, "Campaign Matters; Is 'Liberal' A Dirty Word In New York?" *New York Times*, August 21, 1989; http://www.nytimes.com/1989/.

42. Michael Isikoff, "Drug Buy Set Up for Bush Speech," *Washington Post*, September 22, 1989, http://www.washingtonpost.com/wp-srv/.

43. Ibid.

44. Recent research also indicates that from 1994 to 2008 the probability that a district attorney would file a felony charge against an individual increased from one in three to two in three. John F. Pfaff, "The Micro and Macro Causes of Prison Growth," *Georgia State University Law Review* 28, 4 (Summer 2012): 1237–71.

45. Jo Mannies, "Bond-Nixon Contest Is Hijacked by Crime Rivals for U.S. Senate Seat Argue Over Who Is Tougher Other Issues Get Pushed Aside," *St. Louis Post-Dispatch*, October 18, 1998.

46. Ibid.

47. "The Budget Message of the President," 1966, https://www.gpo.gov /fdsys/pkg/BUDGET-1996-BUD/pdf/BUDGET-1996-BUD.pdf.

48. Department of Justice Appropriations Act, 1996, PL 104–134, as stated in section 114.

49. *Overhauling the Nation's Prisons: Hearing on the Violent Crime Control and Law Enforcement Act of 1994 Before the S. Comm. on the Judiciary*, 104th Cong. (1995) (statement of Timothy P. Cole).

50. Ibid.

51. Ibid.

52. "Crime Bill Boosts Already Healthy Private Prisons," *Bloomberg News*, August 29, 1994, http://articles.baltimoresun.com/1994-08-29/.

53. Ibid.

54. William J. Sabol, Katherine Rosich, Kamala M. Kan, David P. Kirk, and Glenn Dubin, "The Influences of Truth-in-Sentencing Reforms on Changes in States' Sentencing Practices and Prison Populations," Urban Institute, Justice Policy Center, April 2002, 6, http://www.urban.org/sites/

55. Ibid., 11, table 1.5. In 1995, Donna Lyons and Adelia Yee found that five state legislatures addressed privatization of prisons: Connecticut passed enabling legislation authorizing the commissioner of corrections to improve the operation of the state's correctional facilities by entering into contracts with government or private vendors for prison management; Oregon authorized contracts with public or private entities for correctional facilities; New Mexico legislation provided for expanding use of private contracts for correctional

facilities; and Florida similarly provided for expanding private correctional contracts for bed space. Arizona passed a law clarifying requirements for private prison contracts, which includes addressing liability and responsibilities. Donna Lyons and Adelia Yee, "Crime and Sentencing State Enactments 1995," *NCSL State Legislative Report* 20, 16 (November 1995), https://www.ncjrs.gov/pdffiles1/Digitization/161460NCJRS.pdf.

56. Abner Mikva, "Fifth-Eighth Cleveland-Marshall Fund Lecture: 'The Treadmill of Criminal Justice Reform.' " *Cleveland State Law Review* 43, 5 (1995): 5–11.

57. Greg Krikorian, "Federal and State Prison Populations Soared Under Clinton, Report Finds," *Los Angeles Times*, February 19, 2001, http://articles.latimes.com/2001/feb/19/news/mn-27373.

58. Ibid.

59. U.S. Department of Justice, "Prison Construction Keeping Pace With Population Growth," Bureau of Justice Statistics, August 7, 1997, https://www.bjs.gov/content/pub/press/CSFCF95.PR.

60. Ibid.

61. Suzanne M, Kirchhoff, "Economic Impacts of Prison Growth," Congressional Research Service, April 13, 2010, 15, https://fas.org/sgp/crs/misc/R41177.pdf.

62. Correctional costs amount to $80 billion. Tracey Kyckelhahn and Tara Martin, "Justice Expenditure and Employment Extracts, 2010—Preliminary," Bureau of Justice Statistics, www.bjs.gov/index.cfm?ty=pbdetail&iid=4679. The Brennan Center estimates the $260.5 billion number by adding the estimated judicial and legal costs ($56.1 billion), police protection costs ($124.2 billion), and corrections costs ($80 billion).

63. Data between 1850 and 1870 on the number of people in prison are not as accurate as the statistics collected starting in the 1920s. BJS notes that this was a period in which many states were establishing state prisons and reformatories. It may be that part of the large growth between the 1850 rate of 29 per 100,000 and the 1880 rate of 61 per 100,000 is due to growth of the system rather than lack of inclusiveness.

64. Lauren-Brooke Eisen and Inimai Chettiar, "The Reverse Mass Incarceration Act," Brennan Center for Justice, October 12, 2015, 10, https://www.brennancenter.org/publication/reverse-mass-incarceration-act.

65. From 2011 to 2014 the prison population fell by 53,9623 prisoners, and during the same period California's prison population fell by 35,187 prisoners. By dividing California's drop by the total drop, one can see that California accounts for 65 percent of the fall in prisoners. Bureau of Justice Statistics, Corrections Statistics Analysis Tool (CSAT)—Prisoners, "Prisoners Under the Jurisdiction of State or Federal Correctional Authorities," December 31, 1978–2014, http://www.bjs.gov/index.cfm?ty=nps.

66. Danielle Kaeble and Lauren Glaze, *Correctional Populations in the United States*, 2015, Bureau of Justice Statistics, 2016, 12. (2,145,000 people are behind bars in jails, state prisons, and federal prisons).

67. Gary Fields and John R. Emshwiller, "As Arrest Records Rise, Americans Find Consequences Can Last a Lifetime," *Wall Street Journal*, August 18, 2014, https://www.wsj.com/articles/.

68. "In U.S., Concern About Crime Climbs to 15-Year High," Gallup Poll, March 2–6, 2016, http://www.gallup.com/poll/190475/americans-concern -crime-climbs-year-high.aspx.

69. Jeremy Travis, Bruce Western, and Steve Redburn, eds., *The Growth of Incarceration in the United States: Exploring Causes and Consequences* (Washington, DC: The National Academies Press, 2014).

70. Administrators of adult correctional facilities reported 8,763 allegations of sexual victimization in 2011, a statistically significant increase over the 8,404 allegations reported in 2010 and 7,855 in 2009. U.S. Department of Justice, Office of Justice Programs, Bureau of Justice Statistics, "PREA Data Collection Activities," June 2015, https://www.bjs.gov/content/pub/pdf /pdca15.pdf.

71. Michael Mitchell and Michael Leachman, "Changing Priorities: State Criminal Justice Reforms and Investments in Education," Center on Budget and Policy Priorities, October 28, 2014, http://www.cbpp.org/sites/default /files/atoms/files/10-28-14sfp.pdf.

72. Herman B. Leonard, "Private Time: The Political Economy of Private Prison Finance," in *Private Prisons and the Public Interest*, ed. Douglas McDonald (New Brunswick, N.J.: Rutgers University Press, 1990), 78.

73. Cited in "The Downside of Private Prisons," *The Nation*, June 15, 1985.

74. E. Ann Carson and Elizabeth Anderson, "Prisoners in 2015," Bureau of Justice Statistics, December 2016, https://www.bjs.gov/content/pub/pdf /p15.pdf.

75. James J. Sephan, "Census of State and Federal Correctional Facilities, 2005," Bureau of Justice Statistics, October 2008, http://www.bjs.gov/content /pub/pdf/csfcf05.pdf.

76. Private prisons are illegal in Oregon, and legislation also prohibits the Oregon Department of Corrections from sending prisoners to out-of-state private prisons. When Oregon passed the bill in 2003, it had a clause that automatically repealed it in 2009. That date has repeatedly been extended. The original law is located in Oregon Laws 2003, Chapter 422. It was slightly tweaked and extended to January 2014 (Oregon Laws 2009. Chapter 611). It was extended again to January 2018 (Oregon Laws 2013, Chapter 7). North Dakota also has similar legislation. North Dakota HB 1350, 2001. N.D. CENT. CODE ANN. §12-47-37 (2001).

77. Carson and Anderson, "Prisoners in 2015."

78. E. Ann Carson et al., "Prisoners Series,1999–2015." Bureau of Justice Statistics, https://www.bjs.gov/content/pub/pdf/p15.pdf.

79. Carson, "Prisoners in 2014."

80. GEO Group's U.S. corrections and detention division oversees the operation and management of approximately 75,000 beds in sixty-four correctional and detention facilities. GEO Group, "Management and Operations," https://www.geogroup.com/Management_and_Operations; CCA houses nearly 70,000 inmates in more than seventy facilities, the majority of which are company-owned, with a total bed capacity of more than 80,000. Their 2015 annual report noted that they own or manage seventy-seven facilities. CCC, "Who We Are," http://www.cca.com/who-we-are; MTC safely secures more than 25,000 offenders in eight states at twenty-four facilities. MTC, "Corrections Overview," http://www.mtctrains.com/corrections/corrections -overview; Emerald Companies list seven private detention centers. Emerald Companies, "Locations," http://emeraldcm.com/ecm/locations/; LaSalle currently manages eighteen facilities with a total inmate capacity of over 13,000 and leases one facility to a law enforcement agency. LaSalle Corrections, "About Us," http://www.lasallecorrections.com/about-us/.

81. The GEO Group, Inc, Annual Reports (2006–2016), http://investors .geogroup.com/News#subcollapse300. Corrections Corporation of America, Annual Reports (2006–2016), http://www.cca.com/investors/financial -information/annual-reports.

82. Ibid.

83. Snap, Inc,." NASDAQ | SEC Filing. Snapchat stated revenue was at $404 million. http://secfilings.nasdaq.com/filingFrameset.asp?FilingID=11 863680&RcvdDate=2%2F16%2F2017&CoName=SNAP INC&FormType=S -1%2FA&View=html. Airbnb revenue was at around $1.7 billion. "Airbnb Expects $2.8B in 2017 Revenue, $8.5B by 2020," *PitchBook News*, https://pitchbook .com/news/articles/airbnb-expects-28b-in-2017-revenue-85b-by-2020. Pandora revenue was stated at $1.38 billion. "Pandora's Annual Revenue by Source 2016 | Statistic," *Statista*, https://www.statista.com/statistics/190918 /revenue-sources-of-pandora-since-2007/. Dallas Cowboys' revenue was stated at $700 million. Mike Ozanian, "Dallas Cowboys," *Forbes*, https://www.forbes .com/pictures/mlm45geihk/1-dallas-cowboys/#334f12133d55.

84. Carson and Anderson, "Prisoners in 2015."

85. *Report of the Subcommittee on Privatized Immigration Detention Facilities*, Homeland Security Advisory Council, 2016, 6; https://www.dhs .gov/sites/default/files/publications/DHS%20HSAC%20PIDF%20Final%20 Report.pdf.

86. Bethany Carson and Eleana Diaz, "Payoff: How Congress Ensures Private Prison Profit With an Immigrant Detention Quota." Grassroots Leadership.org, April 2015. http://grassrootsleadership.org/reports/payoff

-how-congress-ensures-private-prison-profit-immigrant-detention-quota#1
-keyfindings

87. CoreCivic 2016 Annual Report at p. 33, available at https://www.sec
.gov/Archives/edgar/data/1070985/000119312517053982/d310578d10k.htm.

88. J. Travis, B. Western, and S. Redburn, ed., *The Growth of Incarceration
in the United States: Exploring Causes and Consequences* (Washington, DC:
National Academies Press, 2014).

89. Jeremy Travis, interview by Lauren-Brooke Eisen, November 13, 2015.

90. Carl Takei, "The Wal-Mart Model: Not Just for Retail, Now It's for Private
Prisons Too!", *Speak Freely* (ACLU blog), September 29, 2014, https://www
.aclu.org/blog/wal-mart-model-not-just-retail-now-its-private-prisons-too.

91. Michael Jacobson, interview by Lauren-Brooke Eisen, December 9,
2015.

2. How the Government Privatized

1. Eugene Linden, "Entrepreneurs Can Do Everything Government Can
Do, Only Better," *Inc.*, December 1, 1984, http://www.inc.com/magazine
/19841201/1060.html.

2. Bruce Benson, *The Enterprise of Law: Justice Without State* (Oakland,
Calif.: Independent Institute, 2011), 179.

3. Theodore J. Gage, "Getting Street-Wise in St. Louis," *Reason*, August
1981, 18, https://www.unz.org/Pub/Reason-1981aug-00018?View=PDF.

4. Ibid.

5. Ibid.

6. Benson, *The Enterprise of Law*, 210.

7. Gage, "Getting Street-Wise in St. Louis," 23.

8. The cooperative behavior among homeowners with similar values and
the financial ability to maintain their homes and neighborhoods reduced
crime. The study also found that the privatization of streets deterred crimes
against people and opportunity for crimes such as assault and auto theft.
Oscar Newman, *Community of Interest* (Garden City N.Y.: Anchor Press,
1980), 137, 140.

9. Benson, *The Enterprise of Law*, 201; Charles T. Clotfelter, "Public
Services, Private Substitutes, and the Demand for Protection Against Crime,"
American Economic Review 67 (December 1977): 868.

10. James S. Kakalik and Sorrel Wildhorn, *Private Police in the United States:
Findings and Recommendations* (Santa Monica, Calif.: Rand Corporation,
1971), 1.

11. J. Peter Grace ran his family's $5 billion specialty chemicals and
health care company, which was founded in Peru in 1854 by his grandfather,

William R. Grace, as a shipping and trading company. Kenneth Gilpin, "J. Peter Grace, Ex-Company Chief, Dies at 81," *New York Times*, April 21, 1995.

12. The commission was a public body created by executive order under the Federal Advisory Committee Act of 1972. The Grace Commission included Roger E. Birk, president of Merrill Lynch & Company; James L. Ferguson, chairman of the General Foods Corporation; William M. Agee, chairman of the Bendix Corporation; Willard C. Butcher, chairman of the Chase Manhattan Bank; Coy G. Ecklund, chairman of the Equitable Life Assurance Society of the United States; and Donald E. Procknow, president of the Western Electric Company. David Burnham, "Questions Rising over U.S. Study and Role of Company Executives," *New York Times*, September 28, 1982.

13. PR Newswire, "J. Peter Grace Outlines Nation's Economic Crisis in Speech to Cleveland Sales and Marketing Executives," May 23, 1983.

14. Gilpin, "J. Peter Grace, Ex-Company Chief, Dies at 81."

15. Caroline Rand Herron and Michael Wright, "Nuclear Plant Gets A Flat 'No,' " *New York Times*, Jan 15, 1984.

16. Donna Selman and Paul Leighton, *Punishment for Sale: Private Prisons, Big Business, and the Incarceration Binge* (Lanham, Md.: Rowman & Littlefield, 2010), 54.

17. Ronald Reagan: "Statement on the President's Commission on Privatization," September 3, 1987, compiled by John T. Woolley and Gerhard Peters, The American Presidency Project, http://www.presidency.usb.edu/.

18. Report of the President's Commission on Privatization , March 1998, 79, http://pdf.usaid.gov/pdf_docs/PNABB472.pdf.

19. Ibid., 146.

20. Ibid.

21. Ibid.

22. Ibid., 152.

23. James Sterngold, "85 percent U.S. Stake in Conrail Sold for $1.6 Billion," *New York Times*, March 27, 1987.

24. Robert Poole, "Ronald Reagan and the Privatization Revolution." June 8, 2004, Reason Foundation, http://reason.org/news/.

25. Ibid.

26. Bill Wolpin, "Special Report: 2011 Privatization Survey," *American City & County*, June 1, 2011, http://americancityandcounty.com/administration/finance/government-privatization-survey-201106.

27. Robert Jay Dilger et al., "Privatization of Municipal Services in America's Largest Cities," *Public Administration Review* 57 (January–February 1997), 21, 22.

28. Jonathan Levin and Steven Tadelis, "Contracting for Government Services: Theory and Evidence from U.S. Cities," *Journal of Industrial Economics* 58 (2008): 507, 511.

29. Joe Kent, "The Town That Privatized Everything," International Society for Individual Liberty, June 18, 2014, https://joekent.liberty.me /the-town-that-privatized-everything/.

30. Waste Business Journal, *Waste Market Overview & Outlook 2012* (Third Edition); http://www.wastebusinessjournal.com/overview.htm

31. California Research Bureau and Julia Lave Johnston, "Can You Save Money and Still Save Lives? The Debate over Fire Department Privatization," *California Agencies* 286 (2001): 16, http://digitalcommons.law.ggu.edu /caldocs_agencies/286.

32. Benson, "The Enterprise of Law," 179(citing Robert W. Poole, Jr., *Cutting Back on City Hall* [New York: Universe Books, 1978], 27).

33. Roger Fairfax, "Outsourcing Criminal Prosecution?: The Limits of Criminal Justice Privatization," *University of Chicago Legal Forum* (2010): 265, 281.

34. Roger A. Fairfax Jr. "Delegation of the Criminal Prosecution Function to Private Actors," *UC Davis Law Review* 43 (2010): 411, 415.

35. Keith Fogg, "IRS Makes Novel Use of Outside Contractors—To Audit Microsoft," *Forbes*, November 24, 2014, https://www.forbes.com /sites/.

36. Benson, "The Enterprise of Law," 2.

37. Ibid., 223; Sara Terry, "Rent-a-Judge: A Fast Way to 'Day in Court,'" *Christian Science Monitor*, February 9, 1982, http://www.csmonitor.com /1982/0209/020935.html.

38. Benson, "The Enterprise of Law," 223.

39. Ibid.

40. Anne S. Kim, "Rent-a-Judges and the Cost of Selling Justice," *Duke Law Journal* 44 (1994): 166, 189.

41. Mikhael Weitzel, "History of Army Contracting," U.S. Army, April 4, 2011, http://www.army.mil/article/54337/History_of_Army_Contracting/. For statistics of use, see "Contingency Contracting Throughout U.S. History," Defense Procurement and Acquisition Policy, http://www.acq.osd.mil/dpap /pacc/cc/history.html.

42. Jeremy Scahill, "Bush's Shadow Army," *The Nation*, March 15, 2007.

43. David Isenberg, "Contractors in War Zones: Not Exactly 'Contracting'," *Time*, October 9, 2012, http://nation.time.com/2012/10/09/contractors -in-war-zones-not-exactly-contracting/.

44. David Isenberg, "Contractors in War Zones: Not Exactly 'Contracting'," *Time*, October 9, 2012, http://nation.time.com/2012/10/09/contractors -in-war-zones-not-exactly-contracting/.

45. John W. Whitehead, "Privatizing the War on Terror: America's Military Contractors," *Huffington Post*, January 17, 2012, http://www.huffingtonpost .com/john-w-whitehead/.

46. Department of Defense, "Contractor Support of U.S. Operations in the U.S. CENTCOM Area of Responsibility," 1, http://www.acq.osd.mil /log/PS/.CENTCOM_reports.html/5A_January_2017_Final.pdf.

47. "Lockheed Martin Annual Report 2015," 3, 11, http://www.lockheed martin.com/content/dam/lockheed/data/corporate/documents/2015 -Annual-Report.pdf.

48. Jeremy Wilson, "America's Private Sector Army," *This Week*, February 7, 2014, http://theweek.com/articles/451720/americas-private-sector-army.

49. Matt Apuzo, "Ex-Blackwater Guards Given Long Terms for Killing Iraqis," *New York Times*, April 13, 2015.

50. Even Kuross, "The Rise of Private Military Companies," *Fair Observer*, August 13, 2014, http://www.fairobserver.com/region/north_america/.

51. Brian Forst, "The Privatization and Civilianization of Policing," in *Criminal Justice 2000, Vol. 2, Boundary Changes in Criminal Justice Organizations* (Washington, D.C.: National Institute of Justice, 2000) 19, 26.

52. Truett A. Ricks, Bill G. Tillett, and Clifford W. Van Meter, *Principles of Security* (Cincinnati: Anderson, 1981), 5.

53. Forst, "The Privatization and Civilianization of Policing," 19, 27.

54. Ibid., 27.

55. Ibid., 19, 26.

56. Ibid., 19, 28.

57. Beverly A. Smith and Frank T. Morn, "The History of Privatization in Criminal Justice," in *Privatization in Criminal Justice: Past, Present, and Future*, ed. David Schichor and Michael J. Gilbert (London: Routledge, 2001), 6–20.

58. David Amsden, "Who Runs the Streets of New Orleans?", *New York Times*, July 20, 2015.

59. Nicolas Elliot, "The Growth of Privatized Policing," Foundation for Economic Education, February 1, 1991, https://fee.org/articles/the-growth -of-privatized-policing/.

60. In the Public Interest, "How Privatization Increases Inequality," September 2016, 5, https://www.inthepublicinterest.org/wp-content/uploads /InthePublicInterest_InequalityReport_Sept2016.pdf.

61. Ashley Parker and Philip Rucker, "Trump Taps Kushner to Lead a SWAT Team to Fix Government with Business Ideas," *Washington Post*, March 26, 2017.

3. Prisoners as Commodities

1. Ian Fisher, "Bartering Inmate Futures," *The Nation*, October 29, 1995.

2. "Changing Faces, Common Walls: History of Corrections in Kentucky," 17th ed., National Criminal Justice Reference Service, 1988, https://www .ncjrs.gov/pdffiles1/Digitization/113548NCJRS.pdf.

3. An Act Further to Regulate the Penitentiary, 1825 Ky. Acts, chap. 115, § 12 (passed during first session of the legislature on January 10, 1825); Stephen Mihm, "America's Rocky Relationship with For-Profit Prisons," *Bloomberg*, August 26, 2016, https://www.bloomberg.com/view/; William C. Sneed, M.D., *A Report on the History and Mode of Management of the Kentucky Penitentiary, From Its Origin, in 1798, to March 1, 1860* (Frankfort: Senate of Kentucky, 1860), 164.

4. An Act Further to Regulate the Penitentiary, 1825 Ky. Acts chap. 115, § 6.

5. "Changing Faces, Common Walls," 4.

6. Michael A. Hallett, *Private Prisons in America: A Critical Race Perspective* (Chicago: University of Illinois Press, 2006), 2.

7. David M. Oshinsky, *"Worse Than Slavery": Parchman Farm and the Ordeal of Jim Crow Justice* (New York: Free Press Paperbacks, 1996), 40.

8. Hallett, *Private Prisons in America*, 2.

9. Alex Lichtenstein, *Twice the Work of Free Labour: The Political Economy of Convict Labour in the New South* (London: Verso Press, 1996), 41–42.

10. Robert Zieger, *For Jobs and Freedom: Race and Labor in America Since 1965* (Lexington: University Press of Kentucky, 2007).

11. David Shichor, *Punishment for Profit* (Thousand Oaks, Calif.: Sage, 1995), 36.

12. Zieger, *For Jobs and Freedom*, 47.

13. Donna Selman and Paul Leighton, *Punishment for Sale* (New York: Rowman & Littlefield, 2010), 9.

14. Statement of the American Federation of State, County and Municipal Employees on the Privatization of Corrections Before the Subcommittee on Courts, Civil Liberties and the Administration of Justice of the Judiciary Committee of the U.S. House of Representatives, November 13, 1985.

15. The James family would be in charge of the Louisiana corrections system for the next thirty-one years. "History of Angola Prison," http://www.angolamuseum.org/history/history/#sthash.wFRe6PJ4.dpuf.

16. Shichor, *Punishment for Profit*, 40.

17. The ship was named the Waban, and it arrived near San Quentin on July 14, 1852, with forty to fifty convicts. "Unlocking History: Explore San Quentin, the State's Oldest Prison," *Inside CDCR*, 3.

18. Shichor, *Punishment for Profit*, 40.

19. Mihm, "America's Rocky Relationship with For-Profit Prisons."

20. "Unlocking History," 3.

21. Ibid.

22. Sharon Dolovich, "State Punishment and Private Prisons," *Duke Law Journal* 55, 3 (December 2005); 439.

23. Ashley Nellis, "The Color of Justice: Racial and Ethnic Disparity in State Prisons," The Sentencing Project, June 14, 2016, 3, file:///C:/Users

/eisenl/Downloads/The-Color-of-Justice-Racial-and-Ethnic-Disparity-in
-State-Prisons.pdf.

24. The Hawes-Cooper Act (H.R. 7729) was passed on January 19, 1929.

25. The Ashurst–Sumners Act, P. L. No. 74–215, 49 Stat. 494 (1935); see
Jennifer Rae Taylor, "Constitutionally Unprotected: Prison Slavery, Felon
Disenfranchisement, and the Criminal Exception to Citizenship Rights,"
Gonzaga Law Review 47 (2012): 365, 381.

26. Morgan O. Reynolds, "Factories Behind Bars," National Center for
Policy Analysis, September 1996; http://www.ncpa.org/pub/st206?pg=3; see
Taylor, "Constitutionally Unprotected," 365, 381.

27. Charles Fields, "Hawes-Cooper Act 1929," in *Encyclopedia of Prisons and
Correctional Facilities,* ed. Mary Bosworth (London: Sage, 2005), 395–398.

28. James Austin and Garry Coventry, "Emerging Issues on Privatized
Prisons," National Council on Crime & Delinquency, February 2001, https://
www.ncjrs.gov/pdffiles1/bja/181249.pdf.

29. Bureau of Justice Statistics, *Children in Custody, 1982/83 Census of
U.S. Juvenile Detention and Correctional Facilities* (Washington, D.C.: U.S.
Department of Justice, September 1986).

30. *Brown v. Plata,* 131 S. Ct. 1910, 1923 (2011).

31. Paul Taylor, "Should Private Firms Build, Run, Prisons? States, Short
of Funds, Consider Innovative—but Controversial—Examples," *Washington
Post,* May 7, 1985.

32. *Ruiz v. Estelle,* 503 F. Supp. 1265, 1277 (S.D. Tex. 1980).

33. Selman and Leighton, *Punishment for Sale;* see also Michael Hirsley,
"Tennessee Tempted by Prison Plan," *Chicago Tribune,* November 17, 1985.

34. Bureau of Justice Statistics, *Jail Inmates 1986* (Washington, D.C.:
Department of Justice, 1987), 3, table 9.

35. Howard Kurtz, "Michigan Will Release 500 from Overcrowded Prisons;
14,000 U.S. Inmates Have Had Sentences Cut Short Since 1980," *Washington
Post,* September 17, 1983.

36. Bureau of Justice Statistics, *Prisoners in 1986* (Washington D.C.:
Department of Justice), 5.

37. Selman and Leighton, *Punishment for Sale,* 43.

38. Bureau of Justice Statistics, *Prisoners in 1983* (Washington D.C.:
Department of Justice), http://www.bjs.gov/content/pub/pdf/p83.pdf.

39. Dolovich, "State Punishment and Private Prisons," 456.

40. Austin and Coventry, "Emerging Issues on Privatized Prisons."

41. David J. DelFiandra, "The Growth of Prison Privatization and the
Threat Posed by 442 U.S.C. § 1983," *Duquesne Law Review* 38 (2000): 594.

42. Martin Tolchin, "Companies Easing Crowded Prisons," *New York
Times,* February 17, 1985.

43. Ibid.

44. Ibid.

45. Aric Press, "The Good, the Bad, and the Ugly: Private Prisons in the 1980s," in Douglas McDonald, *Private Prisons and the Public Interest* (New Brunswick, N.J.: Rutgers University Press, 1990), 22.

46. Ibid.

47. Peter Kihss, "New York Group Opposing Bond Issues for Prisons," *New York Times*, June 28, 1981.

48. "State Board Certifies Defeat of Bond Issue for Building Prisons," *New York Times*, December 13, 1981.

49. "The Downsides of Private Prisons," *The Nation*, June 15, 1985.

50. The bill would have required the attorney general to establish a correctional facility in Alaska for federal prisoners ineligible for parole. It did not pass and was never enacted. H.R. 7112 (97th): Arctic Penitentiary Act of 1982, https://www.govtrack.us/congress/bills/97/hr7112.

51. "The Downside of Private Prisons."

52. "Ibid.

53. Mary Bosworth, "Encyclopedia of Prisons and Correctional Facilities," Sage Knowledge, 2005, http://www.sage-ereference.com/view/prisons/n76.xml?hidePageNum&print.

54. "Company Organized to Manage Jails," United Press International, May 29, 1983.

55. Selman and Leighton, *Punishment for Sale*, 59.

56. "Disaster of the Day: HCA," *Forbes*, December 15, 2000.

57. DelFiandra, "Comment: The Growth of Prison Privatization," 591; "Disaster of the Day: HCA."

58. Tali Arbel and Tom Murphy, "HCA raises $3.79 billion in 3rd IPO," Associated Press, March 9, 2011.

59. Austin and Coventry, "Emerging Issues on Privatized Prisons," 16.

60. Megan Mumford, Diane Whitmore Schanzenbach, and Ryan Nunn, "The Economics of Private Prisons," October 20, 2016, http://www.hamiltonproject.org/papers/the_economics_of_private_prisons.

61. Martin Tolchin, "Privately Operated Prison in Tennessee Reports $200,000 in Cost Overruns," *New York Times*, May 21, 1985.

62. CCA charged the county $21 a day for each prisoner except for a $12-a-day fee for a handful of county inmates who were serving weekend sentences of forty-eight hours for driving while intoxicated.

63. "Crime Pays," *60 Minutes* (transcript), 17, 11 (November 25, 1984): 8.

64. Ibid., 12.

65. Michael Hirsley, "Tennessee Tempted by Prison Plan," *Chicago Tribune*, November 17, 1985.

66. "Convict Slain in Tennessee Prison Riots over New Uniforms," *San Diego Union-Tribune*, July 3, 1985.

67. Peggy McGarry, interview by Lauren-Brooke Eisen, December 15, 2015,

68. Michael Hirsley, "Tennessee Tempted by Prison Plan," *Chicago Tribune*, November 17, 1985.

69. "Prison Offer," *Orlando Sentinel*, September 15, 1985.

70. Hirsley, "Tennessee Tempted by Prison Plan."

71. Bill Rawlins, "Company Offers $100 Million to Operate Tennessee Prisons," Associated Press, September 13, 1985.

72. Hirsley, "Tennessee Tempted by Prison Plan."

73. David A. Vise, "Private Company Asks for Control of Tenn. Prisons; 99-Year Contract Bid Gets Mixed Reception," *Washington Post*, September 22, 1985.

74. 1986 Tenn. Pub. Acts chap. 932, at 1208.

75. When the offer to take over the state's prisons were made, Tennessee was hosting a conference on private prisons. The *New York Times* article notes that "news of the offer became a chief topic of conversation at the conference on private prisons being held here by the National Association of Criminal Justice Planners." Martin Tolchin, "Company Offers to Run Tennessee's Prisons," *New York Times*, September 13, 1985.

76. Selman and Leighton, *Punishment for Sale*, 62.

77. McDonald, *Private Prisons and the Public Interest*, 1.

78. "Crime Pays," 8.

79. Martin Tolchin, "As Privately Owned Prisons Increase, So Do Their Critics," *New York Times*, February 11, 1985.

80. Statement of Ira P. Robbins, Barnard T. Welsh Scholar and Professor of Law and Justice, The American University Washington College of Law, House Judiciary Subcommittee on Courts, Civil Liberties and the Administration of Justice Concerning the Privatization of Prisons and Jails, November 13, 1985.

81. Statement of Edward I. Koren, staff attorney with the ACLU's National Prison Project, House Judiciary Subcommittee on Courts, Civil Liberties and the Administration of Justice Concerning the Privatization of Prisons and Jails, November 13, 1985.

82. Statement of Dave Kelly, President, Council of Prison Locals, American Federation of Government Employee, House Judiciary Subcommittee on Courts, Civil Liberties and the Administration of Justice Concerning the Privatization of Prisons and Jails, November 13, 1985.

83. Testimony of Richard Crane, Vice President of Legal Affairs for Corrections Corporation of America, House Judiciary Subcommittee on Courts, Civil Liberties and the Administration of Justice Concerning the Privatization of Prisons and Jails, November 6, 1985.

84. Discussion between Congressman Mazzoli and Richard Crane, House Judiciary Subcommittee on Courts, Civil Liberties and the Administration of Justice Concerning the Privatization of Prisons and Jails, November 6, 1985.

85. Statement of Ira P. Robbins, Barnard T. Welsh Scholar and Professor of Law and Justice, The American University Washington College of Law, House Judiciary Subcommittee on Courts, Civil Liberties and the Administration of Justice Concerning the Privatization of Prisons and Jails, November 13, 1985.

86. Robert William Kastenmeier, House Judiciary Subcommittee on Courts, Civil Liberties and the Administration of Justice Concerning the Privatization of Prisons and Jails, November 13, 1985.

87. Statement of Richard Crane, vice president of legal affairs, CCA, House Judiciary Subcommittee on Courts, Civil Liberties and the Administration of Justice Concerning the Privatization of Prisons and Jails, November 13, 1985.

88. "CCA Prospectus, 1986," filed October 1, 1986, 4.

89. Ibid., 13.

90. The daily rate includes a capital cost component for prisons CCA has constructed and includes insurance to indemnify the government against any claims by prisoners. Greg Earl, "Corporate Correction: From Corporate Fantasy to a Growth Industry," *Australian Financial Review*, October 19, 1988.

91. Norval Morris, "The Contemporary Prison: 1965-Present," in *The Oxford History of the Prison: The Practice of Punishment in Western Society*, ed. Norval Morris and David J. Rothman (Oxford: Oxford University Press, 1995), 228.

92. Philip Mattera, Mafruza Khan, and Stephen Nathan, "Corrections Corporation of America: A Critical Look at Its First Twenty Years," Grassroots Leadership, December 2003. The market share figure is from Charles W. Thomas, "Private Adult Correctional Facility Census," December 31, 1997, www.crim.ufl.edu/pcp. Thomas's absolute numbers are not entirely reliable because he measured capacity based on signed contracts rather than on actual occupied beds, but for relative measures such as market share his estimates are reasonably reliable.

93. James J. Stephan, "Census of State and Federal Correctional Facilities, 2005," Bureau of Justice Statistics, October 2008, https://www.bjs.gov/content/pub/pdf/csfcf05.pdf.

94. Richard A. Oppel Jr., "Private Prisons Found to Offer Little in Savings," *New York Times*, May 18, 2011.

95. Selman and Leighton, *Punishment for Sale*, 72.

4. The Prison Industrial Complex

1. Shane Bauer, "My Four Months as a Private Prison Guard," *Mother Jones*. July-August 2016.

2. Chad Rubel, "No Larger Captive Market Than This One," *Marketing News*, May 8, 1995.

3. Keely Herring, "Was a Prison Built Every 10 Days to House a Fast-Growing Population of Nonviolent Inmates?", *Politifact*, July 31, 2015, http://www.politifact.com/truth-o-meter/statements/2015/jul/31/cory-booker/was-prison-built-every-10-days-house-fast-growing-/.

4. "President Eisenhower's Farewell Address," January 17, 1961, http://www.pbs.org/wgbh/americanexperience/features/primary-resources/eisenhower-farewell/.

5. Joel Dyer, *The Perpetual Prisoner Machine: How America Profits from Crime* (Boulder, Colo.: Westview Press, 2000), 30.

6. Eric Schlosser, "The Prison-Industrial Complex," *Atlantic Monthly* 282, 6 (December 1998): 51–77. "The Prison Industrial Complex" is the title of a recorded 1997 speech by social activist Angela Davis. One could argue that she coined the phrase, although Schlosser's article is widely read and quoted today.

7. Peter Wagner and Bernadette Rabuy, "Following the Money of Mass Incarceration," Prison Policy Institute, January 25, 2017, https://www.prisonpolicy.org/reports/money.html.

8. Jail Bed Space.com, Homepage, 2017, http://www.jailbedspace.com/jbs/.

9. Rena Singer, "View and Space Lousy, but the Realty Sells 'Bed Brokers' Find Prisoners to Fill Empty Cells in Underpopulated Jails," *Philadelphia Inquirer*, September 7, 1997.

10. Ibid.

11. Tracy Kyckelhahn, "State Corrections Expenditures, FY 1982–2010," revised April 30, 2014, http://www.bjs.gov/content/pub/pdf/scefy8210.pdf.

12. Elizabeth Dickinson, "The Future of Incarceration," *Architect*, June 12, 2008, http://www.architectmagazine.com/design/buildings/the-future-of-incarceration_o.

13. DLR Group, "About," http://www.dlrgroup.com/about/.

14. Michael Sorkin, "Drawing the Line: Architects and Prisons: A Call for Architects to Refuse to Design Chambers of Living Death," *The Nation*, August 17, 2013.

15. CCA 2015 Annual Report, http://www.cca.com/investors/financial-information/annual-reports. TransCor generated total revenue of $4.1 million in 2015 and $4.4 million in 2014. The other five privatized transportation companies are PTS of America, U.S. Prisoner Transport Services, Black Talon Enterprises, GEO Transport (GEO Group), and In-Custody Transportation.

16. TransCor America, "About," https://www.transcor.com/about-transcor/transcor-history/.

17. Alex Friedmann, "For-Profit Transportation Companies: Taking Prisoners, and the Public, for a Ride," *Prison Legal News*, September 15, 2006, https://www.prisonlegalnews.org/news/.

18. *Robin Darbyshire v. Extraditions International, Inc.*, filed in U.S. District Court for the District of Colorado, Case No. 02-N-718; "Private Transport Company Settles Female Prisoner's Sexual Assault Suit," *Prison Legal News*, January 15, 2004, https://www.prisonlegalnews.org/news/2004/jan/15 /private-transport-company-settles-female-prisoners-sexual-assault-suit/; Chastity Pratt Dawsey, "State Sheds Little Light on Troubled Prison Transport Firm," *Bridge Magazine*, November 29, 2016; http://www.mlive.com/news /index.ssf/2016/11/state_sheds_little_light_on_tr.html.

19. Colin asked that his name be changed for this book.

20. Colin, interview by Lauren-Brooke Eisen, March 3, 2016.

21. Ibid.

22. Michael Mitchell and Michael Leachman, "Changing Priorities: State Criminal Justice Reforms and Investments in Education," Center for Budget and Policy Priorities, October 28, 2014, 8, http://www.cbpp.org/sites/default /files/atoms/files/10-28-14sfp.pdf.

23. Peter Wagner and Bernadette Rabuy, "Following the Money of Mass Incarceration," Prison Policy Institute, January 25, 2017, https://www.prisonpolicy .org/reports/money.html.

24. Schlosser, "The Prison-Industrial Complex."

25. Jack Smith IV, " 'Video Visitation' Is Ending In-Person Prison Visits— And Prisons Are Going to Make a Ton of Money," *Business Insider*, May 5, 2016, http://www.businessinsider.com/video-visitation-is-ending-in-person -prison-visits-2016-5. The Virginia Department of Corrections charges $30 per thirty-minute session, but JPay reports that a thirty-minute session in one North Dakota prison costs only $12.95, http://jpay.com/Facility-Details /North-Dakota-Department-of-Corrections/Missouri-River-Correctional -Center.aspx.

26. Elizabeth Cree, interview by Lauren-Brooke Eisen, March 2, 2016.

27. Tim Barker, "Prison Services Are Profitable Niche for Bridgeton Company," *St. Louis Post Dispatch*, February 15, 2015.

28. Jeremiah Bourgeois, "Prison Dilemma: When Profit Undermines Safety," The Crime Report, June 29, 2016, https://thecrimereport.org/2016/06/29 /prison-dilemma-when-profit-undermines-safety/.

29. Ariel Schwartz, "This Controversial Device Is Changing the Way Inmates Interact with the Outside World," Tech Insider, July 29, 2015, http:// www.techinsider.io/apple-of-prison-techs-real-story-2015-7.

30. Lauren Galik, Leonard Gilroy, and Alexander Volokh, "Annual Privatization Report 2014, Criminal Justice and Corrections," Reason Foundation, June 2014, 21, http://reason.org/files/apr-2014-criminal-justice .pdf.

31. Rupert Neate, "Welcome to Jail Inc: How Private Companies Make Money Off US Prisons," *The Guardian*, June 16, 2016.

32. Nadia Pflaum, "Should the Profit Motive Figure Into Prison Healthcare?", *Nonprofit Quarterly*, April 10, 2015, https://nonprofitquarterly.org/2015/04/10/should-the-profit-motive-figure-into-prison-healthcare/.

33. David Royse, "Medical Battle Behind Bars: Big Prison Healthcare Firm Corizon Struggles to Win Contracts," *Modern Health Care*, April 11, 2015, http://www.modernhealthcare.com/article/.

34. Phaedra Haywood, "Corizon Paid $4.5M to Settle Inmate Lawsuits," *New Mexican*, June 28, 2016.

35. Maura Ewing, "The Corizon CEO on Losing Its Contract With Rikers: 'You Win Some, You Lose Some'," The Marshall Project, June 16, 2015, https://www.themarshallproject.org/2015/06/16/ceo-of-private-medical-provider-corizon-on-losing-its-contract-with-rikers#.YLe2EIzYa.

36. Reggie Wilkinson, interview by Lauren-Brooke Eisen, February 9, 2016.

37. Greg Smith, "Rudy Giuliani's Law Firm Paid Big Money to Lobby for Prisons," *New York Daily News*, July 12, 2016.

38. Dyer, *The Perpetual Prisoner Machine*, 3.

39. United States Department of Labor, Bureau of Labor Statistics, "Employment and Wages," 2015, http://www.bls.gov/oes/current/oes333012.htm; and first line supervisors of correctional officers, http://www.bls.gov/oes/current/oes331011.htm.

40. Bureau of Labor Statistics, "Occupational Outlook Handbook, 2016–17 Edition, Correctional Officers and Bailiffs," http://www.bls.gov/ooh/protective-service/correctional-officers.htm.

41. E. Ann Carson et al., "Prisoners in 2015," Bureau of Justice Statistics, 2016, 16, https://www.bjs.gov/content/pub/pdf/p15.pdf.

42. Eric Schlosser, interview by Lauren-Brooke Eisen, August 10, 2016.

5. Private Prisons and the American Heartland

1. Bob Thompson, interview by Lauren-Brooke Eisen, December 17, 2015.

2. Ibid.

3. April Hattori, "Lack of Prisoners Brings Appleton, Minn., Facility Head-to-Head with Default," *Bond Buyer*, January 6, 1993.

4. Darrell K. Gillard, "Prisoners in 1992," Bureau of Justice Statistics Bulletin, May 1993, 1, https://www.bjs.gov/content/pub/pdf/p92.pdf.

5. Michael Jacobson, *How to Reduce Crime and End Mass Incarceration: Downsizing Prisons* (New York: New York University Press, 2005), 70.

6. Peter Kilborn, "Rural Towns Turn to Prisons to Reignite Their Economies," *New York Times*, August 1, 2001.

7. James J. Stephan, "State Prison Expenditures in 1996." Bureau of Justice Statistics, 1999, http://www.bjs.gov/content/pub/pdf/spe96.pdf.

8. National Association of State Budget Officers, *2000 State Expenditure Report* (Washington, D.C.: NASBO, 2001), 62.

9. Calvin Beale, "Cellular Rural Development: New Prisons in Rural and Small Town Areas in the 1990's." Paper presented at the annual meeting of the Rural Sociological Society, Albuquerque, New Mexico, August 18, 2001.

10. Tracy Huling, "Building a Prison Economy in Rural America," in *From Invisible Punishment: The Collateral Consequences of Mass Imprisonment*, ed. Marc Mauer and Meda Chesney-Lind (New York: The New Press, 2002), 7.

11. Rhonda Hillbery, "They Built It, but Inmates Didn't Come: Minnesota's Town's Private Prison, Built to Create Jobs, Has Attracted No 'Clients', " *New York Times*, February 23, 1993.

12. Bob Thompson, interview by Lauren-Brooke Eisen, December 17, 2015.

13. Ibid.

14. Don Terry, "Town Builds a Prison and Stores Its Hopes There," *New York Times*, January 3, 1993.

15. Interview with Lauren-Brooke Eisen, December 17, 2015.

16. Ibid.

17. The Associated Press, "Puerto Rican Prison Inmates Leave Minnesota," *Saint Paul Pioneer Press*, March 2, 1995.

18. Conrad deFiebre, "Big House on the Prairie Hits Big Time; Five Years Ago, the Appleton prison Was the Most Troubled Industry for Miles. But Now Home to More Than 550 Inmates, It Is Considered by Some to Be a Model of Public-Private Partnership," *Star Tribune*, January 5, 1997.

19. Alan Pendergast, "The Jail for Hire," Westword, Aug. 8, 1996, http://www.westword.com/news/this-jail-for-hire-5056553.

20. Ron Ronning, interview by Lauren-Brooke Eisen, December 17, 2015.

21. Bob Thompson, interview by Lauren-Brooke Eisen, December 17, 2015.

22. Judith A. Greene, "Lack of Correctional Services: The Adverse Effect on Human Rights," in *Capitalist Punishment: Prison Privatization and Human Rights*, ed. Andrew Coyle, Allison Campbell, and Rodney Neufeld (Chicago: University of Chicago Press, 2003), 59.

23. John Miller, "Idaho Inmates in Minnesota Likely Will Be Forced to Go Elsewhere," Associated Press, February 24, 2006.

24. Betsy Z. Russell, "Exporting Inmates Not Solving Problem, Costs Will Come to Almost $6 Million a Year," *The Spokesman-Review*, November 13, 2005.

25. Steven Donziger, "The Hard Cell," *New York Magazine* 30, 22 (June 9, 1997): 28.

26. Conrad deFiebre, "Big House on the Prairie Hits Big Time," *Star Tribune*, January 5, 1997.

27. Conrad deFiebre, "Prison in Appleton Is Now State's Largest," *Star Tribune*, October 11, 1997.

28. Ron Jackson, "Hinton: Seeing Dollar Signs Prison Profits Unlock Town's Fiscal Future," *The Oklahoman*, July 9, 2000.

29. "Warden to Take over Prison," Western Empire, *Denver Post*, August 9, 2000.

30. Dale Wetzel, "Closing of MN Prison Shouldn't Affect ND," Associated Press, December 26, 2009.

31. "Transfer Complete of Idaho Offenders From Minnesota to Texas," *U.S. State News*, June 1, 2006.

32. Tom Cherveny, "Prairie Correctional Plans to Lay Off 120," *West Central Tribune*, October 3, 2009.

33. Mark Steil, "Tough Economy Forces Shutdown of Appleton Prison." Minnesota Public Radio News, January 8, 2010, http://www.mprnews.org /story/2010/01/08/appleton-prison-closing.

34. Chris Havens and Kevin Giles, "State May Use Private Prison," *Star Tribune*, November 24, 2009.

35. Tom Cherveny, "Appleton Will Not Hold Alaska Inmates," *West Central Tribune*, August 11, 2009.

36. Kevin Giles, "Appleton Prison Won't Get Pennsylvania Inmates," *Star Tribune*, January 7, 2010; Peter Jackson, "Out of Prison Space, Pa. Looks to Other States," Associated Press, November 22, 2009.

37. Havens and Giles, "State May Use Private Prison."

38. Steil, "Tough Economy Forces Shutdown of Appleton Prison."

39. "CCA to Cease Operations at Prairie Correctional Facility," *Market News*, December 4, 2009.

40. Carolyn Lange, "Closed Appleton Prison Could Receive Federal Contract," *West Central Tribune*, September 9, 2010.

41. Carolyn Lange, "Swift Co. Reaches Tax Settlement with Prairie Correctional Facility," *West Central Tribune*, March 17, 2010.

42. Andy Mannix, "Appleton's Economic Future Hinges on Fight to Reopen Prison," *Star Tribune*, February 20, 2016.

43. Andy Mannix, "Town Has High Stakes in Prison Debate," *Star Tribune*, February 21, 2016.

44. Morris Falk, "Local Commentary—Closing of Prairie Correctional Facility May Be Temporary," *Morris Sun Tribune*, December 4, 2009.

45. CCA letter to states from CCO Harley Lappin, February 14, 2012, http://big.assets.huffingtonpost.com/ccaletter.pdf.

46. Ibid.

47. Michael Jacobson, *Downsizing Prisons: How to Reduce Crime and End Mass Incarceration* (New York: New York University Press, 2005), 66.

48. Marc Lifsher, "Busting Into the Prison Business—Corrections Corp. of America Casts Longing Eyes on California," *Wall Street Journal*, May 27, 1998.

49. Erin Sullivan, "Jail Sells," *Metroland*, May 14, 2000, http://www.alternet.org/story/9149/jail_sell.

50. Alexander T. Tabarrok, *Changing the Guard: Private Prisons and the Control of Crime* (Oakland, Calif.: Independent Institute Press, 2003), 78.

51. Leslie Berestein, "Private Prison Industry Experiences Boom," Copley News Service, May 11, 2008.

52. 2015 CCA Annual Report, Form 10-K, p. 20, https://materials.proxyvote.com/Approved/22025Y/20160314/10K_277713/#/1/.

53. GEO Group 2015 Annual Report, Form 10-K, p. 7, https://www.sec.gov/Archives/edgar/data/923796/000119312516478864/d43877d10k.htm.

54. Justin Elliott, "Behind Montana Jail Fiasco: How Private Prison Developers Prey on Desperate Towns," Talking Points Memo, October 12, 2009, http://talkingpointsmemo.com/muckraker/behind-montana-jail-fiasco-how-private-prison-developers-prey-on-desperate-towns.

55. "Who Benefits When a Private Prison Comes to Town?", NPR Staff, November 5, 2011.

56. Pat Dawson, "The Montana Town That Wanted to Be Gitmo," *Time*, May 3, 2009.

57. Alex Friedman, "Improbable Private Prison Scam Plays Out in Hardin, Montana," Prison Legal News, December 15, 2009, https://www.prisonlegalnews.org/news/2009/dec/15/improbable-private-prison-scam-plays-out-in-hardin-montana/.

58. Associated Press," Jail with Checkered Past Takes in Native American Inmates to Fill Empty Cells, *The Guardian*, October 9, 2014; Matt Hudson, "Hardin Jail Struggles to Overcome $40 Million in Debt," *The Independent Record*, December 13, 2015.

59. Matt Hudson, "Lacking Prisoners, Hardin Jail Closes Again," *Billings Gazette*, April 29, 2016.

60. Matt Hudson, "BIA Preparing Lease on Two Rivers Prison in Hardin," *Billings Gazette*, February 13, 2017.

61. Douglas Clement, "Big House on the Prairie," Federal Reserve Bank of Minneapolis, January 2002, https://www.minneapolisfed.org/publications/fedgazette/big-house-on-the-prairie.

62. John M. Eason, "Prisons as Panacea or Pariah? The Countervailing Consequences of the Prison Boom on the Political Economy of Rural Towns," *Social Science* 6, 1 (2017): 17.

63. Ibid.

64. Camille Camp and George Camp, *The Corrections Yearbook, 1998* (Middletown, Conn.: Criminal Justice Institute, 1998), 150, 401.

65. "Occupational Outlook Handbook, Correctional Officers and Bailiffs," Bureau of Labor Statistics, https://www.bls.gov/ooh/protective-service/correctional-officers.htm.

66. Michael Denhof and Caterina Spinaris, "Depression, PTSD, and Comorbidity in United States Corrections Professionals," Desert Waters Correctional Outreach, 2013, 8, http://desertwaters.com/wp-content/uploads /2013/09/Comorbidity_Study_09-03-131.pdf.

67. Huling, "Building a Prison Economy."

68. Susana Kim, "Whole Foods Suppliers Defend Using Prison Labor," ABC News, October 5, 2015, http://abcnews.go.com/Business/foods -suppliers-defend-prison-labor/story?id=34258597.

69. Beth Schartzapfel, "Modern-Day Slavery in America's Prison Workforce," American Prospect, May 28, 2014, http://prospect.org/article /great-american-chain-gang.

70. Graham Lee Brewer, "Board of Corrections Approves Private Prison Rental," *The Oklahoman*, May 5, 2016.

71. Ryan S. King, Marc Mauer, and Tracy Huling, "Big Prisons, Small Towns: Prison Economics in Rural America," Sentencing Project, February 2003, 4, http://www.sentencingproject.org/wp-content/uploads/2016/01 /Big-Prisons-Small-Towns-Prison-Economics-in-Rural-America.pdf.

72. Deborah M. Tootle, "The Role of Prisons in Rural Development: Do They Contribute to Local Economies?", April 2004, 11, http://realcostofprisons .org/materials/Prisons_as_Rural_Development.pdf.

73. There is a "wide diversity in types of living arrangements," including those of homeless individuals, college students, children in shared custody arrangements, and military personnel. Prop. 2020 Census Residence Criteria & Residence Situations § 15(a)-(d), 81 Fed. Reg. 42577 (June 30, 2016).

74. Erika L. Wood, "One Significant Step: How Reforms to Prison Districts Begin to Address Political Inequality," *University of Michigan Journal of Law Reform* 179 (2015): 49.

75. U.S. Census Bureau, "Frequently Asked Questions: How Are Census Data Used?", https://ask.census.gov/faq.php?id=5000&faqId=979.

76. Marie Gottschalk, *Caught: The Prison State and the Lockdown of American Politics* (Princeton, N.J.: Princeton University Press, 2015), 254–55.

77. Ibid., 256.

78. H.R. 3838—Fairness in Incarcerated Representation Act: All Actions: H.R. 3838—114th Congress (2015–2016), https://www.congress.gov/bill /114th-congress/house-bill/3838/all-actions. This bill was last visited July 15, 2016, and last updated October 27, 2015.

79. Prop. 2020 Census Residence Criteria & Residence Situations § 15(a)- (d), 81 Fed. Reg. 42578 (June 30, 2016). Letter from Justin Levitt, Professor of Law, Loyola Law School, to Karen Humes, Chief, Population Division, U.S. Census Bureau (2015), Subject: "Comment on Census Residence Rule and Residence Situations: People in Correctional Facilities."

80. Ibid.

81. See the Leadership Conference Letter, Sept 1, 2016, http://www
.civilrights.org/advocacy/letters/2016/comments-on.html. Recently, the
Leadership Conference on Civil and Human Rights—a coalition of more
than 200 national organizations, including the NAACP and the ACLU—
submitted a written comment advocating for the rule's change. It accused
the usual residence rule of ignoring "the transient and temporary nature of
incarceration" as well as the "overwhelming public comments in favor of an
updated policy." It suggested an inconsistency between the rule's incarcerated
approach and its approach to other transient living situations (such as overseas military personnel), emphasizing the applicability of the Supreme Court's
"enduring ties" holding in *Franklin v. Massachusetts*, 505 U.S. 788 (1992), as
well as the bureau's own proposed change to accommodate military personnel
("Changing one policy, but not the other, illuminates a glaring inconsistency
in the proposed 2020 Census Residence Rules that the Census Bureau has
not adequately explained."). Finally, the comment calls the rule "unacceptably
discriminatory" to the country's majority black and Latino inmates, whose
census-based absence would continue to dilute the voting power of minor-
ity communities, "render[ing] so many of their young men invisible" and
"perpetuat[ing] the distortion of democracy that results from padding the
population counts of communities with prisons."

82. Don Davis, "Minnesota Prisons Numbers Rising Fifth Fasted in Nation,
but Have Fourth Lowest Rates," *Grand Forks Herald*, September 25, 2015.

83. Andy Mannix, "Decades of New Laws Caused Minnesota's Prison
Population Spike," *Star Tribune*, February 7, 2016.

84. Ibid.

85. Lauren-Brooke Eisen and James Cullen, "Update: Changes in State
Imprisonment," Brennan Center for Justice at NYU School of Law, https://
www.brennancenter.org/sites/default/files/analysis/UpdateChangesin
StateImprisonment.pdf.

86. "CCA Extends Lease of the California City Correctional Center with
the California Department of Corrections and Rehabilitation," CCA press
release, June 13, 2016, https://globenewswire.com/news-release/2016/06/13
/848057/0/en/CCA-Extends-Lease-of-the-California-City-Correctional
-Center-with-the-California-Department-of-Corrections-and-Rehabilitation
.html.

87. Tad Vezner, "Minnesota's Move to Use Private Prison Space Draws
Opposition," *Twin Cities Pioneer Press*, March 22, 2016.

88. United States Census Bureau, "QuickFacts Minnesota," https://
www.census.gov/quickfacts/table/PST045215/27; Minnesota Department
of Corrections, "Adult Inmate Profile as of January 10, 2017," http://www
.doc.state.mn.us/pages/files/9914/8518/3869/Minnesota_Department_of
_Corrections_Adult_Inmate_Profile_2017_January.pdf.

89. ISAAIH, "Action to #StopCCA: Vigil to Say No to Private Prisons in Minnesota," https://www.facebook.com/events/995044937243645/, last visited June 19, 2016.

90. Chadwick Syltie, interview by Lauren-Brooke Eisen, December 18, 2015.

91. Ibid.

92. Vezner, "Minnesota's Move to Use Private Prison Space Draws Opposition."

93. "California's Prison-Guards' Union: Fading Are the Peacemakers," *The Economist*, February 25, 2010, http://www.economist.com/node/15580530.

94. Amanda Carey, "The Price of Prison Guard Unions," Capital Research Center, October 13, 2011, https://capitalresearch.org/article/the-price-of-prison-guard-unions-2/.

95. Ibid.

96. "California's Prison-Guards' Union."

97. Mike Riggs, "Public Sector Prison Unions Are Spending Almost as Much on Campaigns as Private Prison Companies," Reason Foundation blog, August 22, 2012, http://reason.com/blog/2012/08/22/what-does-it-mean-that-public-sector-pri.

98. Ed Krayewski, "Are For-Profit Prisons, or Public Unions, the Biggest Lobby No One's Talking About?", Reason Foundation blog, June 2, 2015, http://reason.com/blog/2015/06/02/are-for-profit-prisons-or-public-unions.

99. Robert B. Gunnison, "Sacramento—Privately Run Prison Planned for Mojave/Firm Says It Can House Inmates Cheaper," *San Francisco Chronicle*, August 1, 1997.

100. Monte Williams, "Down-and-Out Town Sees Survival in a Private Prison," *New York Times*, March 24, 1997.

101. Ibid.

102. Donziger, "The Hard Cell," 26.

103. Ibid.

104. Williams, "Down-and-Out Town Sees Survival in a Private Prison."

105. Thomas Kaplan, "Cuomo Administration Closing 7 Prisons, 2 in New York City," *New York Times*, June 30, 2011.

106. Sarah Foss, "Fight Looming Over Proposed State Prison Cuts," *Daily Gazette*, February 6, 2011.

107. David Howard King, "As Cuomo's Prison Closings Become Reality, Some Question the Specifics," *Gotham Gazette*, July 11, 2011.

108. Ken Steir, "NYS Prison Budget Climbs, Despite Fewer Inmates," City Limits, November 10, 2015, http://citylimits.org/2015/11/10/nys-prison-budget-climbs-despite-fewer-inmates/.

109. Brandi Grissom, "Prison Officials Seeking Ways to Recruit and Retain Guards," *New York Times*, November 13, 2014.

110. Alex Hannaford, "Prison Guard Union Calls on Texas to Curtail Solitary Confinement on Death Row," *Texas Observer*, January 28, 2014.

111. Casey Tolan, *The Largest Chapter of the Texas Prison Guard Union Supports Closing Private Prisons*, Fusion, Aug. 25, 2015, http://fusion.net /story/340579/texas-guard-union-close-private-prisons/.

112. Heather Ann Thompson, "Downsizing the Carceral State: The Policy Implications of Prison Guard Unions," *Criminology & Public Policy* 10, no. 3 (2011): 771.

113. Ibid., 775776.

114. Ron Latz, interview by Lauren-Brooke Eisen, December 18, 2015.

115. Herman "Dutch" Leonard, "Private Time: The Political Economy of Private Prison Finance," in *Private Prisons and the Public Interest*, ed. Douglas McDonald (New Brunswick, N.J.: Rutgers University Press, 1990), 8.

116. Ibid.

117. Ron Latz, interview by Lauren-Brooke Eisen, December 18, 2015.

118. Editorial Board, "The State Should Reopen Appleton as a State-Run Facility Before Considering More Brick-and-Mortar Projects to Expand Existing Prisons," *Star Tribune*, April 15, 2016.

119. Jennifer Brown, "Burlington Struggles After Closure of Its Largest Employer, Kit Carson Prison," *Denver Post*, February 27, 2017.

120. Ibid.

121. Corey Hutchins, "The Feds Are Shutting Down Private Prisons, but in Colorado It's Business as Usual," *Colorado Independent*, August 18, 2016.

122. Matt Tinoco, "Inside the Small California Town with a Lot of Prisons, but Not Much Opportunity," Vice News, https://www.vice.com/read /jailtown-usa-where-americas-prison-industrial-complex-calls-home-203.

123. Eric Schlosser, interview by Lauren-Brooke Eisen, August 10, 2016.

124. Martin Horn, interview by Lauren-Brooke Eisen, March 31, 2015, and follow-up e-mail October 5, 2016.

125. "House Approves Bill for Lease or Purchase of Appleton Prison," *Swift County Monitor-News*, April 14, 2017.

6. The Prison Divestment Movement

1. https://www.facebook.com/yalestudentsforprisondivestment/.

2. Ella Every, interview by Lauren-Brooke Eisen, February 5, 2016.

3. Miles E. Johnson, "Columbia Just Became the First U.S. University to Divest from Private Prisons." *Mother Jones*, July 1, 2015, http://www.motherjones.com /politics/2015/06/columbia-finally-stopped-giving-money-private-prisons.

4. "Top News: G4S 2016 Profit Soars as Revenue Rises; Maintains Dividend," *Morningstar*, March 8, 2017, http://www.morningstar.co.uk/uk

/news/AN_1488958726918640500/top-news-g4s-2016-profit-soars-as-revenue-rises%3B-maintains-dividend.aspx.

5. Ella Every, interview by Lauren-Brooke Eisen, February 5, 2016.

6. Dan Morain, "Divestment Forces Say Pressure Paid Off: South Africa: Advocates of Economic Sanctions Count Mandela's Visit a Victory," *Los Angeles Times*, July 1, 1990.

7. Richard Knight, "Sanctions, Disinvestment, and U.S. Corporations in South Africa," in *Sanctioning Apartheid*, ed. Robert E. Edgar (Trenton, N.J.: Africa World Press, 1990), 67–89.

8. Justin Miller, "Columbia University Was Invested in Incarceration—Until Students Stopped It," *American Prospect*, July 6, 2015, http://prospect.org/article/.

9. Ella Every, interview by Lauren-Brooke Eisen, February 5, 2016.

10. Finnegan Schick, "Students Demand Private Prison Divestment," *Yale Daily News*, March 8, 2016.

11. Joseph Gaylin, interview by Lauren-Brooke Eisen, December 21, 2015.

12. John G. Simon, Charles W. Powers, and Jon P. Gunnemann, *The Ethical Investor: Universities and Corporate Responsibility* (New Haven: Yale University Press, 1972).

13. Jason Song, "UC System Divests $30 Billion in Prison Holdings Amid Student Pressure," *Los Angeles Times*, December 26, 2015.

14. Lindsay Holcomb, interview by Lauren-Brooke Eisen, December 23, 2015.

15. Princeton Prison Divest movement, https://prisondivest.com/2017/01/27/princeton-moving-forward-with-prisondivest/.

16. John Lantigua, "Heated Questions, Muted Answers as FAU Defends Naming Stadium After Prison Company," *Palm Beach Post*, March 1, 2013.

17. Ella Every, interview by Lauren-Brooke Eisen, February 5, 2016.

18. Tina Butoiu, "UC System Divests from Private Prison Industry," *The Guardian*, January 3, 2016.

19. Jorge Rivas, "Black Students Win After Slamming University for Investing $30 Million in Private Prisons," *Fusion*, January 6, 2016, http://fusion.net/story/251804/uc-students-divest-private-prisons/.

20. Frank Smith, interview by Lauren-Brooke Eisen, February 19, 2016.

21. William MacAskill, "Does Divestment Work?", *The New Yorker*, October 20, 2015, http://www.newyorker.com/business/currency/does-divestment-work.

22. Valerie Strauss, "Update: Columbia University Divesting from Private Prison Companies. Why Other Schools Should Too," *Washington Post*, September 13, 2005.

23. Lee Bollinger, "President Issues Statement Supporting Divestment from Private Prisons," Center for Justice, http://centerforjustice.columbia.edu

/2015/05/20/president-bollinger-issues-statement-supporting-divestment
-from-private-prisons/.

24. "Prisons' Dilemma," presentation by Pershing Square Capital
Management, L.P., October 20, 2009, http://thinkprogress.org/wp-content
/uploads/2010/09/Bill-AckmanPresentation.pdf.

25. Katie Rose Quandt, "Corporations Divest Nearly $60 Million from
Private Prison Industry." *Mother Jones*, April 28, 2014, http://www.motherjones
.com/mojo/2014/04/investment-corporations-divest-60-million-private
-prison-cca-geo-group.

26. Robert Steyer, "New York City Pension Fund to Explore Divesting from
Private Prison Companies," Pensions and Investments, September 8, 2016,
http://www.pionline.com/article/20160908/ONLINE/160909867/new
-york-city-pension-fund-to-explore-divesting-from-private-prison-companies.

27. "Private Prison Divestment Campaign Tool Kit: Cutting All Ties with
the Private Prison Industry," Enlace, November 2012,

28. Comptroller Stringer and Trustees, "New York City Pension Funds
Complete First-In-The-Nation Divestment From Private Prison Companies," 2017.
https://comptroller.nyc.gov/newsroom/comptroller-stringer-and-trustees
-new-york-city-pension-funds-complete-first-in-the-nation-divestment-from
-private-prison-companies/.

29. Dan Carillo, interview by Lauren-Brooke Eisen, February 29, 2016.

30. American Friends Service Committee, "Investigate: The Prison Industry,"
2017, http://investigate.afsc.org/screens/prisons.

31. "The Banks That Finance Private Prison Companies," In the Public
Interest, November 2016, 3, https://www.inthepublicinterest.org/wp-content
/uploads/ITPI_BanksPrivatePrisonCompanies_Nov2016.pdf.

32. Ibid., 5.

33. Ibid., 29.

34. Joseph Gaylin, interview by Lauren-Brooke Eisen, April 7, 2017, and
follow-up email April 14, 2017.

7. The Politics of Private Prisons

1. Bernie Sanders, "Stand with Bernie Against Private Prisons," 2016,
https://go.berniesanders.com/page/s/private_prisons.

2. Donald Trump, "Full Transcript: MSNBC Town Hall with Donald Trump,"
2017, http://info.msnbc.com/_news/2016/03/30/35330907-full-transcript
-msnbc-town-hall-with-donald-trump-moderated-by-chris-matthews?lite.

3. Hillary Clinton, "Remarks at Columbia University on Criminal Justice
and Mass Incarceration," February 14, 2016, https://www.hillaryclinton.com
/post/remarks-columbia-university-criminal-justice-and-mass-incarceration/.

4. Hamilton, Keegan. "How Private Prisons Are Profiting from Locking Up U.S. Immigrants." Vice News, October 6, 2015, https://news.vice.com /article/how-private-prisons-are-profiting-from-locking-up-us-immigrants.

5. Justin McCarthy, "Americans Divided on Priorities for Criminal Justice System," Gallup, October 14, 2016, http://www.gallup.com/poll/196394 /americans-divided-priorities-criminal-justice-system.aspx.

6. U.S. Department of Justice, "Smart on Crime: Reforming the Criminal Justice System for the 21st Century," 2013, http://www.justice.gov/ag /smart-on-crime.pdf.

7. Dean DeChiaro, "Private Immigrant Detention Firm Gave $45K to Trump Fundraising Group," *Roll Call*, August 25, 2016, http://www.rollcall .com/news/politics/private-immigrant-detention-firm-gives-45k-pro-trump -fundraising-group#sthash.FDNoyKZ4.dpuf.

8. Casey Tolan, "America's Second-Largest Private Prison Company Accused of Illegally Donating to Pro-Trump Super PAC," *Fusion*, November 1, 2016, http://fusion.net/story/364862/geo-group-trump -super-pac-donation/?utm_source=twitter&utm_medium=social&utm _campaign=socialshare&utm_content=theme_top_desktop.

9. Ibid.

10. S. 842, 107th Cong. § 2(9)(2001); H.R. 1764, 107th Cong. § 2(9)(2001).

11. Hearing on the Private Prison Information Act of 2007, Part II, Thursday, June 26, 2008, https://judiciary.house.gov/_files/hearings/printers/110th /43153.PDF.

12. Corrections Corporation of America, Written Statement for a Hearing on H.R. 1889—"The Private Prison Information Act," Submitted to the House Judiciary Committee on Crime, Terrorism, and Homeland Security, Thursday, June 26, 2008, https://archive.org/stream/PrivatePrisonInformationAct /Private%20Prison%20Information%20Act%20Part%20II_djvu.txt.

13. H.R. 2470—Private Prison Information Act of 2015, https://www .congress.gov/bill/114th-congress/house-bill/2470?q=%7B%22search%22%3A %5B%22H.R.+2470%22%5D%7D.

14. Human Rights Defense Center, "Private Prison Information Act of 2013," December 19, 2013, http://privateprisoninformationactof2013.blogspot.com/.

15. Justice Is Not for Sale Act, S. 2054, https://www.govtrack.us/congress /bills/114/s2054/text.

16. GEO Group, "The GEO Group Completes Company Restructuring and Health Care Divestiture; Began Operating in Compliance with REIT Rules Effective January 2, 2013," News Release, January 2, 2013, http://www.businesswire.com/news/home/20130102005486/en/GEO -Group-Completes-Company-Restructuring-Health-Care.

17. CCA, "CCA Completes Internal Reorganization," News Release, January 2, 2013, http://www.cca.com/investors/news-releases.

18. Matt Stroud, "Why Would a Prison Corporation Restructure as a Real Estate Company?", *Forbes*, January 31, 2013, http://www.forbes.com/sites /mattstroud/2013/01/31/why-would-a-prison-corporation-restructure-as -a-real-estate-company/#6f1e20bc2cca.

19. Ending Tax Breaks for Private Prisons Act of 2016, http://www .finance.senate.gov/imo/media/doc/Wyden%20Final%20Prison%20 REIT%20langauge%20MCG16353.pdf; United States Senate Committee on Finance, "Wyden Introduces Bill to Stop Private Prisons from Exploiting Tax Incentives for Profit," Press Release, July 14, 2016, http://www.finance .senate.gov/ranking-members-news/wyden-introduces-bill-to-stop-private -prisons-from-exploiting-tax-incentives-for-profit.

20. Mike Ludwig, "Senate Bill Would End Tax Breaks for Private Prison Companies," Truthout, July 19, 2016, http://www.truth-out.org/news/item /36879-senate-bill-would-end-tax-breaks-for-private-prison-companies.

21. Tax Policy Center, "Tax Policy Center Briefing Book," http://www .taxpolicycenter.org/briefing-book/how-does-corporate-income-tax-work.

22. "Corrections Corporation of America—An Innovative Yield Strategy," May 18, 2015, http://seekingalpha.com/article/3192346-corrections-corporation -of-america-an-innovative-yield-strategy.

23. Private Corrections Institute, Nonprofit Religious Organizations Oppose Prison Privatization Push in Florida," Press Release, February 1, 2012, https:// prisondivest.com/2012/02/01/non-profit-religious-organizations-oppose -prison-privatization-push-in-florida/. The groups that formed this coalition include the ACLU of Florida, Advocare, Citizens United for Rehabilitation of Errants (CURE), Critical Resistance, Florida Justice Institute, Human Rights Defense Center, In the Public Interest, Justice Strategies, National African American Drug Policy Coalition, Ohio Justice Policy Center, Private Corrections Institute, Samuel DeWitt Proctor Conference, The Sentencing Project, Southern Center for Human Rights, Unitarian Universalist Association of Congregations, United Church of Christ/Justice and Witness Ministries, and United Methodist Church General Board of Church and Society.

24. H 768, Leg. (Vt. 2015).

25. Jonathan Levitt, "One Tiny State's Movement to Ban Private Prisons," January 22, 2013, http://www.counterpunch.org/2013/01/22/one-tiny-states -movement-to-ban-private-prisons/.

26. H 28, accessed February 17, 2016, http://legislature.vermont.gov/bill /status/2014/H.28.

27. Ricardo Lara, Dignity Not Detention Act, A.B. 1289, Reg. Sess. (Ca. 2015).

28. George Joseph, "California Pushes to End Private-Prison Management of Immigrant Detention Centers," *The Atlantic CityLab*, August 26, 2016, http://www.citylab.com/crime/2016/08/california-pushes-to-end-private -prison-managment-of-immigrant-detention-centers/497474/.

29. Reynaldo Leanos Jr., "California's Governor Vetoed a Bill That Would Stop Privately Run Migrant Detention. What Now?", PRI's The World, September 30, 2016, https://www.pri.org/stories/2016-09-30/californias -governor-vetoed-bill-would-stop-privately-run-migrant-detention-what.

30. Letter from Gov. Jerry Brown to members of the California State Senate, September 28, 2016, https://www.gov.ca.gov/docs/SB_1289_Veto _Message.pdf.

31. CoreCivic Annual Report, 2016, 31, https://www.sec.gov/Archives/edgar /data/1070985/000119312517053982/d310578d10k.htm.

32. Lichi D'Amelio, "Ending the Barbarity," *Jacobin*, August 24, 2016, https://www.jacobinmag.com/2016/08/private-prisons-department-justice -directive-obama/.

33. George Zoley, GEO Group Fourth Quarter 2015 Earnings Conference Call, February 17, 2016, https://www.sec.gov/Archives/edgar/data/923796 /000119312516473567/d46403dex992.htm.

34. The 2016 GEO Group Annual report states that the Bureau of Prisons contract accounted for 14.0 percent of their total consolidated revenues, ICE accounted for 23.1 percent their total consolidated revenues, and the U.S. Marshals Service accounted for 10.1 percent of their total consolidated revenue. 2016 GEO Group Annual Report, 10-K, p. 36, https://www.sec.gov /Archives/edgar/data/923796/000119312517056831/d320699d10k.htm.

35. CoreCivic Annual Report, 2016, https://www.sec.gov/Archives/edgar /data/1070985/000119312517053982/d310578d10k.htm.

8. Shadow Prisons: Inside Private Immigrant Detention Centers

1. Department of Homeland Security, "Agency Financial Report, Fiscal Year 2016," https://www.dhs.gov/sites/default/files/publications/dhs_agency _financial_report_fy2016.pdf.

2. DHS Immigration Enforcement, "Annual Flow Report," December 2016, https://www.dhs.gov/sites/default/files/publications/DHS%20 Immigration%20Enforcement%202016.pdf.

3. GEO Group Inc., Form 8-K—EX-99.3, February 25, 2014, http://getfilings .com/sec-filings/140225/GEO-GROUP-INC_8-K/d681898dex993.htm#ixzz 4JRcSztah.

4. Bethany Carson and Eleana Diaz, "Payoff: How Congress Ensures Private Prison Profit with an Immigrant Detention Quota," Grassroots Leadership, April 2015, 4, http://grassrootsleadership.org/sites/default/files /reports/quota_report_final_digital.pdf.(Noting that GEO and CCA owned 72 percent combined.)

5. Julia Edwards, "U.S. to Review Use of Private Immigration Prisons, Shares Slide," Reuters, August 29, 2016, http://www.reuters.com/article/us-usa-prisons-immigration-idUSKCN1141W7.

6. Bob Libal, interview by Lauren-Brooke Eisen, August 10, 2016.

7. U.S. Immigration and Customs Enforcement, "Fiscal Year 2014 ICE Enforcement and Removal Operations Report," draft report, 9, https://assets.documentcloud.org/documents/1375456/ice-draft-report.pdf.

8. Seth Freed Wessler, "This Man Will Almost Certainly Die," *The Nation*, January 28, 2016, http://www.thenation.com/article/privatized-immigrant-prison-deaths/.

9. Fact Sheet: Prisoner Operations 2017, U.S. Marshals Serv. 1 (2017), https://www.usmarshals.gov/duties/factsheets/prisoner_ops.pdf; Hannah Kozlowska, "The private-prison industry has one big client that no one talks about," *Quartz*, June 13, 2017, https://qz.com/1002854/the-private-prison-industry-has-one-big-client-that-no-one-talks-about/. Various sources offer contradicting statistics. A USMS fact sheet reflecting data from 2017 reports that 18 percent of its prisoner population is in private facilities. In an article discussing the USMS's reliance on private prisons, Quartz reports a higher number: one-third of USMS's inmate population is in private facilities. Quartz attributes its numbers to Freedom of Information Act responses acquired by In The Public Interest and the ACLU and shared with Quartz. Using this information, Quartz explains that 35 percent of USMS population is in private prisons, with 18percent in federal private prisons, and 46percent in state or local private prisons. The source of the discrepancy in information between USMS and Quartz is not immediately clear and speaks to a general lack of transparency and data regarding inmate populations.

10. Office of the Inspector General, U.S. Department of Justice, "The Department of Justice's Reliance on Private Contractors for Prison Services 3 (2000), https://oig.justice.gov/reports/plus/a0116/final.pdf.

11. U.S. Department of Homeland Security Immigration and Customs Enforcement, Office of Detention Oversight Compliance Inspection, "Enforcement and Removal Operations ERO San Antonio Field Office, Laredo Processing Center, Laredo, Texas," July 14–16, 2015, http://www.documentcloud.org/documents/2823329-2015-ODO-Inspection-Laredo-Processing-Center-TX.html.

12. Ruth Ellen Wasem, Hearing of the U.S. House of Representatives Committee on the Judiciary, "Asylum Abuse: Is It Overwhelming Our Borders?", December 12, 2013, http://judiciary.house.gov/?a=Files.Serve&File_id=5D634F9D-D515-4545-A3F7-F8E6C83DA86D.

13. Ibid.

14. Michael Wishnie, interview by Lauren-Brooke Eisen, October 23, 2016.

15. Juliet Stumpf, "The Crimmigration Crisis: Immigrants, Crime, and Sovereign Power," *American University Law Review* 56, 2 (December 2006): 381, 367–419.

16. Dolovich, Sharon, "State Punishment and Private Prisons," *Duke Law Journal* 55, 3 (December 2005): 457.

17. Aric Press, "The Good, the Bad, and the Ugly: Private Prisons in the 1980s," in *Private Prisons and the Public Interest*, ed. Douglas McDonald (New Brunswick, N.J.: Rutgers University Press, 1990), 28.

18. Anti-Drug Abuse Act of 1988 § 7343(a)(4), P. L. No. 100–690, 102 Stat 4181, 4470, amending INA § 242(a)(2), codified at 8 USC § 1252(a)(2) (1992).

19. H.R. 3355, Violent Crime Control and Law Enforcement Act of 1994, 103rd Congress (1993–1994), https://www.congress.gov/bill/103rd-congress/house-bill/3355.

20. Marie Gottschalk, *Caught: The Prison State and the Lockdown of American Politics* (Princeton, N.J.: Princeton University Press, 2015), 220.

21. "Nation in Brief: Texas: Jailbreak Reveals Transferred Inmates" *Los Angeles Times*, August 10, 1996.

22. Richard Green, "Oregon in the Market for Six Prisons: Not-in-My-Backyard Attitude Won't Prevail," *Seattle Times*, August 30, 1996.

23. Jo Ann Zuniga, "Inmate Types, Escape Plans Draw Concerns," *Houston Chronicle*, August 18, 1996.

24. Sue Anne Pressley, "Texas County Sued by Missouri over Alleged Abuse of Inmates," *Washington Post*, August 26, 1997.

25. Sam Howe Verhovek, "Video Puts Texas Prisons in New Light," *Spokesman-Review*, August 24, 1997.

26. Pressley, "Texas County Sued by Missouri over Alleged Abuse of Inmates."

27. Steve Olafson, "DA slams FBI over Its Actions in Jail Case: Agency Accused of Double Standard," *Houston Chronicle*, October 15, 1999.

28. Cheryl W. Thompson, "Prison Firm Settles Suit by D.C. Inmates in Ohio," *Washington Post*, March 2, 1999.

29. Tribune News Services, "6 Inmates Escape from Private Prison," *Chicago Tribune*, July 26, 1998.

30. Rusty Miller, "Six Inmates Escape Ohio Prison," Associated Press, July 27, 1998, http://www.apnewsarchive.com/1998/.

31. Loie Fecteau, "Private Prisons: Are They the Answer?", *Albuquerque Journal*, September 27, 1998.

32. Michael Coleman, "Private-Prison Inmate Stabbed to Death," *Albuquerque Journal*, January 14, 1999.

33. David Flaum, "CCAs Parent Faces 8 Shareholder Lawsuits," Memphis Commercial Appeal, June 9, 1999.

34. Michael Erskine, "CCA: Novelty Draws Media Glare Private Prisons Receive Intense Scrutiny, Undue Criticism, Quinlan Says," Memphis Commercial Appeal, August 16, 1999.

35. Richard Jones, "State Inmates in Private Prison File Suit: Federal Lawsuits Allege Guards Tortured, Violated Civil Rights of Wisconsin Prisoners in Tennessee," *Milwaukee Journal Sentinel*, August 12, 1999.

36. Peter Slevin, "Prison Firms Seek Inmates and Profits; Management Woes, Loss of Business Noted," *Washington Post*, February 18, 2001.

37. Charles H. Haddad, " 'Private Prisons Don't Work': For-Profit Facilities Face a Barrage of Criticism—And Overbuilding Has Cut Into Profits and Hurt Stock Prices," *Bloomberg*, September 11, 2000, https://www.bloomberg.com/news/articles/2000-09-10/private-prisons-dont-work.

38. Alan Elsner, "Private Prisons Face Financial, Political Pressure," Reuters, February 28, 2001.

39. Haddad, "'Private Prisons Don't Work.'"

40. Ibid.

41. Immigration and Nationality Act (INA), P. L. 101–649, sections 212(a), 237(a) and 238(a) (1990).

42. Judith Greene and Alexis Mazón, "Privately Operated Federal Prisons for Immigrants: Expensive. Unsafe. Unnecessary," Justice Strategies, September 13, 2012, 16, http://www.justicestrategies.org/sites/default/files/publications/Privately%20Operated%20Federal%20Prisons%20for%20Immigrants%209-13-12%20FNL.pdf.

43. ACLU, "Warehoused and Forgotten: Immigrants Trapped in Our Shadow Private Prison System," June 2014, 3, https://www.aclu.org/sites/default/files/assets/060614-aclu-car-reportonline.pdf.

44. Leslie Berestein, "Tougher Immigration Laws Turn the Ailing Private Prison Section Into a Revenue Maker," *San Diego Union-Tribune*, May 4, 2008.

45. David A. Fox, "CCA Reverse Split to Occur by May 2001," *Nashville Post*, December 14, 2000.

46. Nathan James, "The Federal Prison Population Buildup: Overview, Policy Changes, Issues and Options," Congressional Research Service, 2013, 51, https://www.ncjrs.gov/App/Publications/Abstract.aspx?id=263699.

47. Nathan James, "The Federal Prison Population Buildup: Options for Congress," Congressional Research Service, 2016, 1, https://fas.org/sgp/crs/misc/R42937.pdf.

48. Steven Logan. "Quarterly Earnings Teleconference Transcript," October 2001.

49. Rania Khalek, "How Private Prisons Game the System," *Alternet*, December 1, 2011, http://www.salon.com/2011/12/01/how_private_prisons_game_the_system/.

50. Corrections Corporation of America, Annual Report, Form 10-K, December 31, 2004, 16, https://www.sec.gov/Archives/edgar/data/1070985 /000095014405002154/g93600e10vk.htm.

51. Wil S. Hylton, "The Shame of America's Family Detention Camps," *New York Times Magazine*, February 4. 2015, http://www.nytimes.com /2015/02/08/magazine/the-shame-of-americas-family-detention-camps .html?_r=1.

52. Fernando Del Valle, "New Detention Center: Willacy Facility to House Illegal Immigrants," *Valley Morning Star*, June 22, 2006.

53. "They [detainees] are reportedly housed so tightly that when they lie in their bunks, their feet can touch the bunk next to them. Prisoners told us the overcrowding and lack of constructive activity drives many of them mad. Fights frequently break out." ACLU, "Warehoused and Forgotten," 7, 37.

54. Forrest Wilder, "Jailbait: Prison Companies Profit as Raymondville's Public Debt Grows," *Texas Observer*, October 20, 2006.

55. Daniel Blue Tyx, "Goodbye to Tent City," *Texas Observer*, March 26, 2015.

56. Aaron Nelsen, "Prison: Willacy Unit Is to Reopen," *San Antonio Express News*, March 9, 2007.

57. Melissa del Bosque "How a South Texas County Bet on Immigrant Incarceration and Got Burned," *Texas Observer*, January 31, 2017.

58. "New inmates . . . were routinely forced to stay in Special Housing Unit [SHU] cells, or solitary confinement. The contract stipulated that 10 percent of the beds be SHU units, so as the facility became more crowded, solitary confinement became the only place to put detainees." ACLU, "Warehoused and Forgotten," *supra* note 54.

59. Rebecca Cohen, "Last Week's Texas Prison Uprising Wasn't a Surprise: Inmates Had Threatened to Riot for Months," *Mother Jones*, February 25, 2015, http://www.motherjones.com/politics/2015/02/willacy -prison-uprising-immigrants.

60. Ibid.

61. U.S. Census Bureau, "2011–2015 American Community Survey 5-Year Estimates," U.S. Census Bureau, 2015.

62. Tyx, "Goodbye to Tent City."

63. The county also boasted a 500-bed detention center operated by MTC under a U.S. Marshals contract, and a 1,000-bed state jail, operated by CCA. Today, MTC operates three ICE facilities: IAH Secure Adult Detention Facility in Texas, Imperial Regional Detention Facility in California, and the Otero County Processing Center in New Mexico.

64. Associated Press, "Ex-Tent Prison in South Texas, Site of 2015 Riot, to Be Sold," *U.S. News*, March 11, 2017.

65. Nelsen, "Prison: Willacy Unit Is to Reopen."

66. "Raymondville Working on Permit Approval to Demolish Prison Tents," KRGV 5, April 14, 2017, http://www.krgv.com/story/35232533/raymondville -working-on-permit-approval-to-demolish-prison-tents.

67. H.R. 2892, Department of Homeland Security Appropriations Act, 2010, 111th Congress (2009–2010).

68. Public Law 111–83, October 28, 2009; Department of Homeland Security Appropriations Act, 2010.

69. National Immigration Forum, "The Math of Immigration Detention," 2013, 4, https://immigrationforum.org/blog/themathofimmigrationdetention/.

70. Nick Miroff, "Controversial Quota Drives Immigration Detention Boom," *Washington Post*, October 13, 2013.

71. Department of Homeland Security Oversight Hearing, May 2014, https://www.c-span.org/video/?319614–1/homeland-security-department -oversight-hearing.

72. Carson and Diaz, "How Congress Ensures Private Prisons Profit."

73. Geoffrey Ramsey, "Honduras: Home to the Most Violent City in the Hemisphere?" *Christian Science Monitor*, January 18, 2012.

74. National Immigrant Justice Center, "Costly Family Detention Denies Justice to Mothers and Children," (May 2015) https://www.immigrantjustice .org/sites/default/files/Family%2520Detention%2520Bed%2520Quota%2520 Factsheet%25202015_05_15.pdf.

75. H.R. Rep. No. 109–79, at 38 (2005).

76. Julia Preston and Randal Archibold, "U.S. Moves to Stop Surge in Illegal Immigration," *New York Times*, June 20, 2014.

77. Ibid.

78. CCA, "CCA Expands Existing Intergovernmental Service Agreement to Manage the South Texas Family Residential Center in Dilley, Texas," Press Release, September 24, 2014, http://www.cca.com/press-releases/cca -expands-existing-intergovernmental-service-agreement-to-manage-the -south-texas-family-residential-center-in-dilley-texas.

79. John Burnett, "How Will a Small Town in Arizona Manage an ICE Facility in Texas," NPR, October 28, 2014, www.npr.org/2014/10/28/359411980/how -will-a-small-town-in-arizona-manage-an-ice-facility-in-texas.

80. Tanner Clinch, "Texas Prison Is Big Business for Eloy," *Casa Grande Dispatch*, July 4, 2016.

81. Ibid.

82. Chico Harlan, "Inside the Administration's $1 Billion Deal to Detain Central American Asylum Seekers," *Washington Post*, August 14, 2016.

83. Ibid.

84. Aaron Schrank, "Dilley's Immigrant Jail Is a Cash Cow for Private Prison Company, but What About Dilley?", Texas Public Radio, December 21, 2016, http://tpr.org/post/dilley-s-immigrant-jail-cash-cow-private-prison-company -what-about-dilley#stream/0.

85. Associated Press, "South Texas Immigration Detention Center Set to Open," December 15, 2014, CBS News, http://www.cbsnews.com/news /south-texas-immigration-detention-center-set-to-open/.

86. Molly Hennessy-Fiske, "Immigrant Families in Detention: A Look Inside One Holding Center, *Los Angeles Times*, June 25, 2015.

87. This facility is currently the largest detention center in the country. Associated Press, "South Texas Immigration Detention Center Set to Open."

88. Julia Preston, "Detention Center Presented as Deterrent to Border Crossings," *New York Times*, December 15, 2014.

89. César, "CCA Earns $36 Million from Family Detention" (crImmigration blog), May 14, 2015, http://crimmigration.com/2015/05/14/cca-earns -36-million-from-family-detention/.

90. "CCA Reports First Quarter 2015 Financial Results," *Market Wired*, May 6, 2015, http://www.marketwired.com/press-release/cca-reports-first -quarter-2015-financial-results-nyse-cxw-2017255.htm.

91. "CCA Reports First Quarter 2016 Financial Results," *Globe Newswire*, May 4, 2016, https://globenewswire.com/news-release/2016/05/04/836807/0 /en/CCA-Reports-First-Quarter-2016-Financial-Results.html.

92. Edited transcript of GEO Group earnings conference call, April 28, 2016, https://seekingalpha.com/article/3969107-geo-groups-geo-ceo-george-zoley -q1-2016-results-earnings-call-transcript.

93. Flores v. Lynch, No. CV 85–04544 DMG (EX), 2015 WL 9915880, at *6 (C.D. Cal. Aug. 21, 2015), *aff'd in part, rev'd in part and remanded*, No. 15–56434, 2016 WL 3670046 (9th Cir. July 6, 2016). The Ninth Circuit affirmed this holding.

94. Ibid., 7.

95. Emergency Rules: Minimum Standards for General Residential Operations, 40 Tex. Reg. 6229–30 (Sept. 18, 2015).

96. Ibid., (c)(1)–(3).

97. Alexa Garcia-Ditta, "Texas Licenses Detention Center for Child Care, Despite Deficiencies," *Texas Observer*, May 2, 2016.

98. Alexa Garcia-Ditta, "Judge Halts Child Care License for Dilley Detention Center," *Texas Observer*, June 2, 2016.

99. Ibid. The detainee-plaintiffs were joined by the Austin-based nonprofit Grassroots Leadership; both were represented by Texas Rio Grande Legal Aide.

100. Ibid. Judge Crump took issue with the rule's leniency toward facilities that allow unrelated adults to room with children (citing the potential for abuse).

101. "Judge in Texas Blocks Detention Center from Being Licensed as 'Child Care,'" *Think Progress*, June 2, 2016, https://thinkprogress.org/judge-in-texas -blocks-detention-center-from-being-licensed-as-child-care-7d41c86037d6.

102. Center for Migration Studies, "Immigration Detention: Behind the Record Numbers," 2016, http://cmsny.org/immigration-detention-behind -the-record-numbers/.

103. Department of Homeland Security, "Immigration Enforcement Actions: 2012," http://www.dhs.gov/publication/immigration-enforcement -actions-2012.

104. Seth Freed Wessler, "Investigation Into Private Prisons Reveal Crowding, Under-Staffing and Inmate Deaths," interview by National Public Radio, August 25, 2016. http://www.npr.org/2016/08/25/491340335/investigation -into-private-prisons-reveals-crowding-under-staffing-and-inmate-de.

105. Judith A. Greene, Bethany Carson, and Andrea Black, "Indefensible: a Decade of Mass Incarceration of Migrants Prosecuted for Crossing the Border," Grassroots Leadership, July 2016, 6, http://grassrootsleadership.org/reports /indefensible-decade-mass-incarceration-migrants-prosecuted-crossing-border.

106. The CCA website used to have this language, but CoreCivic's 2016 10-K does not mention educating policy makers, https://www.sec.gov/Archives /edgar/data/1070985/000119312517053982/d310578d10k.htm.

107. Rania Khalek, "How Private Prisons Game the System," *Alternet*, December 1, 2011, http://www.salon.com/2011/12/01/how_private_prisons _game_the_system/.

108. Kathryn Johnson, "Appropriations Bills Preserve Profits for Private Prison Companies," *The Hill*, August 22, 2016.

109. ALEC, "About," https://www.alec.org/about/.

110. Laura Sullivan, "Prison Economics Help Drive Ariz. Immigration Law," NPR, October 28, 2010, http://www.npr.org/2010/10/28/130833741 /prison-economics-help-drive-ariz-immigration-law.

111. Ibid.

112. Molly Jackman, "ALEC's Influence over Lawmaking in State Legislatures," *Brookings*, December 6, 2013, https://www.brookings.edu /articles/alecs-influence-over-lawmaking-in-state-legislatures/.

113. "The GEO Group Announces Acquisition of Eight Correctional and Detention Facilities Totaling More Than 6,500 Beds," *Business Wire*, January 26, 2015, http://www.businesswire.com/news/home/20150126005618/en/GEO -Group-Announces-Acquisition-Correctional-Detention-Facilities.

114. "The Geo Group Signs Contract for the Continued Management of Northwest Detention Center," *Business Wire*, October 1, 2015, http:// www.businesswire.com/news/home/20151001005937/en/GEO-Group -Signs-Contract-Continued-Management-Northwest.

115. Lael Henterly, "Hundreds Stand in Solidarity with Detainee Hunger Strikes," *Seattle Globalist*, April 7, 2014, http://www.seattleglobalist.com/2014/.

116. Renee Feltz, "Texas Officials Vote Against British Firm's Plans for Immigration Detention Center," *The Guardian*, June 15, 2016.

117. Associated Press, "With Prison Closure, New Mexico Towns Worry About Economy," http://www.newschannel10.com/story/33013200/with -prison-closure-new-mexico-towns-worry-about-economy; Seth Freed Wessler, "The Feds Will Shut Down the Troubled Private Prison in a 'Nation Investigation,'" *The Nation*, August 15, 2016.

118. Office of the Inspector General, U.S. Department of Justice, "Review of the Federal Bureau of Prisons' Monitoring of Contract Prisons," August 2016, i, https://oig.justice.gov/reports/2016/e1606.pdf.

119. Ibid., ii.

120. Ibid., 42.

121. Ibid., ii.

122. Ryan J. Reilly, "Damning Report Finds For-Profit Prisons Are More Dangerous," *Huffington Post*, August 11, 2016, http://www.huffingtonpost. com/entry/.

123. Contract Prisons, Federal Bureau of Prisons, https://www.bop.gov /about/facilities/contract_facilities.jsp (last visited June 2, 2017); Statistics, Federal Bureau of Prisons, https://www.bop.gov/about/statistics/population _statistics.jsp (last updated June 9, 2017).

124. Nathaniel Meyersohn, "Justice Department Seeks Increase in Private Prison Beds," *CNN*, May 19, 2017, http://www.cnn.com/2017/05/19/politics /private-prisons/index.html.

125. E-mail from Justin Long, Office of Public Affairs, Information, Policy, and Public Affairs Division, Federal Bureau of Prisons, June 12, 2016.

126. Memo from Sally Q. Yates, Deputy Attorney General, to the Acting Director of the Federal Bureau of Prisons, "Reducing Our Use of Private Prisons," August 18, 2016, https://www.justice.gov/opa/file/886311/download.

127. Ibid.

128. Editorial Board, "First Step in Shutting Private Prisons," *New York Times*, August 22, 2016.

129. Editorial Board, "Obama's Break with Private Prisons Doesn't Go Far Enough," *Boston Globe*, August 27, 2016.

130. Bob Egelko, "As U.S. Cuts Ties with Private Prisons, California to Keep Using Them," *Orange County Register*, August 29, 2016, http://www .ocregister.com/2016/08/29/as-us-cuts-ties-with-private-prisons-california -to-keep-using-them/.

131. Hui-Yong Yu and Chris Strohm, "Private Prison Stocks Sink After U.S. Signals the End," *Bloomberg News*, August 18, 2016, http://www.bloomberg .com/news/.

132. Marcia Heroux Pounds, "Boca's GEO Group Expects Contract Renewals Despite Federal Plan to End Private Prison Operation, CEO Says," *Sun Sentinel*, August 19, 2016.

133. U.S. Department of Homeland Security, "Statement by Secretary Jeh C. Johnson on Establishing a Review of Privatized Immigration Detention," Press Release, August 29, 2016, https://www.dhs.gov/news-releases/press -releases.

134. Miriam Jordan, "Immigrant Detention System Could Be in Line for an Overhaul," *Wall Street Journal*, September 27, 2016.

135. Editorial Board, "Prisons Aren't the Answer on Immigration," *New York Times*, September 5, 2016.

136. Sarah Rafique, "Neugebauer: Local Officials 'Expressed Their Dismay' of DOJ's Private Prison Announcement," *Lubbock Avalanche-Journal*, September 16, 2016, http://lubbockonline.com/filed-online/.

137. "Closing Private Detention Centers for Migrants Could Raise More Problems," Reuters, September 8, 2016, http://fortune.com/2016/09/09 /closing-private-detention-centers-illegal-immigrants/.

138. Jordan, "Immigrant Detention System Could Be in Line for an Overhaul."

139. Jorge Rivas, "Private Prisons for Immigrants Not Closing Anytime Soon, Top Official Hints," *Fusion*, September 23, 2016, http://fusion.net /story/350515/ice-closing-private-detention-turn-agency-upside-down/.

140. Elise Foley and Roque Planas, "Homeland Security Panel Wants to Quit For-Profit Immigration Detention," *Huffington Post*, December 1, 2016, http://www.huffingtonpost.com/entry/.

141. Alan Neuhauser, "Homeland Security Panel Rejects Reliance on Private Prisons to House Immigrants," *U.S. News & World Report*, December 1, 2016; U.S. Department of Homeland Security, Homeland Security Advisory Council, "Report of the Subcommittee on Privatized Immigration Detention Facilities," 2016, 10, note 4, http://crimmigration.com/wp-content/uploads /2016/12/DHS-HSAC-PIDF-Report-FINAL-DRAFT.pdf.

142. U.S. Department of Homeland Security, Homeland Security Advisory Council, "Report of the Subcommittee on Privatized Immigration Detention Facilities," 2.

143. Max Siegelbaum, "Immigration Courts in Prisons Raise Issues of Due Process, Public Access," *Tribune Live*, July 31, 2016, http://triblive.com /state/pennsylvania/10796893-74/immigration-prison-court.

144. Ibid.

145. "Backlog of Pending Cases in Immigration Courts as of August 2016," Syracuse University's Transactional Records Access Clearinghouse (TRAC) at Syracuse University, figure 1, http://trac.syr.edu/phptools/immigration /court_backlog/apprep_backlog.php.

146. U.S. Department of Justice, "EOIR Swears in Five Immigration Judges," Press Release, August 2, 2016, https://www.justice.gov/eoir/pr /eoir-swears-five-immigration-judges.

147. Eleanor Acer and Jessica Chicco, "U.S. Detention of Asylum Seekers: Seeking Protection, Finding Prison," Human Rights First, April 2009, revised June 2009, https://www.humanrightsfirst.org/wp-content/uploads/pdf/090429 -RP-hrf-asylum-detention-report.pdf.

148. Scott Pelley, "Trump Gets Down to Business on *60 Minutes*," CBS *News*, September 27, 2015.

9. Public Prisons Versus Private Prisons

1. Richard A. Oppel Jr., "Private Prisons Found to Offer Little in Savings," *New York Times*, May 18, 2011.

2. Laura Krantz, "Vermont Inmates on Lockdown at Kentucky Prison," *VTDigger*, January 21, 2014, https://vtdigger.org/2014/01/21/vermont-inmates -lockdown-kentucky-prison/.

3. Colin (name changed at his request), interview by Lauren-Brooke Eisen, March 3, 2016.

4. Krantz, "Vermont Inmates on Lockdown at Kentucky Prison." Richard Byrne, Vermont out-of-state unit supervisor for the Vermont Department of Corrections told the Vermont House Committee on Corrections and Institutions that the state spends less money per inmate per the CCA contract in part because there are fewer staff and they are paid less.

5. Colin, interview by Lauren-Brooke Eisen, March 3, 2016.

6. Ibid.

7. Larry (name changed at his request), interview by Lauren-Brooke Eisen, February 24, 2016.

8. "Vermont Inmates Allegedly Started Kentucky Riot," *Times Argus*, September16, 2004.

9. Larry, interview by Lauren-Brooke Eisen, February 24, 2016.

10. U.S. General Accounting Office, "Private and Public Prisons: Studies Comparing Operational Costs and/or Quality of Service," 1996, 11, http:// www.gao.gov/archive/1996/gg96158.pdf. "First, several of the studies focused on specialized inmate populations . . . that limited their generaliz-ability to a wider inmate population. Second, methodological weaknesses in some of the comparisons . . . make some findings questionable. . . . Third, a variety of differences in other states and regions could result in experiences far different from those of the states that were studied." Ibid., 3. "In fact, it gets worse. . . . Studies don't simultaneously compare both cost and qual-ity. . . . If we find that a private prison costs less, how do we know that it did not achieve that result by cutting quality?", Alexander Volokh, "Prison Accountability and Performance Measures," *Emory Law Journal* 63 (2013): 339, 361.

11. Corrections Corporation of America, "A Strategic Corrections Partnership with Corrections Corporation of America: A Privatization Plan for Today's Correctional Needs," 6, https://ccamericastorage.blob.core.windows.net/media/Default/documents/CCA-Resource-Center/Strategic_Private_Corr.pdf.

12. Soffiyah Elijah, "Aging in Prison: Reducing Elder Incarceration and Promoting Public Safety," Center for Justice at Columbia University, November 2015, 9, http://centerforjustice.columbia.edu/files/2015/10/AgingInPrison_FINAL_web.pdf.

13. Sasha Volokh, "Are Private Prisons Better or Worse Than Public Prisons?", *Washington Post*, February 25, 2014,

14. Harris Kenny and Leonard Gilroy, "The Challenge of Comparing Private and Public Correctional Costs," Reason Foundation Policy Brief 112 (December 2013); 6, http://reason.org/files/comparing_correctional_costs.pdf.

15. Corrections Corporation of America, "Myths vs. Facts in Partnership Corrections," https://ccamericastorage.blob.core.windows.net/media/Default/documents/CCA-Resource-Center/MYTHS-vs-FACTS.pdf.

16. Rick Seiter, interview by Lauren-Brooke Eisen, October 7, 2016.

17. U.S. Government Accountability Office, "Private and Public Prisons: Studies Comparing Costs and/or Quality of Service," GAO/GGD-96-158,1996, https://www.gpo.gov/fdsys/pkg/GAOREPORTS-GGD-96-158/html/GAOREPORTS-GGD-96-158.htm.

18. Ibid. Only the New Mexico study concluded private prison costs were lower. The other studies were (1) a 1991 Texas Sunset Advisory Commission study comparing the actual costs of operating four male, prerelease, minimum security private facilities and the estimated costs of operating similar hypothetical public facilities in Texas; (2) a 1994 California State University study comparing three male community correctional facilities—a medium security private facility, a high security local police operated facility, and a low to medium security facility operated by a city administration; (3) a 1995 Tennessee state legislature study comparing two state-run and one privately managed multicustody male facilities; (4) a 1996 Washington State Legislative Budget Committee study analyzing public and private facility cost comparisons from other states to determine if privately run facilities were feasible in Washington.

19. Ibid. "The [Tennessee study] analysis showed very little difference in average inmate costs per day among the three facilities—$35.39 for the private facility and $34.09 and $35.45, respectively, for the two public facilities."

20. Ibid.

21. U.S. Government Accountability Office, "Cost of Prisons: Bureau of Prisons Needs Better Data to Assess Alternatives for Acquiring Low and

Minimum Security Facilities Cost," Report GAO-08-6, October 2007, 4, http://www.gao.gov/new.items/d086.pdf.

22. Travis C. Pratt and Jeff Maahs, "Are Private Prisons More Cost-Effective Than Public Prisons? A Meta-Analysis of Evaluation Research Studies," *Crime & Delinquency* 45 (1999): 358, http://www.lwvokaloosa.org/documents /Privatization/Priv-Prison_meta-analysis.pdf.

23. Ibid.

24. James Austin and Garry Coventry, "Emerging Issues on Privatized Prisons," 2001, 22, http://www.ncjrs.gov/pdffiles1/bja/181249.pdf.

25. Ibid., 52.

26. James Austin, interview via email by Lauren-Brooke Eisen, February 21, 2017.

27. The report concludes that "regarding costs and savings . . . the few existing studies and other available data do not provide strong evidence of any general pattern." Douglas McDonald, Elizabeth Fournier, Malcolm Russell-Einhorn, and Stephen Crawford, "Private Prisons in the United States: An Assessment of Current Practice," Abt Associates Inc., July 16, 1998, iv. http:// www.abtassociates.com/reports/priv-report.pdf.

28. Volokh, "Are Private Prisons Better or Worse Than Public Prisons?"

29. Julianne Nelson, "Competition in Corrections: Comparing Public and Private Sector Operations," CAN Corporation, 2005, https://www.bop.gov /resources/research_projects/published_reports/pub_vs_priv/cnanelson.pdf.

30. Douglas McDonald and Kenneth Colinson, "Contracting for Imprisonment in the Federal Prison System: Cost and Performance of the Privately Operated Taft Correctional Institution," Abt Associates Inc., 2005, https://www.ncjrs.gov/pdffiles1/nij/grants/211990.pdf.

31. Nelson, "Competition in Corrections," 45.

32. McDonald and Carlson, "Contracting for Imprisonment in the Federal Prison System," 48.

33. "Having Privately and Publicly Managed Prisons in the Same State Brings Benefits," *Research News at Vanderbilt*, November 21, 2008, https:// news.vanderbilt.edu/2008/11/21/having-privately-and-publicly-managed -prisons-in-the-same-state-brings-benefits-67787/.

34. James F. Blumstein, Mark A. Cohen, and Suman Seth, "Do Government Agencies Respond to Market Pressures? Evidence from Private Prisons," Vanderbilt Law and Economics Research Paper No. 03-16 and Vanderbilt Public Law Research Paper No. 03-05, December 2007, last revised November 20, 2015, https://ssrn.com/abstract=441007 or http://dx.doi.org/10.2139 /ssrn.441007.

35. Erwin A. Blackstone and Simon Hakim, "Prison Break: A New Approach to Public Cost and Safety," Independent Institute, June 30, 2014, http:// www.independent.org/pdf/policy_reports/2014-06-30-prision_break.pdf

36. CCA, "Resource Center," http://www.cca.com/cca-resource-center.

37. MTC, "Privatization in Corrections: Increased Performance and Accountability Is Leading to Expansion," December 2009, https://ccamericastorage.blob.core.windows.net/media/Default/documents/CCA-Resource-Center/MTC_Privatization_in_Corrections-Final.pdf.

38. Arizona Department of Corrections, "Private Versus Public Provision of Services," biennial comparison required per A.R.S. § 41-1609.01(K)(M), December 21, 2011, https://corrections.az.gov/sites/default/files/ars41_1609_01_biennial_comparison_report122111_e_v.pdf.

39. "The public sector is better on some dimensions and worse on others, and there's no evidence that either sector does better at reducing recidivism." Ibid., 364. "Of the studies we reviewed, two (New Mexico and Tennessee) assessed the comparative quality of service between private and public institutions in much greater detail than the other studies. Both studies used structured data-collection instruments to cover a variety of quality-related topics, including safety and security, management, personnel, health care, discipline reports, escapes, and inmate programs and activities. The New Mexico study reported equivocal findings, and the Tennessee study reported no difference in quality between the compared private and public institutions." Blackstone and Hakim, "Prison Break," 9, *supra* note 1.

40. Gerald G. Gaes, Scott D. Camp, Julianne B. Nelson, and William G. Saylor, *Measuring Prison Performance: Government Privatization & Accountability* (Walnut Creek, Calif.: AltaMira Press, 2004), 184.

41. Allen J. Beck and Candace Johnson, "National Former Prisoner Survey, 2008," Bureau of Justice Statistics, May 2012, 5, http://www.bjs.gov/index.cfm?ty=pbdetail&iid=4312.

42. "Sexual Victimization in Prisons and Jails Reported by Inmates, 2011–12," Bureau of Justice Statistics, 2013, 6, https://www.bjs.gov/content/pub/pdf/svpjril112.pdf.

43. Between 2000 and 2009, suicide (29 percent) and heart disease (22 percent) were the leading causes of deaths in jails, accounting for over half (51 percent) of all deaths in jails. Margaret E. Noonan and E. Ann Carson, "Prison and Jail Deaths in Custody, 2000–2009 Statistical Tables," Bureau of Justice Statistics, December 2011, 2, http://www.bjs.gov/content/pub/pdf/pjdc0009st.pdf.

44. Randy James, "Sheriff Joe Arpaio," *Time*, October 13, 2009, http://content.time.com/time/nation/article/0,8599,1929920,00.html#said.

45. Graves v. Arpaio, "Findings of Fact and Conclusions of Law and Order," 2008, 69.

46. Benjamin Weiser and Michael Schwirtz, "U.S. Inquiry Finds a 'Culture of Violence' Against Teenage Inmates at Rikers Island," *New York Times*, August 4, 2014.

47. J. David Goodman, "Mayor Backs Plan to Close Rikers and Open Jails Elsewhere," *New York Times*, March 31, 2017.

48. Pamela Brown and Mary Lynn Ryan, "'Staggering corruption': 46 Correctional Officers Charged in Years-Long Drug Trafficking Sting," CNN, February 12, 2016, http://www.cnn.com/2016/02/11/politics/fbi-georgia-correctional-drug-trafficking/.

49. Joe Gyan Jr., "3 More Former Angola Guards Charged in Beating of Inmate and Alleged Cover-Up," *The Advocate,* November 2, 2016, http://www.theadvocate.com/baton_rouge.

50. CBSNews.com, "Locked Inside a Nightmare," *60 Minutes*, May 9, 2000, http://www.cbsnews.com/news/locked-inside-a-nightmare/.

51. Ibid.

52. Therese Schroder, Security Operations Administrator, Arizona Department of Corrections, "Memo,"August 18, 2010, 2, https://www.afsc.org/sites/afsc.civicactions.net/files/documents/adoc-report-on-kingman-escapes.pdf.

53. Ibid., 5.

54. David Shapiro, "Banking on Bondage: Private Prisons and Mass Incarceration," American Civil Liberties Union, November 2, 2011, 27, https://www.aclu.org/files/assets/bankingonbondage_20111102.pdf.

55. Carl Takei, "Corrections Corporation of America Loses Four Prison Contracts This Month," *Speak Freely* (ACLU blog), https://www.aclu.org/blog/corrections-corporation-america-loses-four-prison-contracts-month.

56. John Burnett, "Miss. Prison Operator Out; Facility Called a 'Cesspool,'" *All Things Considered,* April 24, 2012, http://www.npr.org/2012/04/24/151276620/firm-leaves-miss-after-its-prison-is-called-cesspool.

57. Stephanie Chen, "Pennsylvania Rocked by 'Jailing Kids for Cash' Scandal," CNN.com, http://www.cnn.com/2009/CRIME/02/23/pennsylvania.corrupt.judges/.

58. Alex Friedman, interview by Lauren-Brooke Eisen, April 16, 2017.

59. Volokh, "Are Private Prisons Better or Worse Than Public Prisons?"

60. Citizens for Responsibility and Ethics in Washington, "Private Prisons: A Bastion of Secrecy," February 2014, 12, https://www.scribd.com/document/208365972/Private-Prisons-A-Bastion-of-Secrecy.

10. Wrestling with the Concept of Private Prisons

1. Christopher Rose, "Future of Prisons May Be Private," *New Orleans Time Picayune*, June 14, 1989.

2. Layne Pavey, interview by Lauren-Brooke Eisen, February 11, 2016.

3. Ibid.

4. Ibid.

5. Statement of Ira P. Robbins, Barnard T. Welsh Scholar and Professor of Law and Justice, The American University Washington College of Law, House Judiciary Subcommittee on Courts, Civil Liberties and the Administration of Justice Concerning the Privatization of Prisons and Jails, November 13, 1985.

6. Ira P. Robbins, "Privatization of Corrections: A Violation of U.S. Domestic Law, International Human Rights, and Good Sense," *Human Rights Brief* 13, no. 3 (2006): 12–16.

7. John J. DiIulio Jr., "The Duty to Govern: A Critical Perspective on the Private Management of Prisons and Jails," in *Private Prisons and the Public Interest*, ed. Douglas C. McDonald (New Brunswick, N.J.: Rutgers University Press, 1990), 156.

8. Ira Robbins, "Privatization of Corrections: Defining the Issues," *Judicature* 69 (April–May 1986): 331.

9. Charles Logan, "Propriety of Private Prisons," in *The American Prison: Issues in Research and Policy*, ed. Lynn Goodstein and Doris L. MacKenzie (New York: Plenum Press, 1989), 55.

10. Prisons Ordinance Law (Amendment No. 28), 5764-2004, SH No. 348 (Isr.) (in Hebrew).

11. Editorial, "Private Prisons?", *Jerusalem Post*, June 18, 2006, http://www.jpost.com/Opinion/Editorials/Private-prisons.

12. ALA is a subsidiary of three companies: Lev Leviev's Africa-Israel, the Minerb construction company of Israel, and Emerald Corrections, a Louisiana-based company that operates several private detention centers in Texas.

13. Academic Ctr. of Law & Bus. v. Minister of Fin., HCJ 2605/05, 63(ii) PD 545 [2009] (Isr.), English translation, http://elyon1.court.gov.il/files_eng/05/050/026/n39/05026050.n39.pdf.

14. Ibid., 25.

15. Ibid., 29.

16. Ibid., 30.

17. Abolish Private Prisons, Home page, last visited November 3, 2016, http://www.abolishprivateprisons.org/.

18. Richard Harding, "*Private Prisons and Public Accountability* (New Brunswick, N.J.: Routledge, 1997), 23.

19. Bill Bryson, *A Short History of Nearly Everything* (New York: Broadway Books, 2003).

20. "CCA Awarded New Management Contract with Arizona," *NASDAQ Global Newswire*, December 17, 2015, https://globenewswire.com/news-release/2015/12/17/796420/0/en/CCA-Awarded-New-Management-Contract-With-Arizona.html.

21. In The Public Interest, "Criminal: How Lockup Quotas and 'Low-Crime Taxes" Guarantee Profits for Private Prison Corporations," p. 8 (September 2013);

https://www.inthepublicinterest.org/wp-content/uploads/Criminal-Lockup-Quota-Report.pdf.

22. "How Lockup Quotas and 'Low-Crime Taxes' Guarantee Profits," In the Public Interest, September 2013, 6, https://www.inthepublicinterest.org/wp-content/uploads/Criminal-Lockup-Quota-Report.pdf.

23. Former corrections director (name withheld), interview by Lauren-Brooke Eisen, March 31, 2016.

24. Center for Responsive Politics, "Lobbying Reports," http://www.opensecrets.org/lobby/clientsum.php?id=D000021940&year=2002 and http://www.opensecrets.org/lobby/clientsum.php?id=D000022003&year=2004.

25. Michael Cohen, "How For-Profit Prisons Have Become the Biggest Lobby No One Is Talking About," *Washington Post*, April 28, 2015.

26. Paul Ashton, "Gaming the System: How the Political Strategies of Private Prison Companies Promote Ineffective Incarceration Policies," Justice Policy Institute, June 22, 2001, 17, http://www.justicepolicy.org/research/2614.

27. Center for Responsive Politics, "CCA Federal Lobbying Database 2015," Open Secrets, accessed March 1, 2016, https://www.opensecrets.org/lobby/clientbills.php?id=D000021940&year=2015.

28. Center for Responsive Politics, "GEO Group Federal Lobbying Database 2015," Open Secrets, accessed March 1, 2016, http://www.opensecrets.org/lobby/clientbills.php?id=D000022003&year=2015.

29. Center for Responsive Politics, "GEO Group Federal Lobbying Database 2014," Open Secrets, accessed March 1, 2016, http://www.opensecrets.org/lobby/clientbills.php?id=D000022003&year=2014.

30. CCA, "Political Activity and Lobbying Report 2014," CCA-Political-Activity-Lobbying-Report-2014.pdf.

31. Ibid., 5, table B-1.

32. Ibid., 6.

33. Center for Responsive Politics. "GEO Group Federal Lobbying Database 2015."

34. Center for Responsive Politics, "Revolving Door," Open Secrets, https://www.opensecrets.org/revolving/.

35. Center for Responsive Politics, "Lobbying," Open Secrets, 2016, https://www.opensecrets.org/lobby/clientsum.php?id=D000022003&year=2016.

36. George M. Anderson, "Prison for Profit: Some Ethical and Practical Problems," *America* 183, 6 (November 18, 2000), http://www.americamagazine.org/issue/389/article/prisons-profit.

37. Ibid. Currently, as part of the corrections budget, more than $100 million a year is spent on the private prison industries' six facilities. Five years ago, the amount was barely $3 million.

38. Oklahoma Statute 57, § 570–576 (1985).

39. The Oklahoma Department of Corrections recommended release of 900 inmates, but the governor's office culled the list down to only fifty-eight.

40. Libby Quaid, "Inmate Kills 3 After Early Release in Oklahoma," Associated Press, August 7, 1996, http://www.apnewsarchive.com/1996/Inmate -Kills-3-After-Early-Release-in-Oklahoma/id-03e23d5a9e16b5c6ff3560437 cc5851b.

41. Barbara Hoberock, "Hobson Defends Corrections Chief," Tulsa World Capitol Bureau, August 25, 1996, http://www.tulsaworld.com/archives/hobson -defends-corrections-chief/article_afcbc057-e765-5e8d-a0dc-6281c77e6525 .html.

42. Brian Ford, "Keating Pushes Prison Review," Tulsa World Capitol Bureau, August 28, 1996, http://www.tulsaworld.com/archives/keating-pushes-prison -review/article_2bf9c35c-90c4-53dc-9b0a-e63534f36583.html.

43. Oklahoma State Senate, "Private Prison Official Should Agree Not to Profit from Recommendations," Press Release, September 10, 1996, http:// www.oksenate.gov/news/press_releases/press_releases_1996/pr19960910 .html.

44. "Oklahoma Lawmakers, Corrections Officials Get Prison Review: Keating Backs Report on Overcrowding," *Dallas Morning News*, December 7, 1996.

45. Barbara Hoberock, "Five Private Prisons Seek More Funding," Tulsa World Capitol Bureau, December 8, 1996, http://www.tulsaworld.com/archives /five-private-prisons-seek-more-funding/article_669f0b12-ab71-5b92-9336 -6de93714237f.html.

46. "Oklahoma Lawmakers, Corrections Officials Get Prison Review Keating Backs Report on Overcrowding."

47. Tara Herivel and Paul Wright, eds., *Prison Profiteers: Who Makes Money from Mass Incarceration* (New York: The New Press, 2007), 16.

48. Off the record anecdote, November 13, 2015, from an executive director of a national nonprofit who heard this story directly from the former director of corrections.

49. Cristina Costantini and George Rivas, "Shadow Prisons: A Private and Profitable Corner of the Federal Prison System Thrives After a Long-Ignored Offense Is Prosecuted," *Fusion*, February 4, 2015, http://interactive.fusion .net/shadow-prisons/.

50. Shane Bauer, "My Four Months As a Private Prison Guard," *Mother Jones*, July/August 2016, http://www.motherjones.com/politics/2016/06/cca-private -prisons-corrections-corporation-inmates-investigation-bauer.

51. Richard Gagnon, interview by Lauren-Brooke Eisen, March 23, 2016.

52. Former corrections director, interview by Lauren-Brooke Eisen, March 31, 2016.

53. Reggie Wilkinson, interview by Lauren-Brooke Eisen, February 9, 2016.

54. Leon Neyfakh, "What Do You Do with the Worst of the Worst?", *Slate*, April 3, 2015, http://www.slate.com/articles/news_and_politics/crime /2015/04/solitary_confinement_in_washington_state_a_surprising_and _effective_reform.html.

55. Bernie Warner, interview by Lauren-Brooke Eisen, January 26, 2016.

56. Rick Seiter, interview by Lauren-Brooke Eisen, October 7, 2016.

57. Brigette Sarabi and Edwin Bender, "The Prison Payoff: The Role of Politics and Private Prisons in the Incarceration Boom," In the Public Interest, 2000, 4, https://www.inthepublicinterest.org/wp-content/uploads/Prison _Payoff_Report_WPP_2000.pdf.

58. David Shapiro, "Banking on Bondage," ACLU, November 2, 2011, https://www.aclu.org/sites/default/files/field_document/bankingonbondage _20111102.pdf.

59. Sharon Dolovich, "State Punishment and Private Prisons," *Duke Law Journal* 55 (2005): 437, 528.

60. CCA. "Myths vs. Facts in Partnership Corrections," https://ccamericasto rage.blob.core.windows.net/media/Default/documents/CCA-Resource -Center/MYTHS-vs-FACTS.pdf

61. Mike Tartaglia, "Private Prisons, Private Records," *Boston University Law Review* 94 (2014):1689, 1722; David Fathi, "The Challenge of Prison Oversight," *American Criminal Law Review* 47 (2010): 1453, 1461–62.

62. Christie Thompson, "Everything You Ever Wanted to Know About Private Prisons . . . Is None of Your Damn Business," Marshall Project, December 18, 2004, https://www.themarshallproject.org/2014/12/18/every thing-you-ever-wanted-to-know-about-private-prisons#.O5xljxIJP.

63. ACLU, "Warehoused and Forgotten: Immigrants Trapped in Our Shadow Private Prison System," June 2014, 28, http://www.texasobserver .org/wp-content/uploads/2014/06/060614-ACLU-CAR-ReportOnline.pdf.

64. Thompson, "Everything You Ever Wanted to Know About Private Prisons."

65. Ibid.

66. Friedman v. Corr. Corp. of Am., 2013 WL 784584 (Tenn. Ct. App. Feb. 28, 2013).

67. Prison Legal News v. Corr. Corp. of Am., 2014 WL 2565746 (Vt. Super. Jan. 10, 2014); Prison Legal News v. Corr. Corp. of Am., No. D-1-GN-13-001445 (353d Dist. Ct., Travis County, Tex. Sept. 15, 2014).

68. Thompson, "Everything You Ever Wanted to Know About Private Prisons."

69. Email to Rosa Suarez, July 31, 2015; email to Rosa Suarez, February 26, 2016; email to Rosa Suarez and George Zoley, February 17, 2017.

70. Email from McKinley P. Lewis, communications director, Florida Department of Corrections, February 8, 2016.

71. Email from Michael Weber, April 19, 2016.

72. Email from Pablo Paez, vice president, Corporate Relations at GEO Group, April 26, 2016.

73. Email from Jonathan Burns, Director of Public Affairs. CCA, March 30, 2016.

74. Reggie Wilkinson, interview by Lauren-Brooke Eisen, February 9. 2016.

75. Leonard Gilroy, "California Can Use Private Prisons in Criminal Justice Reform Efforts," *Orange County Register*, October 9, 2016.

76. Adam Liptak, "Justice, 5–4, Tell California to Cut Prisoner Population," *New York Times*, May 23, 2011.

77. Brown v. Plata, 563 U.S. 493, 503 (2011).

78. Foon Rhee, "Breaking Up with Private Prisons Can Be Hard to Do," *Sacramento Bee*, August 19, 2016.

79. Bob Egelko, "As U.S. Cuts Ties With Private Prisons, California To Keep Using Them," *Orange County Register*, August 29, 2016; http://www.ocregister.com/2016/08/29/as-us-cuts-ties-with-private-prisons-california-to-keep-using-them/.

80. Memorandum for the Acting Director, Federal Bureau of Prisons, "Recession of Memorandum on Use of Private Prisons," February 21, 2017, https://www.bop.gov/resources/news/pdfs/20170224_doj_memo.pdf.

81. Megan Mumford, Diane Whitemore Schanzenbach, and Ryan Nunn, "The Economics of Private Prisons," Brookings Institute, Hamilton Project, 2016, 3, https://www.brookings.edu/wp-content/uploads/2016/10/es_20161021_private_prisons_economics.pdf.

82. CCA acquired Correctional Alternatives, Inc. in 2013. GEO Group acquired Dominion Management/McLoud Correctional Services (2000), Correctional Services Corporation (2005), CentraCore Properties Trust (2007), Cornell Acquisition (2010), and LCS Corrections Services (2015). Community Education Center acquired CiviGenics in 2007. Ibid., 3, note 4.

83. Douglas McDonald and Carl Patten, "Governments' Management of Private Prisons," U.S. Department of Justice, January 2004, https://www.ncjrs.gov/pdffiles1/nij/grants/203968.pdf.

84. GEO Group, "Who We Are," https://www.geogroup.com/who_we_are.

85. CoreCivic, Home page, http://www.cca.com/.

86. MTC, "Corrections Position Statement," http://www.mtctrains.com/sites/default/files/MTC_Corrections_Position_Statement.pdf.

87. Alexander Volokh, "Prison Accountability and Performance Measures," *Emory Law Journal* 63 (2014): 339, 365.

88. Ibid.

89. State of Arizona Office of the Auditor General, "Performance Audit, Arizona Department of Corrections Private Prisons," July 2001, http://apcto.org/files/2549/Image/fullarizona.pdf.

90. Mumford, Schanzenbach, and Nunn, "The Economics of Private Prisons," 4.

91. Harding, *Private Prisons and Public Accountability*, 109.

92. Heather Wells et al., "Annual Report Concerning the Status of Private Contract Prisons," December 2013, 1, 3, http://www.doc.state.co.us/sites/default/files/opa/PPMU%20Annual%202013.pdf.

93. Georgia Department of Corrections, "Private Prisons," last accessed Febrauryl6, 2016, http://www.dcor.state.ga.us/Divisions/Facilities/Private Prisons.

94. Department of Management Services, "Private Prison Monitoring," last accessed Februaryl6, 2016, http://www.dms.myflorida.com/business_operations/private_prison_monitoring.

95. Florida Center for Fiscal and Economic Policy, "Are Florida's Private Prisons Keeping Their Promise? Lack of Evidence to Show They Cost Less and Have Better Outcomes Than Public Prisons," April 2010, http://www.fcfep.org/attachments/20100409—Private%20Prisons.

96. Email from Michael Weber, Director and State Coordinator of Division of Specialized Services at the Florida Department of Management Services, April 19, 2016.

97. Mary Ellen Klas, "Florida's Largest Privately-Operated Women's Prison Is in Danger Zone. Lawmaker Wants Gov. Scott to Act," *Miami Herald*, March 23, 2017.

98. Mary Ellen Klas, "Hoodwinked! Lawmaker Says Prison Privatization Is Scamming Florida," *Tampa Bay Times*, March 28, 2017.

99. Ohio Revised Code, 9.06 Private operation and management of initial intensive program prison.

100. ABA, "Key Requirements for the Effective Monitoring of Correctional and Detention Facilities," Res. 104B, 2008, http://www.abanet.org/crimjust/policy/104b.doc.

101. John J. Gibbons and Nicholas deBelleville Katzenbach, "Confronting Confinement: A Report of the Commission on Safety and Abuse in America's Prisons," *Washington University Journal of Law & Policy* 22 (January 2006): 16, http://openscholarship.wustl.edu/cgi/viewcontent.cgi?article=1363&context=law_journal_law_policy.

102. State of New Mexico, New Mexico Corrections Department, Professional Services Contract 14-770-1300-0010 between New Mexico Corrections Department and Corrections Corporation of America, September 2013 through June 2015.

103. Jen Fifield, "Many States Face Dire Shortage of Prison Guards," Pew Charitable Trusts, Stateline, March 1, 2016, http://www.pewtrusts.org/en/research-and-analysis/blogs/stateline/2016/03/01/many-states-face-dire-shortage-of-prison-guards.

104. David Shichor, *Punishment for Profit: Private Prisons/Public Concerns* (Los Angeles, Calif.: Sage, 1995).

105. State of New Mexico, New Mexico Corrections Department, Professional Services Contract 14-770-1300-0010.

106. State of New Mexico Corrections Department, Letter to Monica Wetzel, Warden at New Mexico Woman's Correctional Facility, May 17, 2016.

11. The Future of Private Prisons

1. Matt Flegenheimer and Michael Barbaro, "Donald Trump Is Elected President in Stunning Repudiation of the Establishment," *New York Times*, November 9, 2016.

2. Anjali Sareen, "Trump Immigration Policy Backflip: Deportations 'So Fast Your Head Will Spin' ," *National Memo*, August 23, 2016, http://www.national memo.com/trump-immigration-policy-backflip-deportations-fast-head-will -spin/.

3. "Donald Trump's Speech to the GOP Convention," *The State*, July 21, 2016, http://www.thestate.com/news/politics-government/article91203222 .html.

4. Julie Hirschfeld Davis and Julia Preston, "What Donald Trump's Vow to Deport Up to 3 Million Immigrants Would Mean," *New York Times*, November 14, 2016; Jenna Johnson, " 'I Will Give You Everything.' Here Are 282 of Donald Trump's Campaign Promises," *Washington Post*, November 28, 2016.

5. Robert Ferris, "Trump, Republican Sweep Is a 'Game Changer' for Private Prison Industry," CNBC, November 23, 2016, http://www.cnbc.com/2016/11 /23/trump-republican-sweep-is-a-game-changer-for-private-prison-industry.html.

6. Felice Maranz, "Sessions as Trump Attorney General Positive for Private Prisons: Beacon," *Bloomberg*, November 21, 2016, http://www.bloomberg .com/politics/.

7. Avi Asher-Schapiro, "President Donald Trump May Reverse Obama Policy on Private Prisons; Industry Boosts Lobbying Efforts," *International Business Times*, November 22, 2016, http://www.ibtimes.com/political-capital/.

8. Memorandum for the Acting Director of the Federal Bureau of Prisons, from Jefferson B. Sessions III, "Recession of Memorandum on Use of Private Prisons," February 21, 2017, https://www.bop.gov/resources/news/pdfs /20170224_doj_memo.pdf.

9. Tomi Kilgore, "Trump Presidency Is Providing a Great Opportunity to Buy Prison Stocks," *MarketWatch*, January 20, 2017, http://www.marketwatch .com/story/trump-inauguration-highlights-best-opportunity-to-buy-prison -stocks-in-years-2017-01-19.

10. "CoreCivic CEO on Prison Profits and Trump," CNBC Video, December 20, 2016, http://video.cnbc.com/gallery/?video=3000577783.

11. "CoreCivic Inc's CEO Damon Hininger on Q4 2016 Results," Earnings Call Transcript, February 9, 2017, http://seekingalpha.com/article/4044592 -corecivic-incs-cxw-ceo-damon-hininger-q4-2016-results-earnings-call-transcript.

12. Julián Aguilar, "White House Greenlights a New Immigration-Detention Center in Texas," *Texas Tribune*, April 14, 2017.

13. Since 2006, the national state imprisonment rate has dropped 7 percent, with twenty-eight states reduced their prison populations. Of those, every state but South Dakota also saw crime drop. Lauren-Brooke Eisen and James Cullen, "Update: Changes in State Imprisonment," Brennan Center for Justice, June 7, 2016, https://www.brennancenter.org/sites/default/files/analysis /UpdateChangesinStateImprisonment.pdf.

14. CCA changed its name in late 2016; references herein prior to that time reflect previous name, CCA.

15. Bethany Davis, "Corrections Corporation of America Rebrands as CoreCivic," CCA, October 28, 2016, http://www.cca.com/insidecca/corrections -corporation-of-America-rebrands-as-corecivic.

16. Ibid.

17. Hillenby, "Reputation Management," http://www.hillenby.com/.

18. Danielle Kaeble and Lauren Glaze, "Correctional Populations in the United States, 2015," U.S. Department of Justice, Office of Justice Programs, December 2016, https://www.bjs.gov/content/pub/pdf/cpus15.pdf.

19. Paul Barrett, "Private Prisons Have a Problem: Not Enough Inmates," *Bloomberg Business Week*, September 8, 2016, http://www.bloomberg.com /news/.

20. Carl Takei, "The Wal-Mart Model: Not Just for Retail, Now It's for Private Prisons Too!", *Speak Freely* (ACLU blog), September 29, 2014, https://www .aclu.org/blog/wal-mart-model-not-just-retail-now-its-private-prisons-too.

21. "GEO Group Annual Report," 2016, https://www.sec.gov/Archives /edgar/data/923796/000119312517056831/d320699d10k.htm.

22. In 2009, GEO Group purchased Just Care for $38 million, a provider of "detention health care" that provides medical and mental health services. GEO Group estimated that the acquisition was expected to add $30 million in annual revenues and would enhance GEO Group's ability to market their mental health management services for civil and forensic psychiatric populations throughout the country. "GEO Group Annual Report," 2009, https://www.sec.gov /Archives/edgar/data/923796/000095012310015259/g22198e10vk.htm.

23. GEO Care, responsible for the GEO Group's reentry facilities, day reporting, and youth services, has nearly doubled in three years, from monitoring 70,000 individuals in 2012 to 137,000 in 2015. "GEO Group Annual Report," 2015, https://www.sec.gov/Archives/edgar/data/923796/000119312516478864 /d43877d10k.htm.

24. "GEO Group Annual Report," 2016, 63.

25. Matthew Perlman, "REIT GEO Group Inks $360M Deal for Prison Rehab Provider," *Law 360*, February 22, 2017, https://www.law360.com/articles/.

26. Devlin Barrett, "Prison Firm CCA Seeks to Reduce Number of Repeat Offenders," *Wall Street Journal*, September 12, 2014.

27. "We believe the demand for the housing and programs that community corrections facilities offer will continue to grow as offenders are released from prison and due to an increased awareness of the important role these programs play in an offender's successful transition from prison to society." "CCA Annual Report," 2015, 22, https://materials.proxyvote.com/Approved/22025Y/20160314/10K_277713/.

28. Carl Takei, "CoreCivic's Practices Unchanged Despite Dropping CCA Name," *Tennessean*, December 12, 2016.

29. "CCA Annual Report," 2015, 8.

30. "GEO Group Annual Report," 2016.

31. "GEO Group Annual Report," 2015.

32. Cody Mason, "International Growth Trends in Prison Privatization," *Sentencing Project*, August 2013, 1, http://sentencingproject.org/wp-content/uploads/2015/12/International-Growth-Trends-in-Prison-Privatization.pdf.

33. Kuang Keng Kuek Ser, "Australia and the UK Have a Higher Proportion of Inmates in Private Prisons Than the US," *PRI's The World*, September 1, 2016, http://www.pri.org/stories/2016-09-01/australia-uk-have-higher-proportion-inmates-private-prisons-us.

34. Anastasia Glushko, "Doing Well and Doing Good: The Case for Privatising Prisons," *Policy* 32, 1 (Autumn 2016): 20.

35. The first to be contracted out to G4S was HMP Wolds in 1992. The first to be privately designed, constructed, managed, and financed was HMP Altcourse (in Liverpool) in 1997.

36. The prison in Borallon, near Brisbane, is operated by CCA and has more than 200 beds. Richard Harding, "Private Prisons in Australia," *Australian Institute of Criminology: Trends & Issues in Crime and Criminal Justice*, May 1992, http://www.aic.gov.au/media_library/publications/tandi_pdf/tandi036.pdf.

37. World Prison Brief, "Australia," Institute for Criminal Policy Research, http://www.prisonstudies.org/country/australia.

38. John Stapleton, "Prison Population in Australia Has Climbed," *The Newdaily*, February 18, 2016, http://thenewdaily.com.au/news/national/2016/02/18/australian-prison-population/.

39. Kevin A, Wright, "The Private Prison," in *The American Prison: Imagining a Different Future*, ed. Francis T. Cullen, Cheryl Lero Jonson, and Mary K. Stohr (Los Angeles, Calif.: Sage, 2014), 173–92.

40. Bret Bucklen, interview by Lauren-Brooke Eisen, February 22, 2016.

41. Bret Bucklen email to Lauren-Brooke Eisen, March 20, 2017.

42. Leonard Gilroy, interview by Lauren-Brooke Eisen, November 21, 2016.

43. Leonard Gilroy, "Private Prisons Can Help Florida Reform Its Criminal-Justice System," *Orlando Sentinel*, September 29, 2016.

44. Bret Bucklen, interview by Lauren-Brooke Eisen, February 22, 2016.

45. David W. Chen, "Goldman to Invest in City Jail Program, Profiting if Recidivism Falls Sharply," *New York Times*, August 2, 2012.

46. Emily Gustafsson-Wright, Sophie Gardiner, and Vidya Putcha, "The Potential and Limitations of Impact Bonds: Lessons from the First Five Years of Experience Worldwide," Brookings Foundation, July 9, 2015, 48, https://www.brookings.edu/research/the-potential-and-limitations-of-impact-bonds-lessons-from-the-first-five-years-of-experience-worldwide/.

47. Jim Parsons, Chris Weiss, and Qing Wei, "Impact Evaluation of the Adolescent Behavioral Learning Experience (ABLE) Program," Vera Institute of Justice, September 2016, https://storage.googleapis.com/vera-web-assets/downloads/Publications/rikers-adolescent-behavioral-learning-experience-evaluation/legacy_downloads/rikers-adolescent-behavioral-learning-experience-evaluation.pdf.

48. Leonard Gilroy, interview by Lauren-Brooke Eisen, November 21, 2016.

49. Hanna Kozlowska, "In Australia, a Private Prison Company Gets a Bonus for Every Freed Inmate Who Does Not Come Back," *Quartz*, December 3, 2016, https://qz.com/849774/in-australia-sodexo-owned-private-prison-company-melaleuca-will-get-cash-for-every-freed-inmate-who-does-not-come-back/.

50. Glushko, "Doing Well and Doing Good," 22.

51. Nino Bucci, "Victoria's Ravenhall Prison Operators to Be Paid Up to $2 Million Bonus if Reoffending Reduced," *Sydney Morning Herald*, February 12, 2015.

52. "GEO Consortium Wins Ravenhall Bid," *GEO Insights* 34 (December 2014), http://www.geogroup.com.au/uploads/3/1/0/4/31040789/december_2014.pdf.

53. Reggie Wilkinson, interview by Lauren-Brooke Eisen, February 9, 2016.

54. Bret Bucklen, interview by Lauren-Brooke Eisen, February 22, 2016.

55. Matthew R. Durose, Alexia D. Cooper, and Howard N. Snyder, "Recidivism of Prisoners Released in 30 States in 2005: Patterns from 2005 to 2010," Bureau of Justice Statistics, April 2014, https://www.bjs.gov/content/pub/pdf/rprts05p0510.pdf.

56. O'Lone v. Estate of Shabazz, 482 U.S. 342, 354 (1987) (Justice Brennan, dissenting).

Conclusion

1. Deputy Attorney General Sally Q. Yates, "Phasing Out Our Use of Private Prisons," U.S. Department of Justice, August 18, 2016, https://www.justice.gov/archives/opa/blog/phasing-out-our-use-private-prisons.

2. Editorial Board, "First Step in Shutting Private Prisons," *New York Times*, August 22, 2016.

3. Heather Long, "Private Prison Stocks Up 100 Percent Since Trump's Win," CNN, February 24, 2017, http://money.cnn.com/2017/02/24/investing/private-prison-stocks-soar-trump/.

4. Management and operation of a contractor-owned, contractor-leased, correctional facility, *Federal Business Opportunities*, https://www.fbo.gov/index?s=opportunity&mode=form&id=12d89dfef8cd775fecf26b119b247ff5&tab=core&_cview=0 (last updated June 1, 2017). The solicitation seeks "the management and operation of a contractor-owned/contractor-leased, contractor-operated correctional facility for up to 9,540 beds. . . . Each facility under this requirement must fall within the range of 1,200 to 1,800 contracted beds when filled to 100% of the general population capacity.

5. GEO Group, Inc., press release: "The GEO Group Awarded Contract for the Development and Operation of a New Company-Owned 1,000-Bed Detention Facility in Texas" (April 13, 2017).

6. Julie Hirschfeld Davis and Ron Nixon, "Trump Budget Takes Broad Aim at Undocumented Immigrants," *New York Times*, May 25, 2017, https://www.nytimes.com/2017/05/25/us/politics/undocumented-immigrants-trump-budget-wall.html?mcubz=0.

7. Matthew Ingram, "Trump's Team Said to Be Planning to Privatize Public Broadcasting," *Fortune*, January 19, 2017, http://fortune.com/2017/01/19/trump-public-broadcasting/.

8. Eric Daley, letter to Lauren-Brooke Eisen, March 3, 2016.

9. Id Johnston, "Corporate-Run Prisons a 'Growth Industry' Some Businessmen Claim They Can Do the Job Cheaper . . . and Better," *Los Angeles Times*, March 29, 1985.

10. Suzanne St. Pierre, producer, "Crime Pays," *60 Minutes* 17, 11 (November 25, 1984), 7, CBS Television Network.

11. Ibid., 12.

12. "Prisoners in State and Federal Institutions on December 31, 1984," Bureau of Justice Statistics, National Prisoner Statistics Report NCJ-103768, February 1987, 3, https://www.bjs.gov/content/pub/pdf/psfi84.pdf.

13. Ibid.

14. St. Pierre, "Crime Pays," 12.

Index

Note: Page numbers in italics refer to figures; those followed by n refer to notes, with note number.